CASTE OUT!

The Liberation Struggle of the
Dalits in India

David Haslam

CTBI
Inter-Church House
35-41 Lower Marsh
London SE1 7RL

ISBN 0 85169 250 8

CTBI
Inter-Church House
35-41 Lower Marsh
London SE1 7RL

Typeset and printed by Communications In Print plc,
Basildon, Essex SS13 1LJ.

Cover design by Mark Whitchurch Art and Design.

Cover photograph by John Devaraj, Bangalore 1992, of a sculpture
built by 3000 Dalit children near Bangalore of a woman with her arms
out wide, flying, but also in a crucifix position, called 'Born Free'.

CONTENTS

FOREWORD

by Rt Rev Mano Rumalshah

The caste system is a very serious problem in South Asia today. Its worst effects can be seen in India but it is also prevalent in Pakistan, Sri Lanka and other Asian countries. My own family comes from Pakistan and India, so I speak with a knowledge of both realities.

Casteism demeans people. It demeans those of the so-called 'upper castes' who practice it and are drawn into seeing themselves as some kind of superior race because of it. It demeans those who experience the full brunt of it. They are treated almost as sub-human, they are seen as unfit to live in decent surroundings, do the same work, eat the same food, even drink the same water as the caste people. They are regarded as polluted, and the constant diminishment of their humanity creates for them a miserable existence, passed on from generation to generation. The worst of it all is that casteism gives the impression that it has divine licence, and so discrimination becomes seemingly sanctified.

David Haslam's book, written from a seven-week sabbatical journey which began with a visit to my diocese of Peshawar in north-west Pakistan and took him across the border into India, to the cities of Amritsar, Delhi, Mumbai (Bombay), Bangalore, Chennai (Madras) and Madurai, and to many towns and villages from the north-west of India to the south-east, gives us an outsider's glimpse into India's caste system. It points towards a history of how the system might have evolved, recognising that there are still disagreements among scholars about that history. It describes the debilitating effects of casteism on the Dalits, the outcast people of India, in every aspect of their lives.

The book outlines the responsibility of Indian Governments, past and present, for the current sorry state of affairs, but points out that the British colonial regime must take some of the blame. The Church also does not have clean hands, in fact some say that casteism is one of the most damaging factors within the churches in South Asia, something which greatly hinders our participation in God's mission to the wider society. David Haslam recounts the growing resistance of Dalit people to their oppression, and sees it a sign of real hope albeit also of danger for those Dalit leaders, especially in the multiplicity of Indian villages, who are challenging the caste system.

One vital resource for the churches, both in India and the West, which is emerging from this struggle is Dalit Theology. In the same way that Liberation Theology arose from the fight against poverty and oppression in Latin America, Black Theology has come from of the struggles against apartheid and western racism, and Asian and Feminist theologies have flowed from other battles against injustice, a particular form of theology is developing among Dalits. **Caste Out!** can offer only a taster, we have to find ways of making Dalit theology more available in the West. Perhaps that can be one of the contributions of the 'missionary societies'?

David has considerable experience of struggles for racial justice, both in the anti-apartheid era and more recently as the Secretary for the Churches' Commission for Racial Justice (CCRJ). I first came to know David when I was Education Officer for the CCRJ's predecessor, the Community and Race Relations Unit of the then British Council of Churches. I can testify personally to the difficulty of persuading the churches to deal actively with racism, whether far away in South Africa or close at home within the UK. David Haslam's experience in dealing with structural racism at home and abroad has greatly helped him in identifying the similarities between racism and casteism and those to whom this book is addressed, both in India and Britain, should take him seriously. The Inquiry Report into the death of the south London black teenager Stephen Lawrence has helped British society begin to address the vexed question of institutional racism. Hopefully it will help other societies become more aware of the nature of institutional discrimination and the kind of determined action needed to stamp it out.

This book also raises, perhaps in a slightly tangential fashion, the sensitive question of interfaith relations. How can Christians develop closer contacts with other faith communities without being honest about their views and concerns. This is a real question for theological liberals in western societies. Are all faiths of equal value?, Should we from our more powerful position within the British or western context accuse or criticise those of 'minority' faiths? Will this not give fuel to the enemies of interfaith dialogue? Yet how can we understand each other better if we do not share honest criticism? **Caste Out!** opens up that debate.

I warmly commend the book particularly to those who, like David before he took his Indian journey, know little of South Asia. It gives an insight into one of the most challenging dimensions of the development of world's largest democracy. It is also written in a context where the pace and the nature of 'globalisation' are starting to be vigorously questioned and the rich in the world, both outside and inside India, are growing richer while the poorest suffer more and more. In India the great majority of those poor are Dalits. It is time the rest of the world woke up to this situation, and both urged change upon the Indian authorities, and offered to assist them with the mammoth task they have of overcoming many centuries of caste oppression. In this process, the Churches need to play their part.

Rt Revd Mano Rumalshah, General Secretary, United Society for the Propagation of the Gospel and formerly Bishop of Peshawar.

INTRODUCTION

Who are the Dalits of India? Why should British or European Christians - or others of goodwill - have any interest in them? And even if they have, what can they do to help? This book seeks to answer those questions, or at least begin to do so. Put simply, the Dalits of India are the old 'untouchables', the 'harijans' as Gandhi called them, who constitute some 17% of the Indian population but whose economic, political and cultural influence is comparatively small. With the number of Indians climbing past a billion, we are talking of 170 million people, or 250 million if we include the tribal people who are discriminated against as much as the Dalits. To understand the kind of oppression Dalits face, seven stories are included in the text. Dalits say that every day two Dalits are murdered, two Dalit houses burnt down, three Dalit women raped and fifty Dalits assaulted. The seven stories, indeed the whole book, arise from a sabbatical spent in India in late 1997. The perceptive, brave and courageous people I met there were the inspiration to write it.

'Dalit', as we shall learn, means downtrodden, oppressed, crushed. It is however the first time these downtrodden people have chosen their own name and even to use it is a sign of a new consciousness, a combative identity. It carries connotations of resistance to the ideology of casteism which for very many centuries has kept the Dalit 'out-castes' in chains. Casteism has many similarities with apartheid, with which increasing numbers of people did battle as the twentieth century developed and which was eventually destroyed. Like the Africans of South Africa at the beginning of the twentieth century, the Dalits of India are on the move, and will become an increasingly significant factor in the resistance of the poor of the world to the effects of the market-led dehumanising globalisation which continues to enrich the West.

Westerners in general, and Christians in particular, should take an interest in Dalits for three main reasons. The first is that by and large the colonial administration of the nineteenth and twentieth centuries contributed to and enhanced the oppression of Dalits. The second is that their place and treatment in Indian society is a disgrace, and must be challenged by anyone of any humanity. The third is that the emerging Dalit theology is a new form of the liberation theology which has so affected the thinking of our world - especially in the Church - over the past thirty years, and it has a lot of wisdom for us.

Although Britain by the mid-nineteenth century had won control of the Indian peninsula, there is little sign that the Portuguese, French, Dutch or other European would-be colonists would have treated the 'untouchables' any differently. But the British must carry the main responsibility for collaborating with rather than eradicating caste. The brahmins, the priestly caste who had by then inserted themselves at the peak of India's power structure, were co-opted. They wanted no challenge to the prevailing social and economic system and the British did not produce one.

The missionaries were another story, at least partly. Christianity traditionally appeared in India first not long after Jesus' death with the arrival of Thomas the Apostle in Kerala, in south-west India. The Mar Thoma Church claims to be a direct result of his preaching; however casteism still deeply affects that church and its community (see *God of Small Things* by Arundhati Roy). The Portuguese with their Roman Catholicism were the next major arrivals and although their Christianity was rough and ready and they intermarried fairly freely with Indian women of a variety of castes, the record of Roman Catholicism vis-a-vis casteism is not good. Too many of their missionaries accepted it as an aspect of Indian culture not to be challenged, so churches - and cemeteries - were built in which there were even physical barriers to separate the out-castes.

Protestantism behaved a little better. Some of its leaders, like William Carey, Bishop David Wilson and the American Baptist John Clough were vigorously opposed to casteism and sought to ensure it had no place within the Indian Church. The German missionaries like Ziegenbalg and the Lutheran Graul were also opposed but made concessions. As a result out-castes joined the Protestant churches in increasing numbers, leading to what were called the 'mass movements' or 'spirit movements' of the second half of the nineteenth century and the first half of the twentieth. Dalits were the initiators and catalysts of these mass movements and as a result make up over 75% of the Indian Christian population, an inverse proportion to their proportion among all Indians - of whom Christians are some 2.4%.

It is out of this Dalit-influenced stream of Indian Christianity that Dalit liberation theology has evolved and Christian Dalits have begun to participate actively in the Dalit liberation movements. The plural is important here as there is no single movement as yet. However Christian Dalits are active in the most effective national movements thus far, such as Dalit Solidarity Programmes (DSP), the National Campaign for Dalit Human Rights and the Federation for Dalit Liberation (FeDal), and some give support to political parties with Dalit links, such as the BSP, PT and RPI.

At the same time casteism remains deep within the Indian Church. Many church leaders are from the 'upper castes' - although this is less true in certain areas like parts of AP - and resources such as those in education and health have been used disproportionately to benefit caste people, even those not Christian. Caste Christians are more likely to associate, eat with or marry non-Christians of their own caste than other Christians who happen to be Dalit. There are parallels here with the racism still present in the western churches. Perhaps there is some mutual learning to be done, a common journey to undertake, as we in the West seek to address our sin and focus our repentance in the most effective way.

This book is primarily a 'snapshot'. It does not pretend great knowledge of India, of Hinduism and its various strands, of all the historical and theological nuances. It is the beginning of a journey, for writer and - hopefully - for readers, not an end. There are gaps, unfilled sometimes due to lack of space and sometimes to lack of knowledge. I have been urged to pursue it however by Dalit activists, who have given me advice, correction and encouragement, saying it will be of assistance to them and to their struggle to have this contribution from a sympathetic outsider.

As the world grows smaller and we seek to address its enormous imbalances and to humanise the processes of globalisation, an alliance with the Dalit movements - seeking a new identity, self-respect and justice for their people - could benefit both them and us. The Indian authorities claim caste is an internal matter for Indians to resolve. However, as the radical Indian journalist V.T. Rajshekar says in his book *Dalits: the Black Untouchables of India*, 'the problem of India's untouchables is not India's internal problem but an international problem'. This is increasingly happening as casteism and the situation of the Dalits is appearing in international fora, including the United Nations bodies dealing with human rights, minorities and racial discrimination. The UN Committee for the Elimination of Racial Discrimination were particularly critical of India's most recent report, which failed to deal with the caste issue in any meaningful way. With the re-election of the BJP in October 1999 to head a coalition government the internal situation seems unlikely to change.

Christians and others in the West can ensure the Dalit issue has a high profile and undertake educational campaigning in the West, while assisting Dalit initiatives within India. The struggle against casteism is the new millennium's struggle against apartheid, and we must pray it does not again take nearly a century to resolve. And the struggle is on, from India's national parliament, the Lok Sabha, to the Dalit section, or colony, of the central Indian village where I first heard this Dalit song, sung by an agricultural union organiser -

> We cultivate, but get no food,
> We work on the land, but go hungry,
> We labour in the fields, but the landlords suck our blood,
> We need to struggle together -
> We get nowhere without struggle.

There are many people I would like to thank for various amounts of advice and encouragement. They include Mrs Margaret Allen, Bishop Azariah (former Bishop of Chennai/Madras), Dr Franklyn Balasunderam (with Dr Sathi Clark and others at UTC, Bangalore), Revd Dr Colin Davey of Churches Together in Britain and Ireland, Paul Divakar, Bishop V. Devasahayam of Chennai, Professor Duncan Forrester, Dr Elizabeth Harris, Ms Alison Kaan, Revd Mohan Larbeer, Revd Dr Eric Lott, Revd Isaac Mann, Dr James Massey, Revd Kamber Manickam and other friends at the Tamilnadu Theological Seminary, Ajit Muricken of VAK (Mumbai/Bombay), Bishop George Ninan and colleagues in the Nasik Diocese, Revd Gordon Shaw, Dr Godwin Shiri, Ms Trudy Thorose and Revd Derek Winter. Revd Dr Israel Selvanayagam, Mr Nadir Dinshaw and Revd Bob Scott of the World Council of Churches also deserve particular thanks; they know the reasons why.

Revd David Haslam, December, 1999

ABBREVIATIONS

ADMK	Anna Dravida Munnetra Kazhagam, a Tamilnadu political party
AIADMK	All-India Anna Dravida Munnetra Kazhagam, a Tamilnadu-based political party
AP	Andhra Pradesh, a state in east central India
BC	Backward Classes
BJP	Bharatiya Janata Party
BSP	Bahujan Samaj Party
CBCI	Catholic Bishops' Conference of India
CNI	Church of North India
CPI-M	Communist Party of India - Marxist
CPI-ML	Communist Party of India - Marxist-Leninist
CSI	Church of South India
CISRS	Christian Institute for the Study of Religion and Society
DALET	Dalit Liberation Education Trust, Chennai (Madras)
DARC	Dalit Action Resource Centre, Chittoor, Andhra Pradesh
DMK	Dravida Munnetra Kazhagam (Dravidian Progressive Front), a Tamilnadu political party
DRC	Dalit Resource Centre, TTS, Madurai
DSP	Dalit Solidarity Peoples
EFI	Evangelical Fellowship of India
FeDAL	Federation for Dalit Liberation
INSAF	Indian National Social Action Forum
ISI	Indian Social Institute
LMS	London Missionary Society
MLA	Member of the Legislative (State) Assembly
MPA	Member of the Parliamentary (National) Assembly
MP	Madhya Pradesh (State in central India)
NCCI	National Council of Churches of India
OBC	Other Backward Classes
PAN	Participatory Action Network, Andhra Pradesh
PCRA	Protection of Civil Rights Act
PMK	Pantali Makal Katchi (Tamilnadu Labour Party)
PT	Puthiya Tamilagam (New Tamil Party)
PWG	People's War Group
RPI	Republican Party of India
RTI	Rural Theological Institute, TTS, Madurai
SC	Scheduled Castes
SCF	Scheduled Castes Federation

ST	Scheduled Tribes
TNCs	Transnational Corporations
TTS	Tamilnadu Theological Seminary, Madurai
UP	Uttar Pradesh (State in north India)
UTC	United Theological College, Bangalore
VAK	Vikas Adhyayan Kendra, Mumbai (Bombay)
WTO	World Trade Organisation

1   CASTE AND THE PAST

a)   What is 'caste'?

In one of the James Bond stories our hero is locked in a cell in which one of the walls begins to move gradually inwards. There is no window, the door is double-locked and the walls are all smooth. There seems no way out, as the space for survival gets inexorably smaller. As always however, Commander Bond makes his escape. Being a Dalit is rather like being in one of those cells. Sometimes the wall stops before actually crushing the victim. Sometimes it doesn't. The other analogy that springs to mind is wandering through a maze. You go along this passage and that, turning corners, coming to dead ends, re-tracing your footsteps. You cannot see the centre, or end of the labyrinth. You follow up every new opening, desperately seeking the solution. Eventually you realise there *is* no solution. You're in here for life.

The original description for Dalits was 'untouchable', those whom people of a 'higher' caste actually cannot touch without polluting themselves. They are born into untouchability, and there is no escape. They are confined to the lowest place in society, and its most demeaning jobs. These include cleaning the yards and animal sheds of the 'upper castes', doing their errands, labouring in their fields, drumming for their celebrations and - literally - disposing of their shit. The caste system is built on the concepts of purity and pollution. Some people are purer than others. The highest caste - the brahmins - are the purest of the pure; the other three castes have gradations of purity, the untouchables are wholly impure, and cannot even be allowed to come into contact with caste people.

Still in India many refer to 'upper and lower castes', the latter term sometimes referring to both the fourth caste, the sudras, and also the 'untouchables'. Here however I shall normally refer to 'caste people', which includes all the four castes, and only occasionally use the term 'upper caste', which could imply - falsely - that such people are of greater worth. I shall allude most often to the 'untouchables' by the name they have chosen for themselves, 'Dalits', which signifies that they are outside the caste system, but may also use 'out-caste' in particular contexts. This expression aptly describes people outside the caste system, and also what has been done to them. Today's Dalits however reject caste identity, they aim to be the forerunners of India's 'casteless society'. In this text 'Dalit' is deliberately used with a capital 'D'. In his essay on *Transcending Boundaries*, entitled

1

'From No People to God's People', theologian A.P. Nirmal endeavours to explain the term 'Dalit'. It is a Sanskrit word which includes meanings of 'broken' or split, 'downtrodden' or crushed, 'scattered', 'open' or exposed, 'manifested' or displayed. It has therefore a richness of meaning which can continually be explored. 'Dalit' has superseded 'harijan', which has become discredited. It was the name Gandhi coined for the untouchables. He said it meant 'children of God'; however it also refers to the illegitimate children of temple-women, or devadasis, who are usually Dalits or low-caste women used for sexual satisfaction by men of the brahmin caste. Often no-one knows who is the father of their children, and the latter are referred to as 'harijans'.

Paul Divakar, a long-standing Dalit activist and now a human rights campaigner, says harijan is 'the name that is scorned by our people as the name "nigger" is scorned by the blacks!' He says that for fifty years now 'we have taken the name that our leaders christened - we are proud to say we are DALITS... (this) describes the predicament of those who are alienated from social equality, economic justice and human freedom'.

To be a Dalit however is not just a matter of economic or political oppression. The additional dimension which affects Dalits is the psychological, where they have experienced over 3,000 years of mental oppression, intended to convince them that they are not in fact human beings, but some less-than-human species whose role is to serve the needs of the caste people. As the Roman Catholic Archbishop of Varanasi in northern India said to a 1993 Dalit Consultation 'A Dalit may be poor but that is not the problem, the real problem is the wounded psyche and this must be healed.'

Father Arockiadass, a Jesuit priest, in an essay in *Frontiers of Dalit Theology*, speaks about Dalits in theological terms, they 'are the crucified people; they are the suffering servants of God who struggle to take away the sins of the world; they are the messianic people who would bring salvation to this country'. It is perhaps above all for this latter reason - and the lessons which may be learned are not confined to India - that, says Arockiadass, 'it is imperative for any servant of God to enter into solidarity with (the Dalits), to be with them, feel and think with them and to struggle with them'.

The Dalits themselves however are not just one people. As with the main caste groups there are many subdivisions. Estimates of the number of Dalit sub-groups range from 500 up to 900, many of them situated in specific areas of the country and speaking different languages. The sub-groups have their own names and identities; one large group in Tamilnadu in the south of India, for example, is the 'Paraiyars', from whom we get the English word 'pariah', still used of someone whom no-one wants to know. Clearly this diversity presents enormous problems in building up a wider consciousness and any kind of movement. Furthermore, not all the out-caste people accept the generic term 'Dalit', and some sub-groups are in vigorous competition with others for privileges and advantages. Disagreements among Dalits often take on a caste character, so to create a national Dalit consciousness is a considerable challenge.

In terms of numbers, according to the 1991 census Dalits made up about 17% of the population, which then meant 138 million people. The 1998 minimum estimate was 150 millions, some speak of 200 millions, almost the same population as the United States and nearly four times that of Britain. In Government terms Dalits are referred to as **Scheduled Castes**, and together with the **Scheduled Tribes** they make up 25% of India's population.

Who then are the castes? The **brahmins**, already mentioned, are the priestly class, making up about 5% of the population. They are often lighter-skinned, with sharper features, and have fairly ruthlessly built for themselves a political and economic power-structure which they are very keen to keep. Most of India's leading politicians have been brahmins, including the first Prime Minister Jawaharlal Nehru, his family members Indira and Rajiv Gandhi, and Lal Shastri, although the architect of independence Mohandas K. Gandhi (no relation) was from a sub-caste of the vaishyas. The next main caste group is the **kshatriyas**, traditionally the warrior class, who have often allied with the brahmins in order to maintain control of the society. Then come the **vaishyas**, originally the cultivators but who developed into land-owners and merchants and now occupy much of the commercial, financial and business sectors. Finally there are the **sudras**, who used to be field-labourers but have moved up to become land-owning peasants, or perhaps in urban areas the 'working class', low in the caste system but believing themselves to be markedly superior to the Dalits, regarded as the bottom of the heap.

The brahmins, kshatriyas and vaishyas make up 20-25% of the population, so around 50% consists of the various branches of the sudras, who are also known by the Government as 'Other Backward Classes'. There are various special state schemes to assist Scheduled Castes (SCs), Scheduled Tribes (STs) and Other Backward Classes (OBCs). The Scheduled Tribes are groupings of the original population of India. A 1997 report by Nasik CNI Diocese says tribal peoples total 72 million, and can be roughly divided into five socio-cultural regions in different parts of India. According to the 1991 census there are nearly 400 different communities, speaking 240 languages or dialects. Their occupations range from small-scale farming, fishing and forestry to mobile casual labour and the mining industry. They are potential allies for the Dalits, boxed in as they are near the base of the social pyramid.

The total population of India in 1991 was nearly 850 millions, and rising by 2.4% annually, it is estimated to be over one billion in the year 2000. In fact one sixth of the world's population lives in South Asia, including Pakistan, Bangladesh and Sri Lanka. Looking at the world map it is not a large area, so food, water and work for its teeming millions should be high on the international agenda for the new millennium.

What then is the caste system? We shall look at its origins in the next section, but it is defined by Raja Jayaraman, in his *Caste and Class: Dynamics of Inequality in Indian Society* as 'a type of social stratification in which an individual's social status, that is his or her prestige and honour, are determined by his or her birth into a particular caste... this status is directly linked to his or her caste group within the hierarchy of caste'. Jayaraman goes on to say that each caste is relatively closed, 'the members of which may eat together, and each possessing a distinct name'. It is an unchanging system, there is little opportunity for acquiring status outside the system, and it is founded on the ideology of purity/pollution, which qualities may be attached to persons, material objects or activities, and will regulate relationships between all those within the system. He sees some signs of hope however, as geographical mobility gradually increases, people may leave their home areas, change their names and possibly eventually elude their caste background.

G. Aloysius in *Nationalism without a Nation in India* describes casteism as 'a specific form of ascriptive hierarchy and unequal distribution of power' which is 'sanctified by the dominant religious categories of Karma and Dharma'. Its foundation is the 'status determined by birth legitimised by the dominant Brahminic religio-cultural symbol and belief traditions'. The Indian social scientist Andre Beteille emphasises the pollution dimension, stating that it is not just backwardness which causes poverty in India but 'the stigma of pollution' which appears in the form of social prejudices which weigh heavily against Dalits in 'most competitive situations', i.e. in relation to education and jobs.

4

b)   Casteism and racism

There are more than a few parallels between racism and the caste system. There is an ideology undergirding both, where one group assumes inherent superiority over the other, and treats the other as less than human. In both there has been built up a structure of discrimination, in which one group constantly benefits itself at the expense of the other. This structure has social, political and economic elements to it, and religious and cultural ones too. The ideology of racism was developed during the slave trade, and helped to justify it by positing black people as only half-way between animal and human. Similarly casteism seems to have evolved during a period when the Aryan people were gradually suppressing the indigenous inhabitants of the Indian sub-continent, and vindicated itself by use of the hypothesis that the indigenous and tribal peoples were actually inferior, fit only for slavery and the most demeaning tasks.

A useful mini-definition of racism is 'prejudice plus power', and in many ways the basis of casteism could be described as 'pollution plus power' or perhaps 'purity/pollution plus power'. The 'purity' element is very important for caste people and the whole 'purity/pollution' dynamic is extremely oppressive psychologically for Dalits. As we shall learn, for some caste people even the shadow of a Dalit pollutes, hence the notion of caste purity *becomes* power.

In racism the social element sees black people as those who do not need, or could not adequately benefit from, such services as education, health and housing, so black people in Western societies almost invariably finish up with a lesser share in these sectors. The economic dimension rests on the myths that black people are lazier, less competent, disinterested in improving themselves and not really to be trusted with money, and results in much higher unemployment figures, lower access to finance and a lower standard of living for most black and minority communities. Few black people are found in positions of economic influence.

The political dimension compounds the other spheres of discrimination. In some European countries where black and minority people have lived for generations they are even denied a vote, never mind active participation in the political process. Their numbers are too small for them to influence elections, and few of them are selected for winnable local or national governmental places. The situation is a little better in the United States, where some extrapolations suggest there will actually be a majority of people of colour not too far into the next century. There are a number of prominent minority US politicians. However most of them have had heavily to compromise their views and interests to succeed, and the system usually works on a 'divide and rule' basis. Effective coalitions between African, Hispanic, Asian and Native Americans are not easy to create and difficult to find.

Discrimination also operates in the cultural and religious spheres. In the West cultures such as African, Hispanic, Caribbean, Asian, Kurdish or Turkish are seen as exotic, to be sampled occasionally but not in the same class as European music, theatre, art and literature. There is little knowledge or understanding of the arts of Asia, Africa and Latin America. This came home to me in my visit to Pakistan, India and Sri Lanka. Some of the sculpture, architecture and painting was as good if not better than anything I had seen in Europe, but few in Europe are aware of that. Now, despite all the difficulties, African, Asian and Latin American writers and musicians are proving their worth by gradually overcoming European and North American prejudices, and the same is beginning to happen with Dalits.

As far as the religious field is concerned, racism takes different forms. Within Christianity it operates through the assumptions that only Western theology, liturgy and church practice are really acceptable or meaningful, those that come from Africa, Asia or Latin America are not of the same depth or quality. In both Europe and the US this has forced Christians from black and minority communities to form their own 'black-majority' churches, or African American denominations. Meanwhile black and Asian people in the 'mainstream' churches struggle to make themselves heard, and get their contribution accepted.

Looking beyond Christianity, racism becomes entangled with the perspective of some Christians that Eastern religions are inferior. Islam in particular is full of 'fundamentalists', religious fanatics who go round blowing up buildings and murdering the opposition. There is little sense of the breadth and depth of Buddhism, and its contribution to the culture and history of Asia, or the ecological approach of the Jains, or the social and personal morality and spiritual discipline of many Muslims. During my journey through India, on one train journey my Muslim carriage attendant first insisted on sharing his supper with me, then when later I ventured along the corridor to the washroom, there he was in the little space by the carriage door, cross-legged on his mat, saying his evening prayers. Not many British train attendants behave thus - unless they are Muslim.

Some racist systems have of course justified themselves from what they claim is Christian teaching. The former slave-owners in the South of the

USA, and the Afrikaners of South Africa both claimed to find support for their beliefs of racial superiority in the Bible. They kept their churches unsullied by the pollution of black people, they went so far as to force or encourage the setting up of black, African or 'coloured' churches and sought to ensure that what was taught there helped to 'keep the black man in his place'. Casteism has an even more entangled relationship with religion, which we will come to later.

There are other similarities between casteism and apartheid than the religious undergirding. The latter was based on divide and rule, with non-Europeans being separated into Asians, so-called Coloureds, and Africans - the latter being divided by 'tribe'. In the same way lower caste and outcaste people are divided in India, especially by the use of sub-castes which are strongly based on traditional tasks and sometimes linked with religion. Complications arise at the edges of identity groups, as they did under apartheid. As we shall learn Dalits have certain privileges to offset their disadvantage, but these are denied to Christian Dalits. M.R. Arulraja in *Jesus the Dalit* describes a case where a junior official designated a Dalit student as one sub-caste because of his Christian faith, and therefore not entitled to his course place. The student felt constrained to deny his Christianity, so a more senior officer quashed the first decision and allocated the boy to another sub-caste, which enabled him to continue his studies.

There is an ongoing debate, and some disagreement, as to whether there is any relationship between casteism and discrimination by colour. The word **varna**, which is the system by which sub-caste groups are categorised, literally means 'colour'. Some commentators point to the parallels with the way invading 'Aryans' colonised the aboriginal inhabitants, and make comparisons with Australia or north America. It is said that Dalits can be slightly darker in colour than caste people. Salman Rushdie in *Midnight's Children* has characters using the term 'blackie' when referring to outcaste people. I was interested to note the 'Marriage' advertisements in some church newspapers in India where young women or men - as well as listing their educational qualifications, family backgrounds, jobs and salary - were frequently described as 'fair'. It may well be that colour is largely irrelevant in India, but it may be important in trying to describe the Indian reality to those outside. The same applies to discrimination by race or ethnicity. Dr B.R. Ambedkar, scholar, lawyer and politician - and hero of many Dalits - rejected any analysis by race, and this may well not be helpful in the context of India, but it does assist people in the West better to understand the nature of casteism. Some Dalits also feel they need access to international bodies for tackling racial discrimination and are therefore willing for what happens to them to be described in these terms.

Casteism and racism also breed the double, or triple, oppression faced by women. Black women in Europe say they experience subjugation twice over, being both black and a woman. Dalit women say for them it is threefold - female, Dalit and poor. European racism denies many women a proper education, a decent job, promotion according to merit, effective health care and genuine opportunity. Too often men expect black women to make a home, bring up a family and hold down a job, or struggle with social security. Gender is a factor which is becoming increasingly important in the struggles against oppression, whether it is racism we are dealing with, or casteism. Where then does casteism originate, what are its roots?

c)   The religious roots of caste

There are differing views on the origins of Hinduism, and therefore of the caste system. The word itself seems to have been used first to describe those originating from the Indus valley, now primarily in Pakistan. It achieved prominence largely through its use by the British colonialists. According to the introduction to Swami Dharma Theertha's *History of Hindu Imperialism* (1992) the word 'Hindu' does not appear in the 'so-called Hindu Sastras and Sacred Writings'. The Swami argues that the British administrator 'mass-converted' the Indian people by 'simply enumerating in his census operations all Indians other than Muslims or Christians as "Hindus".' There is discussion as to whether there were one or two cultures from which Hinduism evolved. One would have been the ancient Indus Valley civilisation, at its height between 2500 and 1500 BCE, and the second the Aryan culture which appeared during the second millennium BCE.

Gavin Flood in *An Introduction to Hinduism* (1996) says that the traditional 'Aryan migration' thesis is that the Aryans came from north of modern-day Pakistan, that is Afghanistan, northern Iraq and southern Russia. They were on the whole taller, lighter skinned and with more clear-cut features than the original inhabitants, and after exploring the plains of north-west India, gradually settled into an agricultural way of life. The alternative 'cultural transformation' thesis is that so-called Aryan culture is a development from the Indus Valley civilisation, and does not come from outside. Hinduism resulted from the interaction between Aryan, Dravidian (i.e. original south Indian) and tribal cultures. Part of the problem of definition, says Flood, is that 'Hinduism does not have a single historical founder.' It has no system of belief encapsulated in credal statements, nor any central authority. It is therefore very different from 'the monotheistic western traditions' of Christianity and Islam. Many Dalits feel that the origins of casteism lie within the processes through which Hinduism was formed.

Dalits believe the Hindu scriptures have been very important in the development of casteism, so a short summary of these follows. Their foundation is the **Vedas**, which evolved between 1500 and 500 BCE. Rather like the Old and New Testaments they were originally transmitted orally. Veda means 'knowledge', according to Flood there is also a sense of 'revelation'. The **Upanishads** are a kind of commentary on the Vedas, they contain hints of protest against some of the Vedic prejudices. Dr James Massey, a well-known Christian Dalit leader, in his *Downtrodden: the Struggle of India's Dalits* (1997), (afterwards known simply as *Downtrodden*), feels that the Upanishads really compound what is said in the Vedas. He quotes a verse from the Upanishads which compares a Chandala, one of the Dalit sub-castes, to a 'dog or swine'. The verse says that those who are of 'pleasant conduct' in this life will be born of a 'pleasant womb' in the next; those who are not will enter a 'stinking womb', that of a dog, swine or Chandala. One of the hymns of the Rig Veda outlines the mythical origin of the castes. It explains, when the Gods made a sacrifice with primeval man as victim, how they divided him - the brahmin was his mouth, the kshatriya his arms, the vaishya his thighs, the sudra his feet. The Dalits are nowhere!

The caste myth also appears in the **Manusmriti**, the thoughts of 'Manu', the patriarch who was traditionally the author of the social laws in the centuries immediately before the birth of Christ, which were then written down during the first few centuries CE. It is necessary also to be aware of the two epic poems, the **Ramayana** and the **Mahabharata**. These include some of the stories of the Aryan people's supposed journeyings and conquests, and also some post-Vedic ideas from the 'renouncers' and from regional devotional traditions. In the Ramayana Prince Rama travels down through India and into modern-day Sri Lanka, as the Aryans themselves may have done. The original inhabitants whom the Aryans are said to have displaced were the Panis and the **Dasas**. The Dasas were darker and more flat-featured than the Aryans, and resisted them the most strongly. That they were eventually defeated is suggested by the fact that 'dasa' came to mean slave. They could well be the forerunners of the Dalits. Hence casteism and untouchability are quite fundamentally rooted in the Hindu scriptures.

The **Bhagavad Gita**, part of the **Mahabharata**, asserts that the four castes were created by Lord Krishna, and suggests that the path to salvation is for everyone to carry out the responsibilities prescribed for them as a member of a particular caste (or, in the case of the Dalits, no-caste). The Gita at one point has Krishna saying that he accepts all having devotion to him, including the fourth Sudra caste, and this is the basis of progressive Hindu movements such as the **Bhakti**, which is based on belief in a personal God. There are also some anti-caste stories in the Hindu scriptures, playing perhaps a similar role to Ruth or Jonah in the Old Testament. The above is of course rather like trying to summarise the Old Testament, the Apocrypha and the New Testament in a few paragraphs, it is the briefest of outlines of a complex collection of scriptures whose history itself remains controversial.

Romila Thapar, in volume one of the Penguin A *History of India*, says that when the Aryans first emerged in India they were divided into three classes, the warriors and aristocracy, the priests and the peasant farmers. 'The colour element of caste was emphasised', she says, and became an important element in north Indian Aryan culture. A division developed between Aryans and non-Aryans. The Aryans were 'twice-born', the first the natural birth, the second into one of the three castes - kshatriyas, brahmins and vaishyas. The sudras consisted of darker Dasas and those of mixed origins. Today those conservative Hindu movements who want to claim all Indians are Hindus seek to block out this history.

Only priests could carry out the essential ritual sacrifices. They had also developed the mysterious powers of bestowing divinity upon the kings, and so cleverly insinuated themselves into the highest rank. The brahmin priests, says Thapar, taught that a person's caste was fixed by birth, and depended on their actions in a previous incarnation. This became the doctrine of **karma** (action), which came to be systematised in **dharma**, a word difficult to translate but best summarised as 'natural law', or 'how things are', which in this case included the caste system.

In *Why I am not a Hindu*, Kancha Ilaiah, a fellow of the Nehru Memorial Museum in Delhi and born into a shepherd caste family, one of the sudra sub-castes, analyses the way in which Hinduism has used religion to maintain the hegemony of the brahmins. He says it has co-opted the Dalit gods and goddesses, and used them to control the out-castes. When this failed it used violence, in fact 'violence has been Hinduism's principal mechanism of control'. He says no other religion has created such a plethora of gods who use both persuasion and violence to 'force the masses into submission'. Ilaiah calls the OBCs **bahujans** - meaning 'majority' - and urges the unification of sudras and out-castes as **Dalitbahujans**. He says this means 'people and castes who form the exploited and suppressed majority'.

Ilaiah explores the role of the various gods and goddesses in the Hindu pantheon and shows how cleverly the system is built up to divide and rule. He notes that the goddess of education and chief God Brahma's wife, Sarawathi, never wrote anything, as brahmins do not allow women to write. 'How is it that the source of education is herself an illiterate woman?' he asks rhetorically, 'this is diabolism of the highest order.' Vishnu, the second god, is blue-skinned, which Ilaiah says is to symbolise association between the brahmins and kshatriyas, and is the one who unleashes violence against those opposing brahminical domination. His wife Lakshmi is the source of wealth and property, while in Indian society even brahmin women are denied the right to property. Ilaiah has many more reasons why he is not a Hindu.

His analysis is echoed by others, including Swami Theertha in *History of Hindu Imperialism*. Theertha speaks of 'Brahminism' rather than 'Hinduism' and says it may be defined as 'a system of socio-religious domination and exploitation of the Hindus based on caste, priestcraft and false philosophy'. Born and bred into brahminism, he says, generation after generation of Indian people now see 'virtue in its sins, wisdom in its deceptions and freedom in its serfdom'. Brahmin imperialism 'knows no remorse.... it would see its victims die under its weight rather than relax its deadly grip'. Theertha goes so far as to say that Hinduism is not a religion, in the sense of Christianity, Islam or Buddhism, it is not possible to say what is Hinduism, there is 'no system of doctrines, no teacher or school of teaching, no single god accepted by all the Hindus'. It is his view that caste did not exist in the ancient Aryan religion nor in the primitive Indian religion nor in Buddhism. It is 'the unique contribution of the Brahmin priests'.

During the first millennium caste was reinforced through 'eating and mating', one simply never dined with or married into families of a different caste. Gradually the vaishyas moved more towards craftwork or embryonic trade and commerce, while the sudras moved up the scale, becoming cultivators. This led to the emergence of an additional category, the 'untouchables', consisting mostly of dasas, who had their own language and lived by hunting and rush-weaving, activities which were looked on with contempt by the 'higher' castes.

A system of domestic slavery also grew up, in which many of the slaves were sudras but could buy themselves out, or a slave-master could free them. Slavery was flexible, but caste was not. The brahmins, kshatriyas and vaishyas remained **dvija**, or twice-born, with the sudras knocking on their door and the dasas on the fringes of society. Castes were based primarily on occupation, and as more forms of work evolved, and foreigners moved in, sub-castes developed and the system became more than a little confusing. Mobility among sub-castes became possible, though never it seemed for the dasas.

As the Aryans spread into the south of India, says this theory, they came up against the Tamils, who had their own language, culture and religious practices. This was part of the Dravidian culture, and there is a theory that the Aryans forced the Dravidians into the role of out-castes also. The influence of the Aryans was seen in the way that, in the centuries between 500 and 1000 AD, throughout India, the brahmins took the highest positions and became the largest land-owners. They controlled the temples, and as these became centres for education, they controlled that also. They maintained the Vedic tradition, which itself enshrined caste. The Tamil religious leaders however ignored caste, and their music, dancing and other practices became an essential part of the temple ritual. Some of the dancing got out of hand, and led to the sexually exploitative **devadasi** system, to which we will refer later. Some sudras whose occupations were not demeaning were acceptable in the temple. Some however, as well as the out-castes, were excluded as their presence would pollute the holy places. The system was extended, says Thapar, to the point where even for the shadow of an out-caste to cross a brahmin's path called for ritual ablution. The concept of pollution became one of the key weapons of casteism.

One alternative to the caste system of Hinduism was the Buddhist faith, built up around Gautama Buddha, born about 566 BC in the north of India. Buddhism taught that the world is full of suffering, caused by human desires, and salvation can only be sought by renunciation of those desires. Buddhism also incorporated the doctrine of **karma**, but rejected caste and, as the setting up of Buddhist monasteries led to an option other than the Hindu temples for education, this was very important. Both Buddhism and Jainism, which evolved around the same period, were started by kshatriyas and rejected brahminism and the authority of the Vedas. Both appealed to 'lower' castes, the vaishyas and the sudras. Buddhism in particular provided an opportunity to opt out of the casteist religion of Hinduism, and this is important in view of the much later action of the Dalit leader Dr Ambedkar, in the 1950s.

Buddhism eventually lost its battle with Hinduism, and died out in much of India. It remained strong in Sri Lanka however, and spread widely through South-East Asia, where it remains the major faith. The arrival of Islam through the influx of Arabs, Afghans and Turks was another factor which led to the decline of Buddhism. Both are proselytising and institutionalised religions, and attracted a similar following. Muslim attacks on Buddhist monasteries constituted one of the factors pushing the Buddhists out to the East. Islam was also anti-caste; many of its early adherents were from the 'lower' castes, seeking an escape from Hindu rigidity. Islam was to some degree accepted by the brahmin leadership, which even allowed a Muslim to become the powerful Sultan of Bengal in the early fifteenth century, something which could have been prevented had the priestly caste so wished.

However, although caste was theoretically not practised by Islam, according to Thapar it remained present. Muslim families of Arab, Turk or Persian extraction had the highest status, followed by Hindu converts in the order of their own caste hierarchy. Commensality - sharing at table - was flexible, but marriage was rigidly controlled by caste, which was by now linked strictly with occupation or profession. In spite of its egalitarian philosophy, says Thapar, 'Islam did not lead to the disappearance of caste', and its capitulation limited its own development. Caste remained the crucial factor in the functioning of economic and political power, and caste purity was retained through an unyielding control of the marriage institution.

d)   The colonial period

The East India Company, which was the initial manifestation of British interest in southern Asia, was formed in 1600. Its early influence in India was minimal, but it got the proverbial foot in the door when its 'ambassador' Sir Thomas Roe negotiated an agreement with the Mughal Emperor. The first headquarters were at Surat, in western India, and moved to Bombay in 1674. In 1640 a factory had been established in Madras, and in 1690 one was opened in Calcutta. As Percival Spear says in the second volume of the Penguin *History of India*, 'the pattern of trade which developed was one of steady rather than spectacular returns'. Other European nations were present, including the Portuguese, the Dutch and the French. However, as the Mughal Empire waned Britain's involvement and interest deepened. Robert Clive's seizure of the city of Arcot in 1751 was a blow to the French and they were finally seen off near Madras in 1760. Clive - clerk, guerrilla, diplomat, kingmaker and plunderer - built on Madras as a base and then headed north, retaking Calcutta - which had been lost to local power - in 1757. Soon afterwards Clive returned to England and Warren Hastings became the key English actor on the Indian stage.

Gradually, as the Mughals declined, the British moved westwards and filled the political vacuum. To the question why they were successful Pearce responds that 'the essential answer is commerce and vested interests', though he comments that the details are very different from what might have been expected. One way and another however British influence spread, assisted by a political and economic collapse so profound that a famine in 1782 killed some 60% of the population. By the end of the eighteenth century, evangelical Christians were pressing for the right to launch missions in India, economically the Utilitarians had helped to break the East India Company's trade monopoly and politically the Radicals - while believing in the superiority of the Western world - had evolved a style of gradual improvement of the social and economic situation, rather than any confrontation. According to Pearce, 'Britain took the line of offering the West to the East without compelling its acceptance', and this affected considerably the development of the Indian state which finally achieved independence in 1947.

By 1836 Britain controlled the whole east coast of India, much of the south and west coast, and the great northern plain from Calcutta almost as far as Lahore. The central and north-east was still held by kings, princes and other local leaders, but mostly in a peaceful relationship. Gradually the East India Company was collapsing, a Governor-General had been appointed and by 1850 had added the title of Viceroy. About this time the railway system was begun, and completed around 50 years later, giving India the best system in Asia. An education system trained Indians for (junior) roles in the bureaucracy and the civil service gradually evolved. Towards the end of Gladstone's period of office (1868-86), his liberalism reached India through the appointment of Lord Ripon in 1880. Ripon attempted to give Indians more responsibility but this was resisted by Europeans. Spear comments 'the racial storm thus aroused subdued Ripon to a compromise'. Had he succeeded, in Spear's view partnership rather than resistance to Indian nationalism might have led to a different denouement in the twentieth century.

The British colonists were loath to take on the caste system. A book produced by a group based in Mumbai (Bombay), Vikas Adhyayan Kendra (VAK), called *At Crossroads: the Dalit Movement Today* (1994), (afterwards known as 'Crossroads'), states that Dalits in Bombay-Karnataka in the nineteenth century 'lived like slaves and serfs'. It says that the British-controlled Government did nothing, for example, for the education of untouchables. It reports that in 1850 a Dalit boy was refused entry to a public school and when he petitioned against his refusal the Government's decision indicates that it believed that to interfere 'with the prejudices of the ages for the sake of one or few individuals' would do great damage to the cause of education.

John Webster, in his historical study *The Dalit Christians*, notes that during the nineteenth century the British introduced practices which removed any rights the Paraiyar people had to property, and as a result they 'became much more vulnerable and landless labour increased'. Indeed, says Webster, 'the British government took no interest in the Dalits during the nineteenth century', apparently wishing to keep the support of the traditional Indian leadership. In 1909 however the Government of India Act created considerable controversy by making representation in the legislature proportional to a religious community's percentage of the local population. This happened during the 'mass movements', a series of large-scale conversions of Dalits to Christianity, which we shall refer to again. Hence says Webster, the British Government 'transformed the religious phenomenon of conversion into a highly charged political issue'. Hindu nationalists became very interested in how many and why Dalits were becoming Christians, and how this might be stopped.

This controversial step by the British led to what Webster calls 'the politics of numbers'. In this the drafters of the Indian constitution classified Dalit Christians 'as Christians rather than Dalits', and saw the Indian Christian 'upper caste' elite as the spokespersons for all Christians - the great majority of whom were Dalit. This left the political and economic future of the Christian Dalits in the hands of a few caste Christian leaders who lacked any political power to use in the interests of their fellow 'casteless' Christians. By and large, says Webster, Dalits 'had more faith in the British than in the caste Hindus'. Dr Ambedkar was actually accused of this by Hindus seeking independence. One of the reasons was the action of some colonial State governments in opening schools, public roads and land ownership to Dalits, against caste opposition. However literacy rates remained poor - though usually better for Christian than non-Christian Dalits.

Aloysius makes reference to the colonialists' unwillingness to address casteism in *Nationalism without a Nation*, he says that pragmatically they built upon it. The administrative system, almost exclusively appointing brahmins to 'decision-making and value-enforcing positions' became the means by which 'the entire country was brought within the uniform sway of the ascriptive ideology of the old order'. Worse, the British administration by upholding caste segregation conferred 'a modern secular legitimacy to the sacral order' and earned the epithet 'wet nurse to Vishnu' from the angry missionaries. This actually impeded change, says Aloysius, 'the impact of colonialism was to arrest the social progress, economic diversification and emergence of culture-based politics, and revert to an environment... of pan-Indian brahminical, feudal consolidation'. The colonial period was a hindrance to the sharpening battle against caste.

Dr Franklyn Balasunderam, in his *Dalits and Christian Mission in the Tamil Country* has a few words of praise for the British, saying that initially they took a certain interest in the amelioration of the 'untouchables' in terms of education, employment and political representation. After 1919 they offered further support - educational concessions, employment in public services and reservation of political appointments. However when in 1932 Dr Subbarayan, the Madras Chief Minister, won a vote in his Legislative Council to allow untouchables to enter Hindu Temples the British Governor-General refused it assent. The Indian Congress Party of Nehru and Gandhi supported the right of temple-entry however, as they wanted the Dalits' support, so finally in 1938 the Governor gave his agreement.

Balasunderam outlines the employment measures taken by the (British-controlled) Government and notes that around 1920 the Dalits welcomed these initiatives, but that later 'they began to feel their condition had not improved at all'. Non-brahmin caste groups had formed the Justice Party in 1916, but gradually it had excluded the interests of the Dalits from its concerns, and the British had not questioned this. Dalits who had converted to Christianity found their situation no better than that of Hindu Dalits. It was at this point that the practice began of treating Dalit Christians as Christian rather than Dalit, and therefore not entitled to the help that the rest of the 'Scheduled Castes' were getting. The Government of India Act 1935 had decreed that 'no Indian Christian shall be deemed to be a member of a scheduled caste'. This position was firmly established in independent India by the President's promulgation of 1950. This situation has bedevilled Dalit Christians to the present day, and even now they are campaigning for recognition as Dalits, due to the double discrimination they experience, as Dalits and as Christians. To choose Christianity means to cut oneself off from the education, employment and other benefits to which Dalits are entitled through the reservation system. It has echoes of the way Christians were treated in certain eastern European countries, prior to 1989.

Hence the failure of the British to tackle issues of caste has contributed to the situation Dalits find themselves in today. It is unfortunate that, with the power they wielded as colonial masters, the British were not able or willing to insist on basic concepts of justice in Indian society, which might have initiated changes making the current difficulties faced by the Dalit community much easier to overcome. This is another of those legacies of Empire which the British people and Government need to address today. Although people today cannot be held directly responsible, penitence needs to be expressed and all must take action to ameliorate the worst results of continuing casteism. Perhaps the situation should also be offered to God, in all its complexity, and prayers said that it may be redeemed, leading to a new, more equal and caste-free society in modern India. Let us now examine the missionary period and how it approached the problem of casteism.

e)   Caste and the missionaries

It is the tradition that the first Christian missionary to India was the apostle Thomas, who is supposed to have arrived in what is now Kerala in south-west India in 52 CE. He is reputed to have established some Syrian churches there, and travelled overland to the east coast, near Madras, where he was killed due to his preaching of this new religion in 68 CE. There is little to prove or disprove this, but Romila Thapar in the Penguin *History of India* says that, considering the level of communication at this time between the Mediterranean and India, 'it is not beyond belief' that one of Christ's disciples reached India.

Certainly, when the Portuguese arrived in 1498, they found a good-sized 'Syrian Orthodox' Christian community had developed. According to John Webster, in *The Dalit Christians*, this church functioned rather like a caste, and did not try to evangelise others, particularly the Dalits. It did however enter into communion with Rome in 1599, though later broke away again. The Roman Catholic Portuguese brought in religious orders to evangelise the Hindus and Muslims. They did win some converts from among the Dalits, but found difficulty in integrating them into the Syrian community.

The Portuguese sought vigorously to convert the brahmins. To deprive them of their power they even destroyed the Hindu temples. In an essay in *Emerging Dalit Theology* Fr Poornam Damel SJ says that only brahmins were taught catechism, creed and Bible, other converts were taught simply devotion. The Roman Catholic authorities instigated a law which said only brahmins could become priests, and this remained until the early twentieth century. Castes were separated at worship, and Damel notes that in a papal bull in 1624 'Pope Gregory XV approved of this caste-based approach to conversion.' John Webster observes that the Catholics, viewing caste 'not as a religious but as a social institution... chose to work within the caste system'. The Catholic view was that the separation of castes was required to avoid defections, 'and save their souls'. This policy did offer some gains, but at a high price.

In the early seventeenth century the Jesuit Roberto de Nobili appeared in Tamilnadu in southern India, and he not only allowed distinctions between the castes within the church but encouraged them. In de Nobili's defence it should be said that he learned the Tamil language and in many ways lived as a Tamil, but his 'inculturation' went as far as adopting the caste system - which raises interesting questions about 'the Gospel and culture'. The Jesuit writer M.R. Arulraja is deeply critical of the casteism of de Nobili, and official Roman Catholicism which backed him. Damel's view is that 'in the aspect of caste, Christianity has been conquered by Hindu culture'.

The first Protestant missionary initiative in India began in the Danish settlement at Tranquebar in 1706. Anglican societies, the Society for the Promotion of Christian Knowledge (SPCK) and the Society for the Propagation of the Gospel (SPG), followed then later the Church Missionary Society (CMS) and others. By and large, says Damel, 'all these missions waged a relentless war on caste', which often meant converts from the higher castes left the church. Protestant mission work began in earnest with the arrival of the Baptist William Carey in 1793 and he actively opposed casteism. He wrote to his sister that year that 'caste is one of the strongest bonds the devil used to bind the souls of men and dreadfully effective it is indeed'. Then in 1847 when two candidates for Methodist ordination refused to renounce caste observance, the District Synod recommended their dismissal and unanimously agreed, according to church records, that no-one should be baptised until they could demonstrate that they had renounced caste, and 'no person holding caste in any respect shall be' either a member or employed in the church.

Hence the early Protestant churches contained a wide variety of people. The Protestant missionaries viewed caste as a Hindu religious institution, Webster says they chose to reject it and 'replace it with something better, probably a class system'. Duncan Forrester's *Caste and Christianity* (1980) suggests there was a consensus not only condemning casteism but seeking to remove it from the churches. Webster says missionaries also took an active role on behalf of Dalit converts to get some of the caste prohibitions lifted, eg. the use of public roads and public wells, and (in the South) women being allowed to cover their breasts. Swami Theertha also draws attention to this action. He says that when the outcaste Christian women influenced by the London Missionary Society (LMS) began to wear the upper cloth like the high caste ladies in the Madras area it created much conflict between the high caste Hindus and the Christians. The local State Government 'ordered that the old practice should not be altered', however the Governor Sir Charles Trevelyan addressed a strong appeal to the Maharajah who eventually backed down. One result of the Christian support for covering the breast, says Theertha, was that Travancore, one of the most orthodox Hindu states, 'became more Christian than any other part of India'.

Andrew Wingate describes the opposition to caste in his research thesis *The Church and Conversion* (1997), part of which explores missionary attitudes and effectiveness during the twentieth century in Andhra Pradesh. In a survey of the American Arcot Mission between 1907 and 1948 he reports the Mission's belief that caste is 'the greatest obstacle Christianity has ever had to overcome' but despite the difficulties especially of 'upper-caste' conversion he says that 'throughout, the renunciation of caste in the convert was insisted upon'. Wingate taught theology at the Tamilnadu Theological Seminary in Madurai between 1975 and 1982, and also spent time in many villages. He returned twice and in 1997 published his thesis which examines in some detail the group conversions of village Dalits in Tamilnadu and Andhra Pradesh, and the individual conversions of caste people. He lists the causes of the conversions under the general headings of psychological, socio-politico-economic, cultural/ecclesiastical and theological. The overall theme is one of liberation. Brian Stanley in his *History of the Baptist Missionary Society 1872-1992* also comments on the importance of the economic factor in conversion.

There are various explanations of why Protestantism challenged caste in a way Roman Catholicism did not. Franklyn Balasunderam, in *Dalits and Christian Mission*, agrees with historians like G.A. Oddie, James Alter and Max Warren, that it was because many nineteenth century Protestant missionaries came with a heritage of social activism. They preached a whole Gospel and had fought for religious liberty and supported the struggle against slavery. They were influenced by the Industrial Revolution, the Evangelical Revival and the French Revolution. While they came with a zeal to convert the 'heathen', says Balasunderam, they also got involved 'with the attempts to improve the condition of the downtrodden..... namely, the Dalits'.

It may have been these efforts to reject casteism, and all it stood for, which led to the Dalit **mass movements**, sometimes called 'group' or 'people's movements', or more recently 'movements of the spirit', an extremely significant phenomenon in India's Christian history. These began in the 1860s and 1870s, in different parts of India, and resulted in such large numbers of converts that the missionaries really did not know what to do with them. It was in fact, says Webster, 'the Dalits, not the missionaries, who took the initiative in launching the mass movements'. A major missionary conference in Bombay in 1892 asked whether these movements were the work of God, but so many missionaries already believed they were that from then on the histories certainly of the Protestant churches and of the Dalit movement became almost inextricably entwined.

Webster states that one of the first movements began among the Mala people in the north-central State of Andhra Pradesh in the 1840s, in an area where the London Missionary Society was working. It was followed by more mass conversions in CMS and Lutheran areas. Then in the northern State of Uttar Pradesh in 1859 a community of Mazhabi Sikhs approached Methodist missionaries and over a twenty-year period all became Christians. The first major mass movement in the Punjab, among the Chura sub-caste, began in the 1870s and continued through to the 1920s. The Indian Christian population there grew from about 4,000 in 1881 to nearly 400,000 in 1931. There was much activity in Uttar Pradesh (UP) among the Bhangi and Chamra people in the 1880s and 1890s, and by 1931 there were 173,000 Christians in UP, mostly Dalits. Further mass movements occurred among Mala Methodists in the 1880s and 1890s and in the Anglican Diocese of Dornakal in the 1920s and 1930s. Overall, due to these movements, Webster states that India's Christian population grew from one and a half million in 1881 to over six million fifty years later.

Dalit historians are gradually uncovering stories of some of these early Dalit Christian leaders. In *Frontiers of Dalit Theology*, a collection of the Papers delivered at the Gurukul Lutheran Theological College Summer School in Madras in 1996 (and afterwards known as *Frontiers*), Shanti Sudha Monica recounts the development of the Baptist Mission in south India between 1835 and 1880, one pioneer of which was Yerraguntala Periah, a Madiga from that area. The first outside missionary had arrived from the United States in 1835, thirty years later there were only 36 converts and the work was almost abandoned. However a previous missionary, Jewett, returned in 1865, along with a new couple, the Cloughs, to the Ongole compound for a last try. Periah was a seeker after a new religion, a new faith, and a distant relative who had already converted had

20

taken him to meet Jewett. He spent four years pondering over Christianity before he - and his wife - were persuaded. They were baptised in 1866, the 37th and 38th converts.

The missionaries, according to Monica, were not really aware of the Indian social system, for example the village self-government and the individual's total dependence on family and community. Also, the converts had no freedom to return to their families and villages. Periah however insisted on going back to his village. He then brought converts to Clough, and encouraged him to come out to the villages and preach. It was this policy which led to the mission's success. The Baptist missionaries wished to develop educational work, but by now Clough was continually consulting with Periah on the way they should work, and what should be next done. Clough and Periah put three principles to their new converts - do not work on Sundays, do not eat carrion (as Dalits had previously done) and do not worship idols. This was a fundamental challenge to the caste system, and some persecution developed because of it. Between 1867 and 1880 about a thousand Dalit villages were contacted, and over a period many were converted en masse thus maintaining their family and community life. This was another result of the new policy. In three days in one area over 3,500 came for baptism. Monica believes Periah was the 'spiritual father' of 90,000 Baptists, and 'four fifths of the present Protestant Christian community in India... emerged out of the mass movement' which he initiated.

In *Downtrodden* James Massey tells the story of Ditt, a Chura, an untouchable sub-caste, who was born around 1843 in the Punjab, north-west India. He was lame, and came to the Revd Samuel Martin in 1872 asking for baptism. Martin did not believe Ditt was sufficiently prepared for Christian baptism, but finally decided to go ahead 'because he could see no scriptural ground for not doing so'. Instead of staying in the mission compound for further instruction Ditt wanted to return to his family. Martin reluctantly agreed. Ditt faced much opposition from his own family and village, but he persevered, and within three months brought his wife, daughter and two neighbours for baptism. For a living he bought hides, and in his travels he preached in many places. Eleven years after his baptism he had brought more than 500 converts into the church. By 1915 almost all the Dalits known as Churas in Sialkot had become Christians. Massey and others tell similar stories of how single Dalit converts, by refusing to remain within the mission compounds, ensured the spread of the Gospel.

Hence Dalits were crucial in the growth of Christianity in India, and without the 'spirit movements' of the nineteenth century it is arguable that the Christian Church would not be more than an elite irrelevance today. There are some suggestions that the Dalits were looking simply for an escape from 'untouchability', but the best analysis suggests it was more than this. True, some of the missionaries offered food, especially during shortages. They also offered education. But most of all many Protestant missionaries in particular offered recognition, acceptance and human dignity.

The story of *Ayyankali*, the First Dalit Leader, about a Dalit born in Kerala in south-west India in 1863, reported in *Nationalism* by Aloysius but also in a pamphlet of this name, provides a further illustration. T.H.P. Chentarassery published the pamphlet in 1996, and in the introduction quotes Swami Vivekananda who in 1897 said after visiting Kerala - probably the most 'Christian' of Indian States - that he had not seen such wickedness anywhere else. 'The poor Paraiyar (pariah-Dalits) cannot walk through the street' where the 'higher' castes walk. The condition of the Dalits was pitiable according to Chentarassery, they were 'agricultural instruments' in the hands of their masters and their children were 'also trained from an early age for the same work'. Their dwellings were miserable huts, their clothing a piece of cloth tied around them; the women were not allowed to cover their bodies above the waist, they were treated as slaves and not allowed to worship in the Hindu temples.

Ayyankali grew up in this situation. He was enthusiastic, bright and enjoyed sports and games. One day, playing with caste youngsters, their football went over the fence of an upper-caste neighbour. The owner was enraged and scolded Ayyangali, telling him he would be in serious trouble if he ever played again with boys of a higher caste. Ayyangali was furious in his turn, he left the scene 'with a firm determination which... shaped the future history of Kerala'. As he grew, Ayyankali saw that education and employment away from the villages was essential.

Chentarassery says that disappointed Dalits, being denied the basic right of education, 'sought the camps of Christian missionaries, embracing the new religion'. This was not, however, simply on the basis of faith, 'but also as a protest against the codes of the Hindus' which were so destructive for Dalits. Hence the motives of the Dalits were mixed, partly faith, partly the desperation for something better, for a recognition of their humanity. Perhaps, in the true practice of Christianity, it is not possible to separate the two.

Dr B.R. Ambedkar (see next section) provides some interesting reflections on the relationship of the missionaries to Dalit aspirations. His views are analysed in a Paper by P. Arockiadass SJ in *Frontiers*. Ambedkar found 'great contradictions' between the teaching and practice of the Church. He attacked De Nobili's work for simply absorbing caste practice, including the prohibition on 'eating and mating' and accepting caste people for baptism just 'so long as they were ready to acknowledge Jesus as Saviour'. He was less harsh on the Protestants, although apparently unaware of the moves towards Dalit liberation initiated by some missionaries. He seems to have believed that Christianity neither helped to change the mind-set of the upper castes nor the attitude of the untouchables, 'that Missions should be so inactive in the matter of the social emancipation of the untouchable is, of course, a very sad thing'.

Ambedkar criticised the Christian missionaries 'who took so much pain to denounce idol worship' but did little to unseat the idol of caste. In conversations with Bishop Pickett, says Arockiadass, he focuses on one of the vital reasons why he (like his antagonist Gandhi) rejected Christianity. He said untouchable converts 'don't care a snap of the finger' what happens to other Dalits as long as those who have become Christians get ahead. 'Indeed their chief concern... is to hide the fact that they were in the same community.' Ambedkar believed that one of the key reasons the Christian faith failed to offer Dalits the total spiritual transformation they needed was because of the doctrine of original sin. He felt that it was a doctrine 'fraught with disaster'; instead of being taught they must tackle their false social and religious environment, people are told their fall is simply due to sin. 'The Indian Christians... are living in the laps of the missionaries, for education, for medical care... if they were dependent on the Government they would be required to mobilise, to agitate, educate and organise... for effective political action.' For without such activity no Government would bother. Says Arockiadass, 'Ambedkar's critique of the Indian church, its abominable missionary methods... its negligence of the socio-political implication of spirituality, its denominational divisions, its dependence on foreign funds, its notions on sin... are so relevant' that the church ignores them at its peril. Hence Ambedkar 'sets the new agenda for Indian theology', giving solid principles to make 'a liberating religion'. No meagre achievement for a non-Christian, and a somewhat devastating critique of the Christian missionary enterprise. For Arockiadoss it goes to prove that 'only a Dalit theology is capable of creating an authentic Church, truly Christian and totally ecumenical'.

There is an interesting 'Postscript' to Franklyn Balasunderam's *Dalits and Christian Mission*, in which he reviews the earlier part of the book which he had written over ten years before. He raises a number of questions. Did the Dalits convert to Christianity primarily for economic reasons? He believes not; conversion was an attempt to 'move up' or 'find a way out of a religion which had kept them in servitude for centuries', and what is more the Dalits had more or less to insist that they be accepted as Christians. 'Some Christian missionaries were not at all interested' in baptising large groups, especially during the famines. There was however a change in missionary attitude in the first half of the twentieth century. Although they still prized their 'caste converts', says Balasunderam, missionaries had begun to understand the Christian Gospel as 'relevant to emancipating the underdogs'.

And, how close were the missionaries to the colonialists? Some 'Third World' theologians suggest that originally their societies were thoroughly harmonious, and it was colonialism and the missionaries which disrupted them. Others imply that it was good that missionaries offered conversion but unfortunate that they treated people as 'objects of charity'. Balasunderam believes that, although the missionary movement was 'individualistic, dichotomic and other-worldly', it did bring to India the Gospel of Jesus. He goes on to say that the dedication of the London Missionary Society Christians in particular to the uplifting of the Dalits could not be disputed. These missionaries operated as if they were involved in 'God's Mission of strengthening the Kingdom of God in the here and now'. They started technical training, orphanages, co-operative banks and community schools. They showed that God's mission is directed to the underdog, it is now the Christian task at the threshold of the new millennium to 'forge solidarity with all forces which stand for humanisation of Dalits' and all those like them. If we are to learn today from the best of the missionary enterprise it will mean solidarity with the poor, the underdog, and challenging the 'upper castes', the rich and powerful of our world.

f) Indian perspectives - Gandhi and Ambedkar

Let us now take a brief look at how some of the Indian leadership has dealt with casteism during this century. There could be an argument over who has been the most influential Indian leader over this period. Many would argue it was Mohandas K. Gandhi, others would say Jawaharlal Nehru, a few might even suggest Nehru's father Motilal, or even his daughter Indira. Hardly anyone, at least from Britain, would mention Bheemrao Ramji Ambedkar, the father of India's Constitution. Ambedkar was a Dalit, Gandhi a vaishya, the Nehrus were brahmins.

Jawaharlal, says A.K. Akbar in Nehru: *the Making of India*, was by religion, as a Kashmiri Pandit, 'the epitome of the Hindu caste system'. He was both brahmin and meat-eater, a man Hindus and Muslims could trust. His father Motilal communicated to him an opposition to casteism, especially the tradition of separate dining. Apparently Motilal's eldest brother would not even allow his own children to be present when he ate so Motilal as a lawyer started taking his meals actually in public, at the High Court! Nevertheless, some years after his birth in 1889, he ensured his son underwent the 'thread ceremony', the second birth of the brahmin. Akbar says Jawaharlal preferred his father's intellect to his mother's traditional faith, but he took religion seriously, understanding its hold on people's imagination. He often expressed his contempt for dogma and communalism, but never renounced his caste status term of 'Panditji'.

Although Nehru's sisters married outside their caste community - which was not just brahmin but Kashmiri brahmin - until then their caste and family marriage system had normally operated quite rigidly. It was not simply religion, according to Akbar, but 'the more powerful instinct of race'. The identity of the fair-skinned brahmins, the sharp nose, the Aryan features had to be maintained. 'It was a small and proud community, in a vast Indian sea.' However there is little mention of caste in the rest of Akbar's nearly 600-page biography, suggesting that it was of no great import for Nehru, although in fairness it should be said that he had much to deal with in seeking to hold the religious communities together. It was the Hindu-Muslim divide which most threatened the unity of India, and ultimately in the wider sense destroyed it.

M.K. Gandhi was born a little before Nehru, in 1869. He spent some of his formative years in South Africa. Even before then however, according to a biographical essay by a Jesuit, Father Susai, in *Emerging Dalit Theology* he had challenged the evils of untouchability. An untouchable 'scavenger' used to come to clean the family latrines, Gandhi complained to his mother that untouchability was not sanctioned by religion. Susai says that on his return from South Africa Gandhi initially took a conservative view of caste, advising only patient reform. By 1920 he seemed to change his views somewhat. He decided untouchability was a great social evil, in his magazine he described it as 'a crime against God and man'. He said it has 'oppressed as nothing else in Hinduism has', and rejected any 'scriptural authority' for it.

Gandhi viewed caste as an essentially religious phenomenon but failed to separate it from the practices of untouchability. He sought to challenge the latter on the basis that all are equal before God, God does not treat some as untouchable while others are not and untouchability was inconsistent with true spirituality. India could not obtain its freedom without eradicating it, how could the British be asked to go while the dreadful treatment of untouchables continued? Gandhi focused his attack on the temples, stating that God would not exist within the temples until the untouchables were allowed in. He renamed the untouchables 'harijans', although as noted above he did not consult them first, and the name was not without its problems. He was delighted when the Maharajah of Travancore, in south-west India, declared that the temples in his state were open to all. Gandhi said that in any reincarnation he would wish to be an untouchable, and was himself barred from many temples for his views.

Dalits believe however that Gandhi was unable to escape from his own casteism, he miscalculated the depth of the caste culture, and how integrated it was with Hinduism. This resulted in a failure to consult with the leaders of the untouchables themselves, especially Ambedkar. He also failed to criticise sufficiently the culture of privilege and self-esteem of the 'upper castes'. He believed the caste system as based on occupation could be maintained, while cleansing untouchability from Hinduism. His critics do not. Unless the law of **varna**, or caste, is removed, they say, untouchability will remain, take it away and Hinduism crumbles. Susai is more sympathetic to Gandhi than many of today's Dalits. He believes Gandhi was a guide and friend to those wishing to destroy casteism. Many however feel Gandhi failed to use his considerable prestige to tackle the root of the problem, rather than simply its various manifestations.

By far the most important leader as far as Dalits are concerned is Dr Bheemrao Ramji Ambedkar. He was born on April 14th 1891 in a village in the Konkan area of Maharashtra. He was a fourteenth child and belonged to the Sakbal Mahar caste, believed to be one of the original inhabitants in that area. His father and grandfather had both served in the British Army, the former was a religious man and taught young Bheemrao the same way of life. He learned about untouchability very young, at school, where his books or belongings would not be touched by caste children. His mother died and his father moved some distance away for work. Once when Bheemrao and his brother went to visit their father, after getting a ride on a bullock cart the driver discovered they were untouchables and tipped them off into the road. Although it was late they could not even get a drink and one of Ambedkar's biographers V. Chandra Mowli says, 'that very day (Ambedkar) determined to dedicate his whole life to the eradication of untouchability'.

Ambedkar was a bright student, he was fortunate in some of the teachers who were responsible for him who even though brahmin gave him much advice and support. It was from one of them he took the name 'Ambedkar'. Some parts of India were still ruled by Maharajahs and princes and another of Ambedkar's teachers recommended him to the Maharajah of Baroda, who gave him a scholarship for his studies at Elphinstone College, Mumbai. He obtained his BA in 1912, and was appointed to the Maharajah's service. The caste people in Baroda however made his life a misery and before long he left. He obtained further help from the Maharajah to study at Columbia University, New York, and subsequently took a PhD at the London School of Economics on *The Problem of the Rupee*. In London, Mowli tells us, Ambedkar spent much of his time in the British Museum, being first to arrive and sometimes having to be physically removed at the day's end. He lived in cheap lodgings, ate chips and bread for supper and spent all his money on books.

In 1917 Ambedkar returned to Baroda and was made Minister of Finance. Chowli says such a thing was unheard of and created a ferocious reaction from the caste people. His civil servants would not touch anything that he had touched, they dropped his papers on the desk and refused to pick them up again. They poured out water for him without ever touching his glass. Finally the house where he was staying was attacked and Ambedkar fled for his life. He returned to Mumbai where a friend gave him an office job, but he soon grew tired and applied to become professor of economics at Sydenham College, Mumbai. Despite some objections from the students he won them over, but felt the call to study further and went back to London. He obtained an MSc, then studied law and became a barrister. He returned to Mumbai, started up a law practice, developed a legal aid system and created a number of community projects for young Dalits. In 1926 the Governor of Mumbai appointed him to the state legislature, and Ambedkar's political career had begun. He was to be the greatest single influence on Dalit people until he died thirty years later, and is still the intellectual and activist to whom Dalit leaders turn today.

Ambedkar and Gandhi clashed head-to-head over their different approaches in the run-up to the elections leading to Indian independence. They were both delegates to the three Round-table Conferences in London called to discuss independence. Ambedkar submitted a scheme for the protection of untouchables in an independent India. He commented about Gandhi, who was representing the Indian Congress Party, that 'Mr Gandhi presents himself as a man full of humility. But...(he) can be very petty-minded... he treated the whole non-Congress delegation with contempt.' Ambedkar wanted a separate electorate for Dalits, Gandhi opposed this utterly. His argument was that the untouchables were not organised, they would be threatened and manipulated by other castes and never escape their untouchability. He stated 'I claim myself in my own person to represent the vast mass of the Untouchables... those who speak of the political rights of the untouchables do not know their India', a statement somewhat insulting to Ambedkar.

A view common among Dalits is that Gandhi did not want a split in Hinduism as elections approached as that might have benefited the Muslim parties. In 1932 after Ramsay Macdonald, the British Prime Minister, agreed a form of separate electorate, Gandhi started a fast to death. In *What Gandhi and the Congress have done to the Untouchables* Ambedkar recounts his predicament, 'no man was placed in a greater or graver dilemma than I. There was before me the duty to save Gandhi from sure death... (over against) the saving for the Untouchables the political rights which the Prime Minister had given them.' He remarks that he 'saved the life of Mr Gandhi' by agreeing to a compromise. This may have been one occasion when Gandhi did not command the moral high ground as did his later fasts against inter-communal violence. It would have been political suicide - even personally dangerous - for Ambedkar to have had any responsibility for the death of Gandhi, so he accepted the so-called 'Poona Pact', winning extra seats for the Dalits but without a separate electorate. Later Ambedkar was to write scathingly that the laws of caste and karma were 'veritable instruments of torture' which Hinduism has used against Dalits. These instruments had 'mutilated, blasted and blighted' Dalit life and were to be found 'intact and untarnished in the bosom of Gandhi'.

In 1935 Ambedkar announced that Dalits would leave the Hindu religion and find another, and finally he and several thousand others converted to Buddhism in October 1956. In the meantime he had set up the Independent Labour Party of India, become a member of the Governor-General's Executive Council, written an enormous number of essays and books, joined Nehru's first cabinet, resigned over the Hindu Code Bill, and lost two elections. In 1956, shortly before he embraced Buddhism, Ambedkar initiated a new party - the Republican Party - but died in December that year, aged 65, before the Party could be launched. It was officially established the next year, but subsequently split, and has been plagued by divisions ever since.

Gail Omvedt, who has lived in a village in south Maharshtra since 1979, has been researching issues of caste, class and gender in India for over twenty years. Writing mainly about the central states of India, she describes the emergence of the Dalit movement in the early decades of the twentieth century. By 1930 some Dalits had established a sense of identity, and were left with two choices, a radical assertion of autonomy from Hinduism, or a re-absorption into it, usually via the 'bhakti' devotional movement. Both led on to other choices, the former for example to take up Gandhi's approach of the idealised caste-free village structure or the communist goal of a 'classless industrialised socialism'. These required analysis as to their present situation and who might be their allies - the Muslims, Nehru's Congress Party, the British? It also required an ideology, a basis of understanding their situation and belief as to how it might be changed. According to Omvedt, Ambedkar provided the ideology and the leadership of the emerging Dalit movement.

Ambedkar was a powerful mind, and a profound intellectual, and provided the Dalit people and their supporters with enormous resources for the liberation struggle. His thinking needs to be drawn on by any, inside or outside India, who wish to understand casteism and offer solidarity to the Dalit people. We shall consider his contribution further in a later chapter but first, remembering that although casteism may be declining in urban areas that the vast majority of Indians live in villages, how does it manifest itself in contemporary India?

2 THE STRUCTURES OF DISCRIMINATION

Arriving with a group of Dalit and non-Dalit church and community workers in the village of Kukkarajupalle in Andhra Pradesh our jeep stopped outside the 'tea-shop' in the caste part of the village. There was no 'olde worlde' frontage, with the china crockery and wooden floors and furniture beloved by habitues of such establishments in rural England. The shop consisted of a small area in front of a one-storey house, under a thatched roof, with a stone bench against the house-wall and a pan heating water on a stone shelf next to the doorway. It provided some kind of centre to the village, a small general store stood nearby and a number of the locals were chatting along the rutted, baked-earth 'high street'.

Our arrival caused some interest, and villagers gathered to watch, Two of my colleagues invited me into the 'shop', to sit with them on the bench. I was aware they were Dalits, and normally Dalits were not allowed to take such seats, but these were confident Dalits of the new generation, and they were not about to subject themselves to the villagers' caste rules. We sat and chatted with the onlookers, though I sensed some tension in the air, especially when I got up to take a photograph. I had been briefed by the group to look for the 'Dalit glass', a glass or metal tumbler which would be located fairly surreptitiously somewhere accessible to the outside of the building. If a Dalit wished to take tea, he or she would come to the outside wall, take the glass, wash it if it were dirty and offer it to be filled by the shopowner.

I was able, in apparent innocence, to include the Dalit glass on my photo. My companions said the caste people would have noticed, and the glass would have disappeared by their next visit. After all such practices had been against the law for decades. Whether it would return remained to be seen. It all felt much like black people in north America or Africans under apartheid going to outside hatches and doorways in the cafes and restaurants of the old South or pre-1990 Johannesburg. The main difference was that here you could not tell people apart, the appearance of caste and Dalit Indian is more or less the same. One vital point to make here is that, although there is an increasing flow from village to city in India, the vast majority of the people remain in villages, and it is what goes on in villages that affects most Indian lives.

Examples of caste practices have appeared already in this book and the issues are also illustrated in the 'Stories' which are interspersed with the

30

sections in this chapter. These are intended to be generally informative rather than specifically illustrative. Some are told in the first person, others more objectively. I shall now identify the patterns and structures of discrimination as they penetrate into every part of Indian society, even the mind. A key source is *The Plight of Dalit Christians* (1997) by Godwin Shiri, Associate Director of the Christian Institute for the Study of Religion and Society, who is not himself a Dalit, but with whom I had an interview in Bangalore where he is based. Shiri was inspired to write the book to provide the evidence of widespread discrimination against Christian Dalits which the judge in the notorious Soosai case said was non-existent. Soosai was a Christian cobbler who was denied the Government assistance for training and obtaining premises received by his fellow non-Christian Dalit cobblers.

Shiri and his colleagues undertook a detailed study of 44 villages on the borders of the two central Indian States of Karnataka and Andhra Pradesh. The villages varied between a few hundred and several thousand inhabitants, and contained between two and 150 Christian families. The method of data collection was largely through field-workers with questionnaires containing over 80 carefully-chosen queries, but follow-up meetings were also held. The area in which the study took place had been a mission field of the London Missionary Society since 1810. It had experienced a century of very slow growth partly due to missionary suspicion about any mass conversion of Dalit 'rice Christians', but when one particular missionary championed a group of oppressed Dalits, this became a turning point and, says Shiri, between the 1920s and 1950s the church 'registered a phenomenal growth with the mass-conversion of Dalits'. In this chapter I have divided the areas of discrimination somewhat arbitrarily into five - social, economic, political and religio-cultural, plus the additional and particular category of discrimination against women.

a)   Social

i)   Access to services

Godwin Shiri lists a number of social restrictions experienced by Dalits, including exclusion from village tea-shops, unavailability of barbers and washermen (or dhobis) and non-admittance to village shops. He found that in 93% of the 44 villages Dalits were refused access to tea-shops, in 91% to barbers, in 98% to dhobis and in 91% to village shops. Barbers and dhobis, themselves poor, were unable to extend their trade to Dalits because if they did so the caste people of the village withdrew trade from them. Christian Dalits had to go to villages or towns where they were not known to get their hair cut. Tailors also did not wish to work for Dalits, but would do so if the cloth they brought was brand new.

In the village stores, where of course they paid the same prices as anyone else, Dalits were expected to follow unwritten rules. They had to keep their distance from caste people and wait till they had finished their purchases, and they should neither touch potential purchases nor question the price. Dalits did not always follow these rules, but when they broke them they were subjected to casteist abuse from the owner. Even in the Government ration-shops nearly two fifths of the Dalits felt unwelcome and faced insults. Strangely however, because Dalits were the local slaughterers, the local caste people who ate meat were quite happy to buy from Dalits. They were also usually welcome in the liquor shops where, says Shiri, one can often see 'a Christian Dalit and a beda (higher caste person) engaged in animated conversation while enjoying their drinks... (afterwards) the caste culture crops up again and the non-Dalit stands apart...'.

Health is another sector where Dalits do not get equal access. In Shiri's survey the Dalits expressed 'total disappointment' over Government clinics and hospitals. In most villages they have either become defunct or places of 'rampant corruption'. Not one village containing Christian Dalits had a good word to say for Government health centres and because of casteism they could not get any treatment at the hospitals. Michael Mahar in his essay on a north Indian village in The Untouchables in Contemporary India tells a story of a Dalit who went to a city hospital for treatment for tuberculosis and returned three days later distraught as no-one had offered to help him. His caste employer cursed both the callous city-dwellers and the Dalit's stupidity and next day took him back to the hospital, marched up to the Admissions desk, guided his employee through the bureaucracy and left him for his treatment while he went off to 'see the sights'.

Roads are another 'public service' from which Dalits can be excluded. In Chentharassey's pamphlet on Ayyankali he describes how the Dalit leader bought a cart and two bullocks and drove them down the street, to the fury of his caste opponents. They issued all kinds of threats, but he ignored them and helped to open the roads to his fellow Dalits. Even if Dalits can walk the village streets they may be forbidden the use of sandals. This is the reason why urban churches in 'twinning arrangements' with Dalit communities are sometimes encouraged to give a pair of sandals to each Dalit, as an invitation freely to use the public roads.

Often the whole Dalit section of the village is separate from the caste section, and usually on the side furthest from the main route into the village. Thus the caste people are able to monitor who goes through into the Dalit section of the village. This is related to a wider problem of Dalits not being expected in certain areas of the village, they should always walk round rather than through the caste section. In the village of Kukkarajupalle referred to above, after our visit to the tea-shop we had to drive another kilometre or more past the well-watered fields of the caste people to the parched Dalit section.

ii) Access to local decision-making

Many of those who work with Dalits comment about the way Dalits are always excluded from participation in making decisions, whether in local communities, churches or at Government-level. When they are present, they are almost always tied in some way to caste people. In the villages this takes the form of Dalits not being expected to sit with the caste people, but either to stand or have their own sitting area a little distant. They should not go near the temple, and if they attend a village play and want - as is customary - to garland the actors they must do it through a non-Dalit middleman.

More importantly they are hindered from exercising their rights to be elected or to sit on the 'panchayat', the village council on which they quite often have reserved seats and sometimes even hold the chair. I was told of one village where, due to the reservation system, the panchayat Chair was to be a Dalit woman. When she took up her position she was largely ignored by the caste members of the council who more or less carried on as if she were not there. Eventually a decision was made about which she objected. Other Dalits supported her in taking the issue to the District sub-controller and the panchayat was informed it was unable to proceed without the Chair's agreement. After a further period of resistance the caste people caved in, at least on this occasion.

This problem can extend to Dalits going to raise problems with officials. Partly to undermine their confidence they are often not asked to sit down. One Dalit community activist told me, half amused and half angry, of visiting a petty bureaucrat who he had known almost as a friend for some years. The man was a member of a sudra sub-caste and kept his visitor standing in his office saying, 'I am sorry I don't have a chair to offer you', even though there were plenty of chairs accessible quite close by. 'If he had given me a seat', said the activist, 'he would have been attacked for it by his colleagues when I'd gone.'

iii)   Eating and mating

In many ways these are the heart of social caste discrimination. There are a whole range of customs around food which preclude Dalits from eating with non-Dalits, or even offering them food. M.R. Arulraja opens his book *Jesus the Dalit* with a vignette of a hungry aid worker arriving at a village reported badly damaged by a cyclone. Meeting four youths outside a partly ruined house he asks for water. They want to know who he is visiting here, but being assured he has no relatives locally they give him a drink. When he asks for food however they say they would love to share their food but insist on knowing his caste. When he says he does not believe in caste they say they are happy to hear that. They offer him a cigarette but point out that if he is not an untouchable and they feed him, the caste people 'will beat us to pulp for having offered you food'.

Godwin Shiri says that inter-dining between Dalit and non-Dalit Christians in his research area was totally non-existent. 'Non-Dalits consider it highly polluting or an anathema to eat or drink anything which is prepared or offered by Christian Dalits.' Where relationships are good non-Dalits might attend a Dalit wedding reception but would not consume any cooked food. In some case Dalits act as servants to non-Dalits, but are forbidden from entering the house; all the work has to be brought out to them. In some cases where the pastors are Dalits they may be invited into the homes of Christian non-Dalits, but 'how cordially they receive them is a different question'.

The reasons for this may be several. For Dalits food is simply a means of survival. As Kancha Ilaiah says, Dalits eat to live. Caste people on the other hand have a different perspective. The idea of eating to live, says Ilaiah 'is exactly the opposite of the brahminical notions of living to eat'. The Dalit gods and goddesses do not require one tenth of the ritual the brahminical gods require. There is always a wide range of foods offered to the brahmin Gods, which is more indicative of what the caste people want to eat, and can afford, than of any known desire of the gods.

Caste inter-marriage is still extremely rare, even sub-caste inter-marriage is uncommon. Bas Wielenga of Tamilnadu Theological Seminary (TTS) says this is primarily about the preservation of control by the upper castes.

If they began to inter-marry their hegemony over land and property would start to be eroded. Wielenga's analysis draws attention to the linkage between patriarchy, caste and class and points out that it is this connection which links kinship with control of resources. Even where intermarriage is beginning to happen patriarchy dictates that the woman takes on the man's caste, so the control may be retained. Wielanga points out that, quite early in his career, Ambedkar seized upon the key strategy of promoting inter-marriage as the best way to try to break down the caste system.

Godwin Shiri reports that in his survey of thousands of Christian Dalits in 44 villages there was no inter-marriage whatever. Non-Dalit Christians would much prefer to find a bride or groom for their son or daughter from the non-Dalit Hindu or Muslim urban communities. Phiri comments that the number of such inter-religious marriages is responsible for the large number of non-Dalit Christians permanently migrating to the cities. John Webster quotes a 1959 study including Christians in the Hyderabad area showing that inter-religious marriages within caste were quite frequent while inter-caste marriages between Christians were extremely rare.

There are many 'Romeo and Juliet' stories about cross-caste love affairs. Paul Divakar tells of a police raid on a Dalit village to collect information on a man who was reported to have fallen in love with a caste girl, because the two of them had disappeared. The police beat up Dalit young people to get information but cannot find the couple. Eventually they get married, but it takes the girl's parents a very long time to accept the husband. Godwin Shiri has a less happy story of a bitter feud in one congregation where the son of the local pastor, a Dalit, and a Christian girl of a Sudra sub-caste had fallen in love. There was furious opposition to any marriage from the girl's parents, and finally they were able to break up the relationship and marry their daughter off to a Christian boy at their own caste level.

Attitudes are gradually changing. Urmila Pawar in *Crossroads* says that Dalit boys in particular are keen to marry caste girls. Dalit families are proud of such relationships and happy for a marriage to take place. Dalit girls however are less positive, fearing that they will be treated as inferior and their lower status will be constantly dragged up by the boy's family. The girls feel they should be offered some protection by the Dalit movements but, as we shall see later, there are few women in these movements in positions of influence. It appears that, in urban areas, inter-marriage is likely slowly to increase. This is less likely to happen in the villages, or the Christian Church either.

iv)   Housing

The separation of the castes within villages is a common features of rural life in India. The Dalits are usually found at the most inaccessible parts and where there is little water or the land is subject to flooding. Balasunderam says that as a rule 'the Dalits lived outside the villages in miserable hovels, filthy to the last degree and surrounded by filth'. The Dalit areas are known as 'colonies' or 'keris' and Shiri demonstrates by a series of sketch maps how the Dalit keris are almost always on the village extremities. The caste people's temples and the mosques are also near the centre, whereas the Dalit temples and churches are at the edges.

Shiri found that 95% of the Christian Dalits in the area he studied lived in huts, while 5% lived in cemented or tiled houses. The huts are one-room structures with mud walls and roofing which is thatched or mud and wood. They have one door and no windows. One corner is a kitchen and the animals may also be tethered within the one room. There is little ventilation and this leads to disease. An outside corner may be used for washing but for natural functions people just go to the fields. Some Dalit households have married children resident also, making them even more overcrowded.

In Shiri's survey two-thirds owned their huts, while a quarter lived on land given by the Government. The rest live on land owned by other people. Only 14% had electricity, in nearly half of the villages he studied none of the Christian Dalit households had electricity. Dalits also have to be careful when it comes to harvesting the trees around their huts. In Kukkarajupalle, where I visited the tea-shop, tamarind trees surrounded the centre of the colony, but they belonged to the caste people and villagers found taking the pods would be beaten.

According to Kancha Ilaiah renting in the cities is no different. Even for 'Dalitbahujans' who are doctors, engineers, civil servants or professors houses or rooms cannot be rented in caste areas. Landlords put up signs saying rental is only for vegetarians, vegetarian being a synonym for brahmin. If Dalits build houses in these neighbourhoods, such houses are 'culturally isolated', even contact among children is discouraged. Ilaiah says one only needs to listen to the experiences of those who have built such houses 'to perceive the nature and extent of casteism in urban centres'.

The *Dalit International Newsletter* of February 1999 reports on cases of corruption in housing in central India which are symbolic of a much wider problem. Of 64 houses in the district of Allagurdam sanctioned and paid for by the authorities in 1984, four caved in, 13 are in very bad condition, four were never completed and six were built but never allocated. The contractor never completed the water or electricity supplies. In the Vemsoor area 360 of the 798 houses the Government paid for, for Dalits and OBCs, do not exist and in several villages in the area it is farmers, landlords, businessmen and political leaders who live in ther houses which were built.

Story 1: Nazir Masih of Shahpur, Dhariwal, NW India

Nazir's father, known as Asa Mal, was born in a village in north-west India. He was a Dalit, his family had no land and were totally dependent on the upper caste landowners for work and food. As he grew up a dream came to him of owning land for his family, and he began to think about how it could be possible. He decided he would have to leave home, and go to a place where no-one knew his origins.

Asa Mal went to an area some miles away and after a struggle was able to save enough money to buy some land, but after many difficulties he lost the land and had to return home. His family had become Christian, and was encouraged by the missionaries to better themselves, but little practical help was offered. After a time he left home again to search for land.

During his search Asa met a Sikh, and became greatly impressed with the Sikh faith. Here was a religion which gave people belief in themselves, and inspired bravery and courage. Sikhs had had to fight for what they believed in, against various oppressors. He found the passage in Luke's Gospel, chapter 22, where Jesus tells the disciples to sell their cloaks for a sword, and leapt on it as justification for his new-found militancy. He put it to the Christian clergy that this was what the Gospel taught for someone in his situation, but did not receive any positive response. He distanced himself from the Christian church, and started to attend the Sikh Temple.

Around 1935 he came to the village now known as Shahpur, which had in the past suffered a plague of snakes, and was therefore unused. Asa Mal decided to settle there with his family, but the upper-caste people opposed him and tried to drive him away. He encouraged his fellow-Dalits to fight for the land. They struggled for fifty years including literally fighting, and defeating, the hired thugs of the upper castes - and finally gained ownership of 100 acres. Eventually Asa Mal went back to the Christian church, and met the missionary who had given him so little practical support in his earlier struggles. The missionary's senior officer was also present and when he heard the story reprimanded his colleague for failing the Dalits when they needed action, rather than words.

One of Nazir's uncles was the first Dalit to become a steward, after many years' service in his local church. There was only one upper-caste family in the church, and they always received Holy Communion first, so they did not have to drink from the same vessel as the 'untouchables'. The uncle 'inadvertently' started to administer communion at the 'wrong' end of the line, so the upper caste family had to receive from the chalice after some of the Dalits had done so. The family left the service in anger, and did not return for several months.

Now Nazir is the leading land-owner in his area and a head teacher in the larger village of Dhariwal, with a school of 1200 students aged 5 to 17. Some of his fellow-Dalits have taken up work in the public services. Like his father Nazir had a vision and with his fellow-Dalits - field labourers, brick-makers, animal shed cleaners and 'scavengers' (see Story 6) - initiated the 'Christian Society for Health and Education'. He donated land and a building was erected which is used as a school, a training centre for health and education, and a conference centre. It also undertakes Christian education because although there are some 100,000 Christians in the region many know little about their faith. The foundation stone was laid in 1993 by the Church of North India Moderator, Revd Dr A.C. Lal. By 1997 the Society had reached its target of 90% of children in school.

Nazir has been on the National Working Committee of Dalit Solidarity Peoples, about which we hear elsewhere in the text and which receives support from the WCC for its work.

v) Education

The origins of the education system lie in the institutions which grew up around the temples two thousands years ago. According to Romila Thapar education was the prerogative of the upper castes, opportunities even for the sudras were very infrequent. Gradually it split into theoretical knowledge, confined to the brahmins, and more practical and technical matters for the rest. Later some of the sub-castes of the kshatriyas and vaishyas developed medical or mathematical knowledge. Some of the former studied commerce, but this was considered demeaning and they were reduced to vaishya status. Education was increasingly linked to the caste system, the best sudras could hope for was technical training and for Dalits there was nothing at all.

Hence Dalits have always been discriminated against in the field of education. Chentarassery's story of Ayyankali recounts how the latter in the first decade of this century was struggling for Dalit children's access to education, and finally got a Government order passed in 1910. There was widespread protest by the caste people and eventually the Dalits had to take matters into their own hands. Ayyankali himself took a child called Panchami to the school at Orruttambalam, resulting in 'a great clash which lasted for seven days and in the end the school was burned down by the caste Hindus'. There were similar confrontations in several other villages and, says Chentarassery, 'several lives and a good amount of wealth were wiped off the face of the earth'. Such events seem to be on a par with those in the 1960s in Little Rock, Arkansas, and other cities in the US South when black students sought to gain entry to white schools and colleges.

Education is of great importance, as Godwin Shiri points out, for any hope of Dalit empowerment. Of the respondents in his survey only 30% were literate, and in only half of Christian Dalit households was anyone literate. This rises to 60% if children are excluded. More worryingly, he found a very high drop-out rate among Christian Dalit children, in some villages none were going to school at all.

Shiri says that the main cause is poverty. Christian Dalit children often start working at the age of seven or eight as cowherds, stable cleaners and house servants. In many cases 'the children were forced to engage in these jobs in settlement of old loans' which landlords had granted their parents. These could be as small as 200 rupees (£3), but due to compound interest the loan could never be paid and the situation amounted to bonded labour. Statistics presented to an Indian Social Institute seminar in Delhi in September 1997 indicated that in rural areas 38% of Dalit boys and 30% of girls stayed away from school for economic reasons. In urban areas it was 40% of boys and 20% of girls.

Another cause for absences was the poor condition of the schools. Some villages had no building at all, others had very poor ones 'with more of a resemblance to a cattle shed'. The teachers, who live in nearby towns, 'were found to be frequently and habitually absent'. All children faced these problems, Dalits faced the additional problems of casteism. Often Dalit children have to sit separately, teachers treat them indifferently and in some cases schools refuse to admit them at all. Caste culture operates in the schools, the non-Dalit children seldom mix with Dalits, says Shiri 'they even take precaution not to physically touch them'. If they do accidentally touch, 'they utter a word or two of self-purification to redeem themselves

39

from being polluted'. This humiliating situation is seldom discouraged in the schools. Under such circumstances 'the Christian Dalit children have little motivation to learn'.

Shiri points out that the London Missionary Society (LMS) originally opened 30 schools in this area but closed them due to difficulties in supervision, despite the desperate need. He is devastating about the church's failures, 'The church's almost insignificant contribution in the field of education is beyond comprehension. The church should give top priority to start schools and vocational technical schools in the area.' He criticises a proposal to relocate the one rural development project the church has.

Kancha Ilaiah writes about his own schooldays, when the teacher's attitude depended on their own caste background. Brahmin teachers hated the Dalitbahujan children, who came dirty from the fields, and were 'good for nothing'. The caste children, on the other hand, came to school washed, their hair carefully oiled and combed. They wore chappals (sandals), whereas those who fed the cattle and made the chappals from their skins have none to wear. The caste children bore the names of the Hindu scriptures, whose names were as alien as Shakespeare. Even the language in the school-books was not that of the communication and production-based society of the lower castes. Our childhoods, says Ilaiah, 'were mutilated by constant abuse and by silence... Our culture was Dalitbahujan, the culture of the school was Hindu. The gap between the two was enormous.'

Ilaiah goes onto describe how, as he progressed, education became more and more alien, 'more and more brahminical and anglicized'. The history books were full of kshatriya kings, 'we read their love stories and their war stories'. Dalits were excluded from history, in fact 'our history was no history at all'. At least in the English textbooks, says Ilaiah, there was acknowledgement of class. In the Telugu textbooks there was nothing of caste, 'the conspiracy of silence is as loud as a thunderclap'. All the teachers were upper caste and however radical and leftist they were, 'all of them kept silent about the question of caste discrimination'. Most of them considered Dalitbahujans did not deserve university places, admitting them would lower the standards of higher education in institutions which were, Ilaiah points out, 'built only by extracting the surplus generated by our own parents'.

Even when Dalit children have completed their secondary education when they return to the village they often have little choice but to become

40

agricultural labourers like the rest, which thoroughly discouraged the whole community. However when I visited the village of Mittamalapalle, as we held our evening meeting in the darkened village square two young men proudly announced they were now at college, and one young girl spent most of the time sitting under a light at the corner of the square determinedly copying into her school-book. Near Thaiyyur a small school had been started by Dalit youth who had themselves been through college. They aimed to do without Government grants as by this means they could retain their independence, and control the teaching posts in the school. Ayyankali's tradition of resistance in the field of education is alive and well.

vi)   Harassment and violence

Violence is perpetrated continuously against Dalits in Indian society, and appeared to be getting worse when the BJP were elected to power in 1998. Many Dalits would say it began when their ancestors were forced from the land three thousand years ago. Wherever Dalits resist their oppression they are likely to incur the wrath of the caste people. Stories 2 and 5 - Ayyangali and Jawarkhar - illustrate this, as does the account above of Ayyankali's battle for education.

Ajit Roy in *Crossroads* recounts chilling statistics from a report of the Commissioner for Scheduled Castes and Scheduled Tribes. Between 1981 and 1986 there were 3,139 murders, 8,501 grievous hurts, 3,998 rapes and 6,279 arson attacks against SC and ST people and the figures demonstrated a steady rise, year-on-year. Then, says Roy, just in the two States of Uttar Pradesh and Madhya Pradesh in the year April 1990 to March 1991 there were 254 Dalit murders and 373 rapes of Dalit women.

Paul Divakar, Dalit activist in Andhra Pradesh, in his Paper *Blessed are the Dalits, for theirs is the Kingdom of God* reinforces the thesis that resistance breeds reaction with his analysis of the Karamchedu massacre in AP in 1985. It arose from a Dalit woman asking an upper caste boy how he could wash his buffalo in the Dalits' drinking water pond. Her question led to a violent response by the caste people which resulted in the deaths of six Dalits from that village. The police and judiciary, according to Divakar, continually fail to support Dalit witness against marginalisation, land loss, atrocities and injustices of all kinds.

The concept of the 'dominant caste' is introduced by the Indian social scientist M.N. Srinivas from his studies of rural village life. He says it is complex, and to do with both land ownership and proportion of the population. Srinivas says that 'a caste may be said to be dominant when it preponderates numerically over the other castes, and when it also wields preponderant economic and political power. A large and powerful caste group can be more easily dominant if its position in the local caste hierarchy is not too low.' He goes on to describe how in one community he observed, where the dominant caste was okkaligas (a sudra sub-caste), when the Dalits began to refuse to beat the drums, remove dead cattle and take away dirty food-plate leaves, the Okkaligas beat them up, burned their huts and forced them to return to their 'duties'.

Godwin Shiri lists the types of harassment his villagers had to put up with - verbal abuse, physical assaults, forced labour, land-grabbing, forcible eviction, molestation and rape of women, and even mass attacks. The very language which non-Dalits use to Dalits is oppressive and demeaning, 'Christian Dalits have to address the non-Dalits with all... respectability, while... even a non-Dalit urchin can address an elderly Christian Dalit as he likes' - a dynamic depressingly similar to black-white relationships under apartheid, where 'boy' and 'girl' were often used even by white youngsters to adult Africans. Insulting twists are often added to names, especially addressed to Dalit women and there are a range of abusive slang phrases about Dalits which are in common use.

The TTS annual report for 1996 describes several examples of harassment against Dalits, from the section on the Dalit Resource Centre (DRC). It notes that there is an increasing trend towards caste riots and reports how one political party advocates attacks on Dalits who are becoming more self-assured and economically advanced. It lists acts of aggression against Dalits in Kodiyankulam, where 300 families were driven from their homes - some of which were destroyed, in Chinthalapatti, where 60 houses were damaged and 25 Dalits injured and in Kunnuvaran Kottai, where 150 Dalit families were abused and exploited. The DRC monitors caste violence, sends students out to support Dalit communities under attack and undertakes training for those who are facing abuse and violence.

In Dalit literature there are endless accounts of attacks on Dalit communities and the lack of an adequate response by the authorities. Jesuit L. Yesumarian in *Emerging Dalit Theology* (1990) tells of the events in Kil-Chembedu, a village in north Arcot in south-eastern India, where in 1987 the Dalits decided to form an association. One of them had the temerity to ride a bicycle through the village, whereupon he was beaten by the caste Hindus with chappals. On reporting the incident to the police, instead of the culprits being punished, a 'peace-talk' was arranged; the caste people subsequently reduced Dalit wages. The Dalits put up a small hut for their association, the caste people destroyed it and built a temple in its place. Two police officers were sent to the village to maintain law and order, but the caste people attacked the Dalit section beating men, women and children. Houses were looted and set ablaze, and the Dalits were scattered to other villages. When they gathered at the police station to protest and demand somewhere else to live they were loaded on to trucks and returned to Kil-Chembedu. The young Dalit leader was subsequently attacked and hospitalised, the perpetrators went totally unpunished. Yesumarian remarks that the police and judiciary are more a part of the problem than of the solution. He concludes that Dalits have to use 'all the available legal and meta-legal methods', protests, demonstrations, mass organisation and mass education. 'When the oppressors of Dalits come to know that the Dalits know their rights that will be the beginning of the Dalits' liberation.'

Knowledge of rights will avail them nothing however if the forces of law and order do not protect them. Roman Catholic priest Anthony Raj describes what he calls an 'ongoing riot' in southern Tamilnadu, where dozens were killed, among both Dalits and caste people, and houses destroyed. When supporters went to ask the Dalits if they needed food, houses or land, the simple response was 'No, we need guns.' One of the worst incidents took place in Laxmanpur Bathe in the north-east State of Bihar in December 1997 when as a result of a land dispute 61 people mostly Dalits - were killed by extreme rightists, including 27 women (8 of them pregnant) and 17 children. According to the National Crimes Records Bureau in 1997 there were 8,500 crimes reported against Dalits, including 261 murders and over 300 rapes. These were expected to top 12,000 in 1998, but they are only the reported incidents and the reality is thought to be considerably worse.

The February 1999 *Dalit International Newsletter* reported that the previous October caste violence had again broken out in southern Tamilnadu, around Ramanathapuram. The Thevar caste had called a rally to urge the repeal of the 1989 Prevention of Atrocities Act. Truck loads of Thevars en route to the rally stopped at Dalit villages and ransacked them. Two women were killed, others injured and many lost their belongings. Muslim shopkeepers, seen as Dalit allies, were also attacked. At more or less the same time the *Indian Express* reported that 48 houses were razed and ten set alight in the Dalit area of a village in southern Maharashtra. 600 caste men attacked the village after reports of a love affair between a married Dalit man and a caste woman. Damage was estimated at five million rupees. The same *Newsletter* gave an account of a Dalit youth beaten by six caste youths in Rajasthan for chewing pan in front of them at a bus stop. The police refused to register a complaint until forced to do so by the local community. The **Human Rights Watch** report *Broken People* (1999), published just as this book was completed, recounts a wide range of atrocities across the whole of the country.

Story 2: Jawarhar of the Dalit Resource Centre, Tamilnadu Theological Seminary, Madurai

I came to the Tamil Theological Seminary (TTS) some years ago, and obtained a qualification in theology. However, as a Dalit, I wanted to be involved in more practical theological work and at present I am an activist with the Dalit Resource Centre, based at the Seminary. Our focus is on youth and women, and we organise at three levels, village, town and District. We aim at the younger generation, aged 16-35, and teach them about the history of oppression in India, the development of the Dalit movement in Tamil Nadu, the work of Dalit leaders and how to use the Protection of Civil Rights and Prevention of Atrocities legislation.

We address local manifestations of discrimination against Dalits, for example use of separate glasses in village tea-shops, refusal of temple entry, denial of the use of land owned by the Dalits and low wages paid by the caste people. For tea-shops to offer separate glasses is illegal and recently we went to the District Collector (the leading local official) and the Police superintendent and listed the local villages using separate tea-glasses. We said, 'If nothing is done we are going round to all these shops to smash their tea-glasses in the street!' Then the police toured the villages, giving out warnings. Only if we threaten direct action do we get any response.

Land ownership is a big problem for Dalits. In the late nineteenth century the British gave 120,000 acres of land to Dalits in Tamil Nadu, but they still do not actually farm much of it. Often they don't even know they own it, and the caste people simply hang onto it. In 1957 Vinhoba travelled round the country, urging the caste people to give land to the Dalits. They said they would, and even gave the Dalits the title documents, but they kept using the land themselves! We got hold of the title-papers of Dalit-owned land in one of the villages where I am working, Dindigul, and have presented them to the District Collector, and the Chief Minister of the State of Tamil Nadu. If nothing happens soon we will start a hunger-strike outside the District Collector's office.

This land at Dindigul is worth about 150,000 rupees. The caste leaders came to me privately and said 'What do you want? We will give you 20,000 rupees to

44

drop this agitation.' I told them that it was not enough, so they came back and offered 50,000! I taped the conversation and took it to the District Collector, who says he will take action against them. I could have made a lot of money out of that. We organised a cycle rally of 150 youth round thirty villages, to demonstrate our determination to have the land which rightfully belongs to us. We took a petition with us, and afterwards we presented it to the District Collector. We carried sticks to advertise the fact that we would defend ourselves.

We have appealed for police protection. They say they have warned the caste people but they are really on the same side. In 1995 in Dindigul a caste person put up a tea-shop on land where there was a Dalit shrine. One of our leaders called Subramaniam made a complaint to the police. After three days the police and some upper caste people went to Subramaniam's house. They went in, and beat him so severely they killed him. Complaints were made but the police involved continued on duty. Our youth met, and organised road-blocks, involving 5,000 people altogether. Only then did the Government act, and suspend the officers concerned. Still no-one has been punished for this murder.

In another example, it has been the custom that when a death occurs in an upper caste family, a Dalit has to go and take the message of the death to family members in other villages - they are given a few drinks to do this. A child in a caste family died and a Dalit was called to take the news around. He said, respectfully, that he was ill and could they find someone else. They came to his house, beat him up and raped his wife. When he went to the police they said, 'Well it's not too serious. We'll see if they will pay you some money in settlement.' Our network found out about this, went to the village and got support there and from other villages to organise a hunger-strike to force the police to take action. The police always believe Dalits can be bought off.

There are a few Dalit police officers but they are under the control of the caste people. They can't do anything. If they step out of line they will be transferred to another station. Even non-Dalit officers who try to act fairly towards Dalits find themselves being transferred. Due to the Reservation laws 18% of the police force should be Dalits, but there are not anything like that number. The caste people come up with all kinds of excuses not to employ us.

The caste people in my area are out to get me now. Recently a friend of mine had borrowed my shawl and was waiting at a bus stop. All of a sudden he realised he was being surrounded by around a dozen men, with weapons. He jumped into a taxi and got away. I never go into the villages alone now, and I always carry a knife. I am theologically trained and would like to be ordained eventually but somehow Dalits never seem to get ordained in my diocese. My parents come from

45

a remote village and very much wanted me to be a pastor. I tell them, 'I am doing Christian work now, the same kind that Jesus did.' But they find this hard to accept. They want to see me in a cassock.

vii)   Burial and death

Even in death Dalits find themselves discriminated against. In some Christian graveyards there are separate areas for caste people and Dalits. In a few cases walls have been built between the two. In many parts of the country pressure is put on Dalits to prevent access to their burial grounds so that caste people can take them over. In villages in the north-western state of Haryana, in the central State of Andhra Pradesh and in Tamilnadu in the south I was told similar stories. Near Shahpur, in Haryana, the Dalit graveyard was surrounded by non-Dalit land, and Dalits were being threatened with beating if they crossed to visit their family graves. They were being encouraged to relocate the graveyard so the present one could be incorporated into a caste estate. 'Untouchable' land is not so untouchable it seems, if it is worth money.

Kancha Ilaiah recounts the differences between the death of Hindus and of Dalitbahujans, which arise from their differing views of the purpose of life. Life for the brahmin is simply a preparation for the death which is the passage to swarga, or heaven. The brahmin must eat all the best foods, prepared in the appropriate way. He - for the brahmin system is patriarchal must also possess a wife, to give him pleasure and provide a son. Ilaiah says that in working towards this death which is passage into the next world the brahmin needs leisure and prayer. Leisure assists in focussing the mind on acquiring eternal life and its pleasures. The brahmin consumes the food produced by the labour of lower castes for the sake of God who ensures his release from this present life. He indulges in sex to guarantee the continuation of life through progeny. Prayer legitimises this life-view and through it the brahmin establishes his hold over the rest of society. When he dies his fellow-priests pray for permanence for his soul in *swarga*. In recent times the brahmins have incorporated modern materialist comforts into this higher form of existence but their real ambition is still for permanence in the world to come.

Hence, says Ilaiah, 'those who have done little except cheating and eating in their lifetimes are made... historically important persons'. Their obituaries and photographs are published, 'newspaper advertisements have become modern methods of "upper" caste celebrations of a person's death'.

And large sums of money are spent, 'even after a Hindu dies, living Hindus go on wasting their... wealth on him'.

For Dalits life is a one-off affair, there is no concept of *swarga*. Life is related to work, and eating is necessary simply for life. Work begins before dawn, eating must wait until some work has been accomplished. Everything humans use or eat is the result of work, and that must always be recognised. Without work we cannot live; leisure and prayer are only of marginal interest to the Dalit. The Hindu priest when performing the death ceremony never concedes an equal place for a Dalit. In fact, says Ilaiah, such a death is simply a means for the priest to make money. Bodies are burnt; this means that whereas caste people sometimes retained paintings, sculptures and these days photographs of their families, Dalits disappear for ever. 'Hinduism left no stone unturned', says Ilaiah, 'to destroy the wisdom, the feelings, the images of the Dalitbahujans, while they were living and also after death'. Dalits share nothing with Hindus in life or death; this situation must be changed not by brahminising the Dalits but by Dalitising the brahmins, to take them beyond themselves into true plurality.

b)   Economic

i)   Land

Land has always been a crucial commodity in India, initially because good and fertile land was not particularly common and later because, as irrigation and fertilisers improved, the population also increased and the demand for food rose. In the sixteenth and seventeenth centuries the Mughal emperors used land to reward those who were loyal and it became a key measure of wealth. Some historians believe that the Afghan Sher Shah laid the real foundations of the Mughal empire in the 1540s. He set up an imperial administration, based it at one centre and, says Percival Spear in the Penguin *History of India*, 'embarked on that essential of traditional Indian government, a reassessment of the land-tax'. The Mughal emperors who followed including Akbar who undertook a geographical survey still used centuries later - benefitted from Sher Shah's foresight. They maintained their rule on the basis of his system until a combination of their own failures, the sallies of new pretenders and the arrival of the British changed India's face.

Clive had little opportunity or desire to tackle the question of land, and for Hastings taxing trade was of first importance. The matter was left to

Cornwallis, who arrived as Governor General in 1786. In one key area of British influence, Bihar and Bengal in the north-east, revenue had been collected through *zamindars*, a mixture of landowner and tax collector and in effect the government's rural agents. They extracted taxes from the peasants and the authorities extracted what they could from them. Cornwallis reorganised and stabilised this process but, according to Spear, he did so in a way which undermined the balance of the rural system, the result being 'stability at the price of justice and good relationships'. After the Indian Mutiny in 1857, to which the injustices of land policy may have contributed, the policy was revised. Indian landowners were treated even more as adjuncts of the administration and given certain responsibilities. This did not work well however, and the British policy of turning land into a commodity for sale and thus failing to enforce its fairer distribution contributed to the parlous state of the Dalits when independence eventually arrived.

Sitting down with Dalit villagers and asking them what are their main problems, land will always be mentioned. Either they have poor land, stony or dry, or they have too little decent land, or they have none at all. In Kukkarajupalle they pointed to their largest piece of land in the distance, on high, rocky ground beyond the area owned by the caste people, more fertile because the water drains down into it. They told how, when the caste people discovered they were learning to conserve the water on the higher land, they tried to prevent them taking their animals up to graze. The agricultural union however stepped in, urging the district authorities to ensure the right of way. The union was also helping the women with their thrift and credit scheme, perhaps to buy the extra animals which more fertile grazing land would support.

The lack of union or other institutional support often leads to Dalits being either prevented from using their land or even losing it altogether. Godwin Shiri in his research found frequent cases of embezzlement of Christian Dalit land by caste landlords or money-lenders. This is often done by cheating them into debt, an issue to which we will return a little later, but also by blocking them from cultivating land which the authorities have granted them. This sometimes happens through court cases, (see Stories 2, 4 and 7), but other times by non-Dalits physically preventing access to the land. One tactic used was to report that, being Christians, the proposed beneficiaries of Government land could not be 'Scheduled Castes'; this comes back to the inequity of the 1950 Presidential promulgation.

Shiri's research showed that in his 44 villages while over 60% of Dalits owned some land, only 29% owned more fertile 'wet land'. Only 4% of

Dalits owned above four acres of wet land, an area providing a basic standard of living. The struggle for land is the struggle for life. In the worst atrocity reported while I was in India, on December 3rd 1997 61 people, including 22 women and 17 children, from Scheduled Castes and extremely backward communities in Bihar were killed by an illegal 'landlord's army', in a dispute over the ownership of land. The State Government declared an emergency but observers commented that the the police would be either terrified of the landlords, or on their pay-roll.

ii)   Employment

Work in India has been caste-based for centuries. Romila Thapar in the Penguin *History of India* says it was quite rigid in the earliest centuries of the Christian era, but with economic development it began to fragment just a little. This process is beginning to pick up speed in contemporary India in that most of those who in desperation leave the rural areas and move to the cities turn into one of the myriads of people selling on the streets, at the bus-stops or around the stations.

In this process they abandon their traditional occupation. Each sub-caste or group in Indian society has always had its own tasks. Kancha Ilaiah explains how as a 'Kurumaa' he was taught in detail about different kinds of sheep, their health care, birth processes, food and shearing. Even the girls needed to learn about sheep, as well as domestic practices. A Kurumaa man hardly stays at home, he sleeps where the sheep are. A Goudaa, who is a toddy-tapper, rises at cock-crow and goes straight to the trees. He has a name for each tree and begins to climb at first light, 'He is the one who gets to see the beauty of nature at sunrise from the tallest tree'. (p.24) Other Dalit groups begin their day in similar ways, however - says Ilaiah - for most of them what they do is not decided by them but by their masters.

The vast majority of Dalits are engaged in agriculture. Shiri in his survey lists the types of work done by the Christian Dalits in his area. 90% are engaged in skinning, 68% as house-servants in caste households, 57% in shoe-making, 32% in slaughtering, 14% in grave-digging and 10% in 'scavenging', to which we shall return. The work of house servants includes cleaning out stables, helping in the fields, drumming at celebrations and conveying news of a death to the extended family. The relationship is almost feudal. Overall 89% of Dalits were engaged in farming of one kind or another.

49

Reservation has helped some Dalits obtain employment, but these opportunities are diminishing with privatisation, and in any case do not apply to Christians. Even if they did, only 10-20% of Dalits work in the organised sector - public and private. Over 80% of Dalits are employed in a non-organised capacity. Their lack of education is a considerable handicap; few have the kind of educational qualifications which would enable them to try for jobs in the organised sector - public or private.

One of the most unpleasant tasks Dalits find themselves required to undertake is known as 'scavenging'. What it actually involves is a daily cleaning of the dry latrines used by caste people, and transporting the human waste, sometimes to dumps quite close to Dalit villages. This practice is the subject of Story 6. The Indian Government legislated a ban on scavenging in 1972, but despite this there are still 700,000 Dalits estimated to be involved in this activity. It has been one of the main practices intertwined with the philosophy of 'untouchability' and pollution.

In 1980 the Government initiated a 'Liberation of Scavengers' scheme, providing for the conversion of dry latrines into water-flush ones and for rehabilitation for scavengers and their families, but somehow the funds never got used for the right purposes. In 1991 it introduced a 'National Scheme of Liberation and Rehabilitation' for scavengers and dependents to finally abolish manual latrine cleaning by 1997, with a five-year budget of 8,000 million rupees. Then in 1994 it established the **National Commission for Safai Karmacharis (Scavengers)** to ensure the programme was completed. According to the Indian authorities the practice of scavenging has now to all intents and purposes died out; however the subject of our Story 6, Wilson, could be excused for not believing this, and Godwin Shiri's 1995/6 survey of 338 families in 24 villages of Andhra Pradsh found that 16% of them were still engaged in scavenging.

Wages are another vital aspect of employment, for many Dalits they are abysmal, and that is when they can find work. Paul Divakar estimates Dalits get only 150-190 days work per year, at 40 rupees a day for men and 25 for women (about 70p and 50p). Shiri finds the rates even lower in rural Karnataka and Andhra Pradesh, 80% of men earn up to 10 rupees a day, and none earn more than 20. For women, 46% earn 6 rupees a day and none earn more than 10. These are subsistence wages with a vengeance.

It probably goes without saying that most agricultural workers are not unionised, though there have been many struggles in this direction. In 1912 in Kerala Ayyankali started to organise the labourers and 1913 saw

50

the first strike, demanding an improvement in wages, reduction of working hours and admission to school for their children. The workers stayed away from the landlords' fields for over a year, a period reminiscent of the Montgomery bus boycott in the early sixties by Martin Luther King's followers. The landlords began to try and sow discord among the strikers and molest their women - a tactic that often seems to recur when Dalits offer resistance. They also encouraged the police to bring baseless charges against the Dalit workers. Eventually the Government intervened and the strike ended in May 1914 with the labourers gaining most of their demands. Story 6 illustrates the contemporary struggle for union organisation in Andhra Pradesh.

Story 3: Wilson and the Theology of 'Scavenging'

I am Wilson; when I was born my parents were so delighted that, like Hannah with her son Samuel, they dedicated me to God. They wanted desperately that I should become a Christian pastor. I did well at my studies, was accepted by the church, and in 1994 enrolled as a student at the United Theological College in Bangalore.

However I am a Dalit, and come from a family of 'Safai Karmacharis' (the English word we use is 'scavengers'). I had become increasingly distressed that large numbers of my people were still involved in scavenging, even though it was outlawed in 1972. 'Scavengers' is the rather polite name given to those who have to clean out each morning the dry latrines used by the caste people in many areas. Despite the ban there are still estimated to be 700,000 Dalits involved in this most demeaning activity. It has been one of the main practices undergirding the philosophy and ideology of 'untouchability' and pollution.

The latrines in question consist of two concrete foot-platforms, each side of a shallow trench. After their use by caste people in the early morning, the Safai Karmacharis are supposed to come along and remove what is there with a steel implement and bucket, then clean out the trench before moving on to the next house. Sometimes it is just easiest to do the job by hand. The contents of the buckets are usually then taken to some disposal point away from where the caste people live but often near to our homes. They are later collected in a large vessel, perhaps drawn by a tractor; when this is loaded the contents quite frequently get splashed around. The vessel is then taken off to deposit its contents in a large pit. For each latrine thus treated a scavenger may receive between two and five rupees (3p to 8p) a month. She or he will therefore have to clean many to reach anything like a living wage.

According to the Indian authorities the practice of scavenging has to all intents and purposes died out. In 1980 the Government initiated a 'Liberation of Scavenging' scheme, providing for the conversion of dry latrines into water-flush ones and for rehabilitation for scavenger and their families, but somehow the funds never got used for the right purpose. In 1991 it introduced a 'National Scheme of Liberation and Rehabilitation' for scavengers and dependents, to finally abolish latrine cleaning by 1997, with a five-year budget of 8,000 million rupees. Then it 1994 it established the 'National Commission for Safai Karmachari' to ensure the programme was completed. States such as Andhra Pradesh, Karnataka, Tamilnadu and Kerala reported that scavenging had been eradicated. However our unofficial checks have shown that this is not the case. A survey we undertook in 51 towns of twelve Districts in Andhra Pradesh demonstrates that where the authorities said scavenging had been eliminated in 43 towns the true figure was only ten.

I helped initiate this and other unofficial surveys on the true situation. There are two main reasons why my people still do what they do - generations of psychological pressure that this is all they are good for and the lack of any alternative employment. I do not know why the scavengers have not been rehabilitated, or where the 8,000 million rupees have gone. I felt strongly that I was called to be involved in the campaign to get the Government to do what it has said it will do and end scavenging, and I got actively involved.

When in 1995 national publicity rewarded our efforts the caste people in the police and security services started to get interested. My college Principal even received a midnight telephone call. He sent me a message and we discussed what had happened. Eventually he suggested that if I wanted to continue with this work it might be better if I took leave of absence from the college.

[Wilson decided to take leave of absence, in order to serve his people, the Safai Karmacharis. He presently carries out his Christian ministry campaigning against the obnoxious practice of scavenging. Someday, he says, he hopes to become a real pastor. Some would say he already is.]

iii)   Debt

The economic relationship between the Dalit and the employer is sometimes akin to slavery. A Dalit Solidarity People's conference in 1995 heard from Professor Yesudasan who said that Kerala was the only Indian state where Dalit human beings were bought and sold like animals, although in other states they had to suffer the bonded labour system. Anthony Raj says that 82% of more than two million bonded labourers are

Dalits. In this system the Dalit family gets into such debt to their master that they can never get out of it. They borrow, especially for marriages, health care or other emergencies, and the rates of interest are such that repayment is always impossible.

In *Venturing into Life*, the story of Tamilnadu Theological Seminary, Dhyanchand Carr tells how through staff and students going to live in a nearby slum the college began to learn of the harsh economic realities of those Dalits who had moved to the city. The money-lenders would charge enormous rates of interest to anyone who wanted to take an initiative. For example, says Carr, women wanting to sell vegetables would need capital of about a hundred rupees. The money-lenders were always around at the places where the vegetables were sold cheaply in bulk early in the morning. They lent at the rate of 10% **per day**. This interest often took 50% of what the woman earned; sometimes she did not even earn back the hundred rupees.

The lender would allow the money to accumulate, but even if on half of the days the woman earned her money back, on the other half she would soon create an accumulated debt too large to pay. She - or her daughters - would then have to offer the money-lender sexual favours, or her few possessions would be taken. Men who drank what they earned finished up the same way. Carr goes on to recount a rather naive effort to negotiate between the debtors and the money-lenders, which initially got many of the poor out of debt but in the end actually enhanced the power of the money-lenders, showing how important is the planning for long-term social change.

Shiri's survey discovered that the debt trap was the greatest cause of continuing forced labour of rural Dalits. He found that 48% were in debt to Government bodies and 56% to private lenders. Government debts are at a lower rate but there is so much bureaucracy involved that the poor often give up. In some villages Shiri found that 90% of the Christian Dalit families were in the hands of money-lenders. Around 70% of debt was contained under 4,000 rupees, but 20% went up to 8,000 and 16% of the debt to private lenders was over 8,000 rupees and therefore virtually impossible to repay. Almost all the money-lenders are of course caste people. Rates varied from 2% per month to 10%.

In some loan arrangments a Dalit family would have to surrender their land title deeds as surety. Shiri found that as many as a quarter of those with private debts had mortgaged their land. Those who had no land 'mortgaged' their working capacity and became bonded labourers. He also discovered that almost all Government loans were for crops, livestock, land or other agricultural purposes, but this was only true of 40% of private loans, most of these were for domestic purposes, including marriages. Shiri comments that in the survey area, 'the debts that Christian Dalits incur for conducting marriages is the major cause for their perpetual indebtedness'.

iv)   Water

Bishop Lesslie Newbigin, in his *South India Diary* published in 1951, tells how he was constantly approached by Dalit people to help get access to wells. On one occasion he approached caste people on their behalf and spoke of the terrible difficulties of the outcastes who had to collect water from a muddy pool into which water from rubbish heaps drained, while there was a deep, clean well nearby. 'The only result of the conversation' said Newbigin, 'was that... the caste people raided the outcaste quarters and beat up the people there.'

When I visited villages and asked what were the problems they faced, water was one of the first things to be mentioned, both for domestic use and for cultivation. Water sources for washing and drinking can include wells, boreholes, ponds, tanks (small reservoirs), streams or canals. All create difficulties of different kinds. Dalits are never allowed access to large water sources at the same convenient places which the caste people use.

In his village research Godwin Shiri found that 76% of Christian Dalits had problems with access to water. He comments that 'the non-Dalits are so fanatically opposed to the Dalits drawing water from their wells that, even in most emergencies, the Dalits are forced to tread long distances to fetch water from a pond or tank'. He notes ironically that the non-Dalits, if they need water, never hesitate to take it from the Dalits' sources presumably it becomes purified in some magical way. Shiri says that in some instances of obtaining water the 'casteist arrogance and contempt shown by the non-Dalits' have sparked considerable violence. He gives an example of the village of Jummaladinne where in 1993 a boy actually from one of the lower castes taking water from a Christian Dalit borehole abused the women who were waiting for water. Some Dalit youths who came by threatened him. He went and called his caste men who returned in a body to the Dalit area or *keri*, physically assaulted ten Dalits and stoned their huts for some two hours. They then imposed a socio-economic boycott for several weeks, causing much hardship, which was only gradually lifted.

Water for cultivation is also vital. I refer in Story 6 to Kukkarajupalle, where activists were helping villagers conserve water on their higher and poor quality ground, something which incensed the caste people when they discovered it. Shiri describes how in the villages he studied most Dalits have 'dry land', which receives just rain water. 27% have 'wet land', which has access to canal irrigation and only 7% have access to tanks or wells. 'Wet land' cultivation can be possible for 10 or 11 months of the year, but 'dry land' for only 4 to 6 months. A tiny number owned water pumps, which were a great boon, but two-thirds of the Christian Dalit community depended entirely on sometimes very erratic rainfall. The control of water by caste people is one of the most symbolic examples of the stranglehold they have on the economic life of Dalit communities.

Story 4: The village of Thaiyyur, Chittoor District, AP

Thaiyyur is a village with about 80 Dalit families, sited in the south of the state of Andhra Pradesh (AP). It consists mostly of baked-mud huts, with a few brick buildings. The economy, like most Indian villages, depends almost entirely on agriculture; there are cows, hens and goats ambling through the lanes, and plots with rice, sugar-cane, and some vegetables around the village boundaries. There are wells, but they are insufficient for full crops all the year round. There is no sanitation. Nearby are the much larger houses of some caste families, who own much of the local land on which some of the Dalits have to work.

In 1974 the Government awarded the Thaiyyur villagers 47 acres of land in order to improve their access to food and their standard of living. They began to cultivate it, but after two or three years the caste people, seeing the improving economic situation of the Dalits and recognising that it could mean an end to cheap labour for them, put in a complaint that the 47 acres were 'common land' and could not be allocated to one group. The dispute meant the Dalits had to stop cultivation, but eventually the caste people's claim was rejected. They then asserted the land had originally been owned by their ancestors and was not the Government's to redistribute. There followed endless legal wrangling. The Dalits got themselves a lawyer and put the case in his hands. He however was in close touch with the caste people, and possibly on their payroll. Anyway he did nothing for the Dalits' case and actually gave them incorrect information.

Another ploy of the caste people was to go out one night and build a shrine in a small copse in the centre of the land. They then claimed this was a shrine at which their families had always worshipped, and therefore the land could not be given to the Dalits. This was despite the clear presence of a Dalit shrine close by,

55

which demonstrated the separate basis of Dalit religion. If the caste shrine had really been there first, such proximity would not have been allowed.

When making a case to the State officials the caste people always used to cite the reference of an adjacent piece of land which did belong to them. Officials can rarely be persuaded to actually come and check on land, so kept saying that it did belong to the caste families. When they were finally persuaded of the correct ownership of the land, they suggested a compromise by which the caste people would keep that part of the land which they had sown with sugar-cane, and the Dalits could have the rest. By now the Dalits had become much more self-confident and said, 'We were allocated 47 acres of land, and 47 acres is what we will have!'

Their confidence had come partly through contact with a group called 'Prajwala' ('Kindling a Spark'), who have been giving them advice and support. There is a great need for legal advice in particular, as the court system is complicated and for some issues the court to be attended is several hours journey away. One of the ways the caste people seek to wear down the Dalits is by forcing them to keep having to go to court, with the legal and travel cost, and the loss of another day's work.

At one point the caste people encouraged their cows to graze on the Dalits' land, destroying their crops. The villagers asked for a meeting with the caste people and told them, 'We are tough, we have to be to survive round here. If you put your cows on this land again, we'll put our cows on your land, and get all our relatives from the surrounding villages to do the same.' The caste cows disappeared back to their own pastures.

The villagers built a track for several hundred yards from the nearby road so there is vehicular access to the land. Finally in September 1997 the court judgement came through that the land was theirs. They immediately began to divide out the land for each family and to sow some crops. There was technically an appeal period of a month, but no-one could think of grounds on which the caste people could again appeal. The senior officer responsible had already given instructions to the relevant official to issue the land-title. However she still resisted doing so and in late October the caste people did register an out-of-time appeal which, nevertheless, will mean yet another trip to court. In November the caste people were again releasing their cows on to the Dalit land during the night, forcing the villagers to hurry out in the mornings to drive the cows from their crops, losing their own working time.

The Thaiyyur villagers are now certain that they will very soon obtain their land title, over 23 years after the Government granted it to them. They plan to put up a statue of the Dalits' hero, Dr Ambedkar, to celebrate their victory. The question has to be asked as to whether the next generation will display the kind of long-suffering patience that the current elders have exhibited, and what will be the result if they do not.

c)   Political

Political discrimination is another form of oppression of Dalits. It is less harsh than under the apartheid system, where Africans did not even have a vote. It is more akin to the situation in the American Deep South in the sixties, where black people could register to vote but were actively discouraged from doing so. Dalits can vote, but there is a great deal of pressure and manipulation in the Indian electoral system. The effects of political discrimination are certainly harsher than any in the UK at the present time, where black and Asian people are free to vote, although their share of representation in terms of MPs is only a quarter of what it should be. The reservation system ensures quite a large proportion of Dalits in the Lok Sabha, but most of them are firmly under the control of the party bosses who put them there. This is the result of the 'Poona Pact' of 1932.

i)   The caste basis of politics

In the *History of India* Romila Thapar suggests that caste and politics have been intertwined more or less since India began, and since the emergence of caste over twenty centuries ago it has gained a greater influence than any political institution even kings and emperors. Kings, though divine, could be removed for failure to protect the social order, and that order included caste as its most fundamental institution. Hence caste has very deep roots in the political power structures of Indian society.

It was this phenomenon, according to some historians, which crucially hindered India from resisting the British incursions in the eighteenth century. The horizontal layers of caste and the vertical division by religion fractured Indian society and prevented the development of the kind of nationalism which might have opposed the British more effectively. Caste weakened India then, as it does now, as for caste people their purity was more important than the good of the nation.

As the colonial period progressed however political forces evolved which sought to overcome the worst divisions in order to press for independence.

Percival Spear draws attention to Ram Mohan Roy, a brahmin who worked for the British in the early nineteenth century and agitated for reform. He initiated the first Indian newspaper, advocated civil and political rights including for women - and campaigned against 'suttee' (the self-immolation of widows) and casteism. Borrowing what was useful from the West, his ideas permeated some of the new British-trained Indian middle-class. The latter maintained their basic religious beliefs, but absorbed and incorporated Western customs. Spear describes it as 'caste in the home, equal rights on the street, the dhoti at ease, the Western suit on duty'. Out of this kind of blend grew a new nationalism. But to gain power, alliances had to be built across caste, and hence was formed the Congress Party, the vehicle by which India achieved independence. Its leadership was always safely in the hands of non-Dalits, but it needed Dalit support to achieve its ends, and in the end it needed a Dalit, Dr Ambedkar, to write the new Constitution.

Kancha Ilaiah says that in the post-colonial period the only two kinds of parties were the liberal democratic (Congress) and the marxist (the Communist Parties). Congress 'talked about the welfare of the Dalitbahujan castes, while all the state resources were cornered by the Hindus'. The relationships between the caste people and the Dalits was like that between the gods Rama and Hanuman, Hanuman being a South Indian Dalit who worked and fought for Rama, but whose place was always 'marginal and subservient'. So it was for Dalitbahujans who joined Congress, their main tasks being to mobilise the masses and organise rallies for the caste leadership. The local Congress leaders were related to the priests and the Government officials, and were able to manipulate the whole socio-political system. Though a liberal democratic party has ruled India for fifty years, says Ilaiah, 'it has not improved unequal caste relations, and the gap between Hindu "upper" castes and the non-Hindu Dalitbahujans... has never been bridged'.

One result of this has been the gradual demise of the Congress Party such that, without the intervention of Sonia Gandhi in the March 1998 election, Congress might have been all but wiped off the political map. The Hindu nationalists, the Bharatiya Janata Party (BJP), due to its clever strategising, probably obtained as much support from Dalits as Congress did. This is particularly unfortunate given that a prime political aim of the BJP is that the caste basis of Indian society shall survive. Dalits however have begun to organise politically and more will be heard later of parties such as the Republican Party of India (RPI) and the Bahujan Samaj Party (BSP).

ii)   The failure of the state

When India obtained independence one of the stated aims of the new leadership was to build a more united nation. However it was soon clear that this would not be done at the expense of the caste system. When Nehru announced his list of ministers for the Interim Government in August 1946 there was no Dalit name. Ambedkar responded by stating that the Scheduled Castes would neither obey nor respect the Nehru Government. Gandhi sent a message saying, among other things, 'Abolish the salt tax. Unite Hindus and Muslims. Remove untouchability', but it was only untouchability which was to be removed, not caste. A year afterwards, however, in the Cabinet list for the first full Government, Ambedkar's name did appear. Three years later he was to resign, believing that Nehru was giving in over the Hindu Code Bill, designed to remove some of the more medieval elements from Hindu social law. Nehru's biographer M.J. Akbar describes this as an unhelpful move, but Ambedkar clearly felt casteism was not being seriously tackled.

It seems that Nehru himself did wish to challenge inequality, and laws were passed seeking to remove untouchability, as Gandhi had urged, and to promote the interests and opportunities of the Scheduled Castes. For Nehru, says Spear, 'Equal rights for all meant not only the outcasts... but the regular castes as well and women as well as men.' Spear's use of 'regular castes' indicates his awareness that casteism itself was not under attack. Spear also notes that the political structures introduced, including universal suffrage, meant that 'no brahmin today can receive election today without low caste votes'. However he goes on to observe that 'caste groupings are in many areas being exploited as ready made political machines'. One reason why this manipulation was so successful was the high illiteracy rate - seventeen years after independence it was still 70%. Nehru said this must be addressed but the Government failed to deliver, thus leaving the Dalits and Other Backward Classes vulnerable to continued political exploitation.

One form this exploitation takes is that of creating 'vote-banks' where political candidates do deals of one form or another with local institutions - villages, churches, voluntary bodies - to deliver the votes of their members in an upcoming election. In several personal interviews with Dalit activists this was mentioned as an ongoing problem. According to Godwin Shiri even local churches could be used in this way, both in the political realm and for preferment within the institutional church. Shiri went so far as to say that caste people used Dalit Christians politically 'like smoking a cigarette, then grinding it out under your foot'.

Kancha Ilaiah describes how at village level the Dalits and sudras are excluded from power. He says the three institutions through which political and economic power operates are 'police, patel and patwari' (police, administrative official and revenue officer). The latter two posts are controlled by the brahmins and kshatriyas, and Dalitbahujans are denied the experience of and involvement in decision-making structures. Women are also excluded. In the early '90s it was decided in the Constitution Amendment Act to set aside 30% of the places on the new 'panchayats' or village councils for women, but women will have to work very hard to actualise the power they nominally have. It will be the same for Dalits, Ilaiah believes, as they try to take up positions which have been designated for them.

It is however the system of 'reservation' in employment, land-grants and access to loans which has been constantly manipulated to benefit caste people at the expense of Dalits. Where employers, even state-linked bodies such as educational institutions, are supposed to fill a proportion of jobs up to certain levels with candidates from the Scheduled Castes or Backward Classes they find many ways of not doing so. The most common claim, using a legal loophole, is that they are unable to find people of sufficient qualifications or experience. This sounds rather like employers in European countries challenged about their low numbers of black or minority employees. In both places employers fail to put into place the mechanisms of recruitment and training which would enable a sufficient supply of such employees while in the USA, at least in the late eighties and early nineties, positive action created a new situation.

When really imperilled by Dalits potentially obtaining power caste politicians threaten violence. I was given several examples of this during my visit. One or two of the Stories illustrate this, including that of Jawakhar. **People's Watch**, a human rights organisation for Tamilnadu based in Madurai, regularly documents human rights abuses, including denials of political rights for Dalits. Its 1996 report contains a section on the monitoring of the 1994 Tamilnadu Panchayats (local councils) Act, which was promulgated in response to the Constitutional Amendment Act and offers reserved constituencies for Dalits and tribal peoples. The report gives detailed examples from four villages of how caste communities have prevented Dalit access to positions of responsibility, usually by threats.

Melavalvu Panchayat had been reserved for Dalits, but the caste community warned them that any Dalit contesting the elections faced social and economic boycott. The Dalit elders submitted but the young people refused and some filed nomination papers. One nominated for panchayat president had his house burned down. The young people then sought police protection, which was offered, but in insufficient numbers. Dalit families began to leave the village in fear, pleading with the youth to withdraw their nominations. The youth did so, but when they returned to their village received further threats. Dalit houses were being stoned, so the youth left for the safety of the city of Madurai. A similar process took place in Keeripatti village, but here violence was not necessary as no Dalits dared to file nomination for panchayat membership.

Both in Keeripatti and another village, Pappapatti - whose panchayat was also reserved for Dalits - the Dalits were dependent for income on working in the fields of the caste community. When told that all work would be denied if nominations were filed, the Dalits acquiesced and no names were put forward. People's Watch told the same story of Nattapangalam panchayat, here three Dalits did file papers but were put under extreme pressure and eventually withdrew. In all four villages listed here the caste people prevented the taking of photographs for voting identity purposes and the authorities were unable or unwilling to enforce the law. Not only are caste people denying Dalits political rights but they do so with threats of various kinds which go unpunished.

The 1995 annual report of the **Dalit Solidarity Programme** (now **Peoples**) gives an illustration from another part of the country of a different way of circumventing the law. A Dalit woman Councillor and her husband were actively involved in Dalit social development and the husband decided to stand for election as panchayat president, as the panchayat controlled a lot of income from the local sugar and cotton mills. He was threatened by the caste community who put up an illiterate Dalit labourer as their candidate, and got him elected. He then followed their every instruction in taking decisions.

Story 5: Ayyangali of Perungudi, near Madurai

I have been an activist in my village since 1978, when I decided I could put up with our treatment as Dalits no longer. In our rural areas casteism is still extremely strong; in many villages Dalit people cannot walk through villages with their sandals on, enter hotels, take water from the village wells or drink tea in the village 'tea-shops'. Nor can we get even our legal rights, as the bureaucracy is full of caste people.

61

In my village, as part of the land distribution programme, the Government in 1980 designated three pieces of land for Dalit housing. Two of them were separate from the caste part of the village, and there was no problem with them, but the other piece was close to some of the caste housing and created a lot of opposition. The caste people put pressure on the land-owner who had sold it to the Government, and he then illegally resold it to a non-Dalit.

We appealed to the Rural Theological Institute (RTI) of the Tamilnadu Theological Seminary, which we knew was sympathetic to Dalits. When the RTI intervened the State officials reviewed the case, and agreed what had happened was wrong. However they failed to get the illegal occupants off the land. For three years we organised petitions and protests, and held fasts, but still nothing changed. The landowner concerned has a lot of influence locally - political and economic - and the official who should have issued the title to the land was under a lot of financial and political pressure not to do so. At one point an order to hand over the land came from higher up, but even this turned out to be a ruse by the bureaucracy.

So in 1983 we decided on an occupation. We approached local action groups, teachers unions, the RTI and leaders from other villages, and at 6 am one morning 5,000 people assembled to reclaim the land. The State brought in thousands of police and protestors were faced with 600 officers with guns, thousands wielding lathi sticks and others armed with tear gas. We were undeterred; we said either the State gets these people off our land or we will. The State officials hoped that as the sun rose and people ran out of water we would disperse, but after several hours under the hot sun, we were still there.

The officials and police wanted to negotiate, rather than evict the illegal occupants, but finally at 2 pm they gave in and signed an undertaking that within sixty days the land would be ours. After 45 days the illegal occupants left, then two months later my house was set alight. Fortunately the baby was disturbed and woke us up, otherwise we might all have been killed as the house was burnt out. No-one has been charged with trying to kill us.

The original owner then took a case to court saying he had not been paid enough for the land, such a 'dispute' prevents any final decision being made. After various appeals this spurious case was finally thrown out in 1991, when the court stated that the price was fair. Again nothing had happened by the end of the year, so in early 1992 150 of our young people decided to hold a 'half-naked protest', just dressed in loin cloths. Then we decided to block the road to the airport, which is quite close. The night before our demonstration the police came and arrested several of our leaders including me. They patrolled the area all night, but the youth went underground then came out in the morning, with women and children, and 500 people blocked the airport road for most of the day.

Despite various promises we still did not get the land title. We next held a mock funeral at the office of the Collector, one of the most important State officials. 500 people joined in a 'funeral lamentation', wailing 'The State is dead; it no longer exists!' The caste people then attacked the Dalits, and the police - instead of simply charging the attackers - registered a case against both parties, again preventing any further movement on the land issue until the charges were resolved. The authorities then asked both parties to sign a statement that the land was under dispute, despite the fact that it was the State who twelve years earlier had allotted the land to the Dalits!

We continued to press for the land title. We could have occupied the land again but this would probably have led to bloodshed, and anyway we wanted to demonstrate that the Government's schemes to improve the situation of the Dalits just do not work. In 1996 the Collector sent out a Circular saying the land was Dalit land, but privately he sent an emissary to the land-owner saying any action he took would not be opposed. This is what we have to put up with! The State could arrest the agitators under the 1989 Protection of Civil Rights Act, for which there are special attorneys, police and funding, but it won't even use its own designated means to enforce its own legislation - this is 'law' for Dalits in India.

The authorities' latest ploy is to suggest that the land - being near to the village school - should be used for public purposes, a children's play area. We have pointed out there is plenty of room already for children to play. Our young people have completely lost faith in democracy and the rule of law. When we fight back against caste oppression the Government squawks 'National Security!' and charges us under the 'Prevention of Terrorism Act'.

In the State of Tamilnadu untouchability is deeply entrenched. It can only be tackled through struggle. Yes, this will create polarisation, there will have to be sacrifice, there will be bloodshed. But despite all the State repression Dalits will go on demonstrating and battling. This is what we will have to do if we want to create a caste-free society in India.

iii)   The role of the police

As suggested in the previous section, the police are not always entirely helpful in upholding the law and in some cases side actively with those breaking it. Jawakhar's story also illustrates this. In the TTS history

Venturing into Life Dyanchand Carr - now the seminary Principal - gives some reminiscences from the development of the Rural Theological Institute (RTI). One of these relates to the hamlet of Ramankulam, which comes under the jurisdiction of Kusavankundu, and is situated near to the farm in which the RTI had made its headquarters. The headman of Kusavankundu was a 'high caste' person, Alagu Pillai. He had gained a tyrannical control over Ramankulam and the police and local officials were in his pocket. RTI members had gone to the elder of Ramankulam, Thiru Pichai, asking if he wanted help in loosening Pillai's grip, but he had told them the Dalit villagers were enjoying peace and prosperity. Later however, when the RTI vigorously confronted Pillai on another issue Thiru Pichai brought out the Ramankulam villagers to support them.

Pichai told the astonished RTI staff that he could not be sure of them before, as they were the same caste and class as Pillai, but when he saw them confront Pillai he knew they could be trusted. Since then, says Carr, the local villagers' self-confidence has increased, and 'the power the police wielded through their intimidatory tactics has been considerably broken' because the people have gained legal knowledge about how to fight illegal arrest and torture. A group of Christian lawyers came together to assist them with their efforts to redeem their fraudulently stolen lands. When fifty people including five RTI staff members were charged by police during protests three lawyers, including Director of 'People's Watch' Henri Tiphagne, spent three years defending them and winning their acquittal.

The police can however be more actively involved in violence. In the 1985 Chundur massacre referred to above, when six Dalits were killed, the police encouraged threatened Dalits to flee in the direction in which upper caste people were waiting to hack them down. While the carnage occurred, says Kancha Ilaiah in *Crossroads*, the police were chewing *pan* and smoking, Dalit women observers said at least one officer was involved in the killings.

The Mumbai-based **Centre for the Study of Society and Secularism** has undertaken monitoring on police activity, on their role with regard to communal relationships as much as oppression of Dalits. In June 1997 the Centre published a Paper by one of its founders, a respected Muslim observer on human rights issues Asghar Ali Engineer, about the Meerut riots a decade earlier when over 150 Muslims had been killed, many at the hands of the police. Engineer's investigations into the various incidents had demonstrated that 25 Muslims youth were shot and thrown into a canal by police at Hashimpura and the same day 60 Muslims had been shot dead at Maliana, ten kilometres from Meerut. He obtained evidence that these plans to 'teach the Muslims a lesson' had emanated from the top of the largely Hindu-dominated police force. Despite the promises of several Chief Ministers of Maharashtra State, and even Prime Minister Rajiv Gandhi, says Engineer 'the people of Hashimpura and Maliana are still waiting for justice, even ten years after the wounds are fresh'. Engineer goes on to point out that this incident raises serious questions about India's criminal justice system, which 'has no respect for human rights values'.

People's Watch in Tamilnadu also closely monitors police activity and has many questions about the current system. One area it has tried to tackle is deaths in police custody, an issue which has also been on the agenda of the **Churches' Commission for Racial Justice** in the UK. The Director Henri Tiphagne has been campaigning for India's **National Human Rights Commission** to demand a report on anyone dying in police custody. There was in fact a requirement that such a report should be received from Government at national or state level within 48 hours of such a death, but it was not happening. People's Watch started to agitate and by July 1997 a monitoring programme had been put in place.

The 1996 'People's Watch' annual report gives several examples of deaths in custody, which make it clear that the police do not always follow the procedures laid down when deaths occur. A number of these concerned Dalits, at least two of whom appear to have died under police torture. Even more worrying however is the report's section on more widespread atrocities against Dalits, in which the police are sometimes directly involved. There was considerable caste tension in the south of Tamilnadu in 1995, and a number of murders of both Dalits and caste people took place. In August 1995, after Dalits from Alantha and Kasilingapuram villages had been involved in self-defence incidents in which caste people had been killed, the police raided both villages. Dozens were arrested, women and children were beaten up, houses were ransacked and looted, and cash and jewels worth 100,000 rupees were taken from Alantha alone.

Subsequently the village of Kodiyankulam became a police target. Although a Dalit village it is quite wealthy and therefore a Dalit power centre. On 31st August 1995 the police superintendent arrived with 600 officers. The villagers came out to greet them and they promptly struck the headman, who collapsed. A young woman student remonstrated and was nearly strangled. An angry youngster threw a stone and the police, having provoked an 'attack', began firing on the unarmed villagers. Fifty were reported to have been wounded. The police then charged into the village with a range of weapons, broke into houses, smashed some electrical goods, stole other goods and jewellery, tore up documents including degree certificates, destroyed foodstuffs and allegedly poisoned the well. A week later, at a large rally in support of the villagers in Chennai police opened fire. Three people were killed and 23 admitted to hospital.

There is always a political element to such rallies, and some at the rally said the trouble had been started by police and/or political agents provocateurs, to warn the Dalits against political activity. In the subsequent events a number of Dalits and caste people were killed and injured, but usually only Dalits got arrested and charged. People's Watch lists a number of other incidents - in January 1996 the police were also reported to have killed several Dalit Christian fishermen, at Tutcorin on the coast.

One of the worst atrocities occurred in the summer of 1997 in Mumbai. Some caste people, possibly with the knowledge of the police, had hung a string of chappals, or sandals, around the stature of Dr Ambedkar in one of the Dalit neighbourhoods. The Dalits had come on to the streets to protest, and urged action by the police. No action was taken, and so a demonstration began. The police subsequently began firing, ten Dalits were killed and several more injured. Some commentators regarded this a 'set-up' to warn the Dalits to keep in their place. The Gundewar Commission into the atrocity held 120 sittings, and presented its report on its investigation to the Maharashtra BJP-Shiv Sena State Government in August 1998, but the report had still not been laid before the State Parliament by the end of the year. In many cases such as this the police seem to act as the arm of the caste people rather than a neutral force.

iv)   Divide and rule

This age-old mechanism of power has been successfully employed against the Dalits past and present. Time and again caste people in the power structures use the 'sub-caste' system to set Dalits against each other, denying them any hope of success in political and economic struggles. Gopal Guru in *Crossroads* introduces the term 'relative deprivation' and describes how it operates, for example among the Mahars, one of the main Dalit sub-castes in Maharashtra. In the vertical dimension the Mahars feel relatively deprived against a reference group like the upwardly-mobile caste people. However horizontally, within their own caste stratum, the reference group is the emerging Mahar elite and there seems to have developed feelings of 'hatred, contempt and jealousy' for those Mahars who have achieved more material benefits. Says Guru 'the feeling of relative deprivation, if assuaged

66

successfully, has an in-built atomising tendency which isolates the Dalits under reference from the larger Dalit masses'. It also prevents the emergence of a consciousness which would make a 'critique of the Indian State and (its) lopsided economic development'.

Hence the mechanism of relative deprivation 'suspends, if not eliminates completely... the development of a homogenous Dalit unity cutting across castes and regions'. The caste people are clever, and the State is also involved. Guru believes 'the State plays an extremely important role in keeping the sense of relative deprivation active among the forces that arise from below'. This is done systematically and shrewdly by transferring resources from the more privileged to the less privileged as a welfarist strategy. The State therefore diffuses its articulate critics and co-opts the most vocal elements into the welfare structures. Guru gives as an example the way in which the Dalit Panther movement was seduced by the Integrated Rural Development Programme which co-opted leaders such as Gaekwad and fragmented the Dalit movement into at least a dozen sub-groups of the Republican Party of India. The operation of relative deprivation atomises the community and prevents the formation of 'a collectively critical subversive consciousness'.

P.G. Jogdand, in the same volume, analyses the failure of efforts to create a unified Dalit Movement. He says there are two stages in the history of the struggle, accommodation and protest. The first focused on submitting petitions to the authorities, the second progressed to collective, direct action. It later developed further in the political, educational and religious dimensions. For success, says Jogdand, any Dalit movement needs to operate at grassroots level, through which more vigorous changes may be brought about.

However, in Maharashtra, 'each splinter faction of the Dalit movement is routinised and functions as a political establishment or business corporation' of whichever is the concerned Dalit group. Leadership ambitions and competition has created a vacuum. Dalit leaders 'do not bother about the welfare of the masses', they live in urban areas and ignore rural communities. Jogdand believes there are three categories who participate in the Dalit movement, the theoreticians or intellectuals, the activists and the 'peripheral participants'. Moreover there is a middle class which 'believes in negotiations and compromises', and launches protests only to gain some benefits for itself. The contemporary Dalit movement has failed to mobilise the masses, says Jogdand, because of its own organisational weaknesses. It has so far been unable to make any serious dent in the system oppressing the Dalit communities.

67

The 1996 report of Dalit Solidarity Peoples makes reference to the caste tactic of 'divide and rule' by religion. It issues a reminder that in 1950 Dalits who were Sikhs, Buddhists, Christians and Muslims were excluded from the Scheduled Caste list which would have entitled them to reservation and other affirmative schemes. Since then Buddhists and Sikhs have been accepted into the list but Muslims and Christians remain outside. This is actually anti-constitutional as the Indian Constitution states there shall be no discrimination on grounds of religion. One example the report gave of the success of the caste people in dividing the Dalits was a rally organised by the Hindu nationalist BJP in Delhi in September 1996, when a Bill was being brought forward to include Dalit Christians among the Scheduled Castes. 6,000 Hindu Dalits marched to oppose the inclusion of their fellow Dalits in positive action programmes.

'How to unite the Dalits who are scattered all over the country, who face language, culture and other barriers?' This is the question of Franklyn Balasunderam, he says it is the 'crucial challenge' facing the Dalits today. Dalits are in different religious and 'sub-caste' groupings, 'how to create in them a Dalit consciousness, make them rise above their political, religious and ideological affirmations and strive for unity/solidarity?' Following Hindu ideology, he says, Dalits have adopted hierarchical distinctions among themselves, some sub-castes will have nothing to do with one another. Balasunderam also points to the BJP as a deeply divisive force in relation to Dalits, and the self-seeking of the Dalit leadership as destructive to their hopes. He states that the world is changing, and 'Dalit solidarity is becoming a reality today', but his comment has a feeling of hope rather than expectation. 'Divide and rule' has been and remains an extremely successful strategy to deny the Dalit movements political power.

Story 6: Participatory Action Network (PAN) & the AP Agricultural Union

PAN is the umbrella for development work among Dalits in a number of villages in a part of Andhra Pradesh (AP). It is linked with similar initiatives in other areas of AP, such as Prajwala, referred to in Story 4. It has arisen out of over fifteen years of work by experienced activists who have evolved certain principles. Firstly Dalit people themselves must be in the forefront of the work to be done. Secondly the work needs to be focused on issues which relate directly to the villagers concerned. Thirdly it has to be evolved carefully so that confrontation is not created until the community is strong enough to face it. Fourthly, unless a support network is built up among a range of villages, Dalit communities can be picked off one-by-one, and permanent change will never occur.

The PAN workers explained that a feeling of self-belief has been suppressed for so long among the Dalits, they have been told for so long that they have no contribution to make, that they are hardly human, that it is very difficult for them to believe they have something to offer. Even better-off Dalits suffer from this syndrome. This is why it is essential they are enabled to take responsibility for new initiatives, no matter how long it takes.

Talking to the PAN workers, and going out with them to visit villages, the issues quickly crystallise around land, access to water, education, wages, transport, and the position of women. Most of India's population lives in villages of between a few hundred and a few thousand people. The better houses are brick-built, may even have two storeys and have running water and sanitation. The poorer ones are baked mud, with one main room which may house livestock also, a shared water-tap or well which may be some distance away and the fields for sanitation.

Arriving in the village of Kukkarajupalle our group stops at the village tea-shop in the centre. Although some of us are Dalits, the size of the group and the presence of a European ensures we are served, although we can see on a stone ledge the tea-glass set aside for Dalits. This has to be taken and washed by a Dalit, who can then be served tea in it while standing outside the tea-shop, a practice which is illegal, which has been publicly condemned by Government, but which still continues.

We then have to drive another half-mile, through the well-irrigated fields of caste people to the Dalit section of the village. Here the huts are poorer, some people are living under plastic sheets, and three families are occupying the Government-supplied training centre as their huts have burned down. We sit down beneath the tamarind trees, looking out towards a distant, dry, stone-covered hillside. I am told this is land which has been given to the Dalits under a Government scheme, but firstly it's very dry and secondly direct access to it is across non-Dalit land. The PAN workers have been teaching the villagers techniques to conserve water on the upper hillsides, so that it does not immediately flow down to irrigate non-Dalit land. This has begun to annoy the non-Dalits, who retaliate by preventing passage to the Dalit land despite the legal right of access. The authorities have been drawn in, but instead of insisting on the Dalits' legal rights propose a compromise, in which human beings can have direct access but animals must make a long detour round. This is useless to the Dalits, they need direct access for their animals' grazing. So the arguments continue.

The tamarind trees under which we sit are owned by a caste family from the main village, even though the Dalits now own the land. Dalits are not allowed to touch the tree, the owners will come when the pods are ready and harvest them.

A Dalit who takes a few, even for personal cooking, is likely to be beaten up by the non-Dalits.

The women say they used to have no access to money so they started a 'thrift and credit' scheme. They each save a tiny amount weekly; those who need it can take out a loan, the rest is put in the bank. Once they get twenty members they can get state help. Some of these schemes now have hundreds of members, ensuring the availability of capital to buy animals, purchase seeds and tools, or improve properties, and giving the women some economic independence. The men did not look entirely happy during this part of the meeting.

Women may also suffer sexual harassment. In one village where a Dalit woman's husband had died a non-Dalit man watched her movements (and those of her four children), then broke into her house one night and tried to rape her. The women's organisation in the village, and the agricultural union, protested to the authorities and the man was arrested and charged, though he was soon out on bail and it remains to be seen if the case ever gets to court. As we leave Kukkarajupalle an older woman comes forward, bows to me, crouches and touches my feet. A PAN member lifts her up, and says that was what the landlords expected whenever they came to the village, it is entrenched in her mind that this is how to treat potentially influential visitors.

We approach the village of Mittamalapalle as dusk falls. A mile short of the village the road becomes too narrow for our four-wheel-drive jeep and we have to walk. As we walk beside the 'tank' or small reservoir I am reminded that the Dalits will probably not have access to this water. The fireflies glitter in the bushes, showing off to one another, and helping me not to keep asking what I am doing trekking across the middle of India in the darkness, when I have been told my bed for the night is still three hours drive away. At one point the track disappears under water, shoes come off and trousers are rolled up. When we finally get to the village meeting one of the first complaints is lack of vehicle access. I sympathise. Another problem is education, though this village has one youth in technical college, another studying for a degree and judging by the hands raised when we ask who can read, a literacy rate above the average. One young girl sits on a step at the back, writing carefully in an exercise book throughout the meeting. I am told the union is helping them with their campaigns for transport and land.

In order to build up a system of wider support some years ago PAN encouraged the development of a union for agricultural workers, peasants and small farmers (known as the APVVU). The local people set up a branch in each village and urged people to join. The membership is primarily Dalit, members pay a tiny annual fee, but as the union has spread and the number of branches multiplied

70

the income has grown to a respectable sum. More importantly, when one village comes up against non-Dalit opposition it is able to call on other 'union branches' for support.

At the end of our visits to the villages there was always a call for some songs. These songs of awareness and liberation are spreading across India, even though the languages in each area are different. There is a rhythm and a repetition which makes them easy to learn, a verse of one - roughly translated appears in the Introduction to this book.

The union organisation now covers several mandals in Chittoor and several other AP Districts and has a membership of over 190,000. It is giving the workers a sense of what a wider organisation might achieve. Hearing about it brings back to me memories of hearing about the Primitive Methodists, and their role in building up a national union of agricultural workers in nineteenth century Britain. Eventually it is hoped that the union will cover the whole state and become self-sufficient, a real manifestation of people's power.

d)   Religio-cultural

A key factor in maintaining subserviency in a dominated human group is to deny it self-respect, access to its own history, language and culture, and any vestige of pride. Religion is a further means of oppression. Such cultural genocide has been practised often by dominant groups - whites in South Africa, Europeans in relation to aboriginal peoples in Australia and the Americas, the English towards the Scots, Irish, Welsh and - more recently - black and Asian communities. Such a process can ultimately deprive social or ethnic groups not only of meaningful relationships with others but of any positive feeling about themselves. The results can be seen, for example, in the high rates of alcoholism and suicide among Australian aborigines and native Americans.

i)   Identity denied

Some of these mechanisms have been used against Dalits. They frequently write or speak of the denial of their history and even their identity, and the manipulation of religion to exclude them from mainstream society. Arvind Nirmal in an essay in *Indigenous People: Dalits* (1994) says 'We were not only "no-people" but we were also "no humans".' Dalits were excluded from social intercourse, they were unfit for human society. Kothapalli Wilson, in the same volume, offers a similar analysis, '(Dalits) think of themselves as sub-human beings... This self-understanding is scored by self-disrespect... Its high-point is self-alienation... the end result is the commencement of a master-slave relationship.' Wilson also draws a direct analogy with Blacks in the West:

> As long as they believed the propaganda of the Whites describing them as inferior... they even hated themselves because of their blackness... The moment they acknowledged the sacredness of their identity as blacks and declared that black is beautiful... the Blackman emerged as an authentic human being.

Kancha Ilaiah describes from his own South Indian experience how the choice of names can be used to demean a person and entrench casteism. He also describes the way history has been taught in India. In higher education it was in English, but at primary and secondary levels in Telugu. In the latter, 'The history books were full of stories of kshatriya kings... Dalitbahujan life figured nowhere in the curriculum. We had been excluded from history.' In higher education the teachers were upper caste and although many were liberal and even radical all kept silent on caste discrimination. What was worse, Dalitbahujan people were paying for this education. Even if Dalits try to escape into English medium schools, when they return home they are 'pulled back into the culture of their respective castes'. The result is that the excluded begin to deny their own identity, and Ilaiah describes how some Dalitbahujan officials, doctors and academics try 'to be more Hindu than the Hindus themselves'.

What is required, says Ilaiah, is that the whole society should be 'dalitised'. To do this everyone has to learn from the 'Dalitwaadas', the Dalit communities, where there is a much greater collective life and consciousness and the material basis is rooted 'not in wealth but in labour power'. There is serious alienation among Dalitbahujans, but it is being overcome by community culture and consciousness. Everything that takes place within the Dalitwaada, pleasure or pain, birth or death, is shared by all. Dalits are trying hard to hold on to this collective consciousness. In a 1994 statement the Indian National Social Action Forum (INSAF) speaks of what it calls 'Cultural Annihilation and Dehumanisation', and how the 'cultural space' of Dalit communities is being increasingly squeezed.

Franklyn Balasunderam urges the reconstruction of Dalit history, but says there are problems, including the fact that contemporary historians are not particularly interested in Dalits and academic historians demand written sources or archaeological evidence. Dalit histories, he says, are 'oral histories based on oral traditions'. As they are a conquered people their history has to be 'reconstructed from hostile sources', and because it is pre-Aryan and pre-Dravidian it is hard to recover. There is also need to examine in depth Dalit rituals, festivals and other ceremonies. The core values of Dalit culture and religion have been denied, the beliefs that ecological, gender and spiritual structures need to be taken seriously, and that power is service and should be rotated rather than retained. Would such values strengthen Dalit identity today, asks Balasunderam, or undermine it in the pressure-cooker of globalisation and the consumer culture?

A further question in this area raised by James Massey in *Dalits in India* is whether Dalits have a common historical identity with tribal peoples, an alliance which would be greatly reinforced if this were shown to be the case. The first Commissioner of Scheduled Castes and Scheduled Tribes, L.M. Shrikant, said the latter should be identified by tribal origin, their primitive way of life, their location in remote areas and general backwardness. The UN Special Rapporteur on Indigenous Peoples has identified four main criteria of indigenous identity: an historical continuity with pre-invasion societies, a self-understanding as distinct from other sectors of those societies, people who form non-dominant sectors of society and those who are determined to preserve and transmit their territory and ethnic identity. Dalits, according to Massey, fulfil at least the first three of these four but ultimately they themselves will have to decide if they see themselves as indigenous. In the meantime some Dalit leaders continue to explore common ground with the tribal communities or 'Adivasis'.

ii)   The place of religion

Many commentators on the situation of the Dalits point to the use of religion in helping to reinforce both psychological and social dimensions of oppression. Anthony Raj in his essay 'Social Foundation for a Dalit Theology' in *Emerging Dalit Theology* has a section on 'Religion, the Legitimiser of an Unjust Order'. He says that through its creation of myths and symbols religion has often provided a 'justification of the domination-subordination relationship' and that in such a context it is essential to critique Hinduism in order to understand caste as 'a system of institutionalised inequality'. Raj says that in all unequal societies where the ruling class want to retain their privileges they have sought the assistance of theologians. Hindu theologians have 'surpassed everyone' in justifying an unjust society. These theologians have consigned the out-castes to oblivion, denied their aspirations and access to 'society's material and cultural resources', and foisted on them shameful occupations and a dreadful existence. Raj concludes, 'It is therefore right and just for every Dalit to disown Hinduism...'.

One of the most concrete ways in which the use of religion contributed to the psychological oppression of Dalits was their exclusion from places of worship. Romila Thapar notes that in the India of 1,000 to 1,500 years ago organised religion controlled by brahmins was 'well-fortified with finance and patronage', and maintained with endowments of villages, land orfrom the craft guilds - capital. Brahmins conducted the worship, other 'higher' castes played music, lit the lamps, provided flowers and cleaned the buildings. The 'unclean sudras, such as the potters and the tanners and outcastes, were not permitted to enter'. Several hundred years later the British and a few Hindus had made supportive moves to those seeking temple access, but little had changed. Bishop Nirmal Minz of the Evangelical Lutheran Church comments in an essay in *Dalit Solidarity* (Das and Massey, 1995) that although there is legislation requiring access to public temples, 'in practice temple entry is not possible for the Dalits in many parts of India, especially rural areas'.

In *Dalits in India* James Massey summarises the roots of casteism in Hinduism but also describes how little changed in the Muslim and Christian (British) periods. Why was this, when both religions rejected casteism in principle? Says Massey, the 'acculturative influence of Hinduism' may be one reason. There are also elements in Islam which support such distinctions. Jews and Syrian Christians have both received privileges from Hindu kings, but have had to 'internalise caste perceptions' to legitimise their status. Sikhism rejected caste distinctions but evidence shows that by the mid-nineteenth century 'the caste hierarchy among Sikhs was well established'. And as we have seen, Protestant and especially Catholic Christians were little better.

Kancha Ilaiah describes how, not only were Dalitbahujans not allowed to enter Hindu temples but they were not supposed to take the *Bhagavadgita* as a holy book into their homes. In any case Dalits were not expected to learn to read, which was a sure means of preventing religious texts entering Dalit consciousness. This harks back to the way African slaves were prevented from learning to read, even after they had been baptised, and to Roman Catholic worship being retained in Latin for many centuries. Ilaiah says that although today some 'lower caste' people can enter temples they cannot really relate to the gods and goddesses allocated to them. In fact the gods and goddesses of the temples 'were basically set against' Dalits. The brahmins 'walked over the corpses of our culture'.

Showing how this exclusion still goes on, V. Devasahayam told a story at a Dalit Women's empowerment conference in 1995. He recounted an incident in Thattur village, in the state of Karnataka. A Dalit woman had worshipped the Hindu monkey god Hanuman since her childhood. There was a Hanuman temple in the village and one day she asked her husband for something for the first time since they were married - she wanted to see Hanuman. He went to the priests to ask permission for his wife to enter the temple just once, to see the idol. They were furious at the couple's effrontery. They took a slipper and soaked it in excreta and forced it into the man's mouth.

iii) Drums and processions

During my visit to India, while staying in a hotel in a small town, I heard the sound of drumming. Hurrying outside I saw two men coming down the road, dressed in old shirts and ragged trousers, producing some very effective rhythms and being followed by a horse and cart. As they passed I saw there was no-one on the cart, simply a large board advertising a film. The drummers were dutifully drawing attention to the board and the horse was dutifully following close behind them. My Indian colleagues told me this was quite a frequent sight; the men were sure to be Dalits hiring out their not inconsiderable musical talent, to publicise some event they might even be unable to attend, for a few extra rupees.

More often they play at caste funerals, not particularly because they wish to but because they are required so to do. They are also expected to go to the relatives of a caste person who has died and give them the bad news. One theologian informed me he was writing about Dalits as 'the people of the drum'. It is their humble role to carry messages for others.

Godwin Shiri reports in his survey in Andhra Pradesh and Karnataka that even most Christian Dalits practise drumming, more than 70% of those questioned. In AP it was nearly 100%. Drum-beating is required when the village council (panchayat) has announcements to make and when there are religious or social festivals. In most cases, says Shiri, all they receive is 'a little alcoholic drink as an incentive'. If a travelling merchant (or cinema) wants to advertise they may get a little cash. Dalits who refuse to drum can face abuse or physical attack. Shiri found that when some

Christian Dalits refused to play for certain Hindu celebrations 'a vicious backlash was unleashed' and when they sought their daily work they were boycotted. I was told a story in AP about Dalit drummers at a funeral where the caste people complained of poor drumming and beat them up, knocking out one man's teeth. Drumming is one of the practices of Madigathana-Okkaluthana, a set of duties which includes cleaning out animal sheds, helping with the harvest and stripping from dead animals for leather, as well as drumming for caste people. For all these services a Dalit receives a small portion of the harvest crop. Drumming had a negative connotation in the past, it was seen as demeaning, even dirty; 'pariah' means drum. However as Dalit consciousness grows drumming is being rehabilitated, and regarded as a positive skill.

Drumming for caste people's celebrations or processions is one thing. Dalit processions are another. Marriage is an important an occasion in Dalit culture as anywhere else but Shiri discovered in his survey area that Christian Dalits are seriously restrained from having marriage or other family processions in the streets. Such processions were banned for over 60% of those questioned in Karnataka. Most of the areas where the bans were strongest were where Christian Dalits were more literate or economically powerful, suggesting that far from these guaranteeing more freedom they represent more of a threat to caste people. However Shiri also reports that the situation is gradually improving, largely due to active pleading, persuasion and struggle with caste leaders. In some villages a marriage procession is allowed but the newly-weds cannot ride in a vehicle or even on a cart, they have to walk.

Other religious processions are more freely allowed. In only half-a-dozen villages were those restricted. Such processions take place at festival times, it appears these are seen as less threatening. If the caste people are holding processions, dramas, or other events, Dalits are not normally expected to take part, unless they are drumming. They can stand round the edge of the audience for a play but if they want to express traditional appreciation by garlanding the actors this can only be done through a caste intermediary. Prevention of participation in or the practice of cultural celebrations and activities is another form of oppressing Dalits, and supposedly keeping them in their place.

Even in Christian processions the Dalit drummers can be kept apart from Christian caste people. Kumud Pawde tells of seeing a Catholic procession in Goa in 1987 where the Dalit Christians were walking in front, holding wooden crosses and beating their drums, taking precautions to keep a certain distance from the main procession. When she enquired she was told that drumming was a Dalit occupation, be they Hindu or Christian, so she observes 'conversion did not change their caste'.

iv) The power of the priesthood

In Hindu religion - as in most others - the priest exercises a good deal of influence. He maintains it through a cultural and religious power structure which makes him essential at key points in the life process.

Ilaiah says that marriages and funerals are two of the very few occasions that Dalitbahujans come into contact with a brahmin priest. The priest comes to murmur prayers and mantras, but in Sanskrit, a language the people do not understand. The end-product of the encounter, according to Ilaiah, 'is that the priest acquires wealth'. At the end of each mantra he uses two words 'samarpayaami', meaning one must give away all one has, and 'swaaha' meaning one ought to eat everything up. It is the priest who gets to eat everything; every marriage ends in an argument about the priest taking rice, vegetables, tamarind, even cashew nuts from people who in some cases have never yet eaten cashew nuts. The priest must also have his fixed fee, irrespective of the economic condition of the marriage party.

For Ilaiah there is no spirituality in the relationship between brahmin priest and people, it is one between exploiter and exploited. It is worse than between feudal lord and serf; at least the lord has some interest in his serf staying alive, if only to provide more labour. At a marriage even the poorest Dalibahujans will have scrimped, saved and borrowed to buy something new for the occasion, but even in their best clothes there is a wide chasm between them and the priest. 'His overgrown belly, his unexercised muscles hanging from his bones, his oily skin, his clean-shaven head (the barber sub-caste can only touch him while shaving...), all must be seen to be believed. The Dalitbahujans celebrating the marriage look as if their blood has been 'siphoned into the priest's body'.

The relationship has a much deeper dimension however. Because they do not understand the ceremony, or the Sanskrit in which it is performed, the people are made to feel separated from God. At the same time the priest instructs them clearly how to behave towards himself. They must sit, stand, and walk round the burning fire. Finally they must touch his feet, a 'brazenly shameful... subtly manipulated, coercive act'. If anyone - often a youth - refuses to touch his feet the priest incites the elders, urging them to bring the young rebel into line. The elders are made to feel that the community is sinning, and that they must force the youth to perform the act of obeisance.

The priest and his family share no experience with the Dalitbahujan family. The latter must work hard together to provide even basic food, housing, clothing and other basic needs. The Dalits must rise before dawn to begin their daily work, looking after animals, toddy tapping, leather work, cleaning (in the caste homes first) and cooking. The priest however rises, takes his bath and reads the scriptures. He asks God for the day's food, knowledge and character. God will undertake all difficult and delicate tasks, the priest therefore leaves everything to God. He then changes into his silk clothing, 'which of course no Dalitbahujan can ever dream of wearing'. Ilaiah is both cynical and angry at the power wielded by Hindu priests over 'lower' caste and out-caste people. It is linked with the purity/pollution syndrome which is so destructive for the Dalits' sense of self-belief and respect.

It is true that today the movement from the rural areas to the towns and cities has to some degree undermined the power of the brahmin priests. The above pattern, while still the norm in most rural areas - where the majority of Indians live - is breaking down in the confusion of urban life. It may however be easier to persuade Dalits to stay in the villages, thus limiting the enormous strain on the urban infrastructure, if priestly power is destroyed, and village Dalits are released from its baneful influence.

Story 7: The Nasik Diocese, Church of North India (CNI)

Nasik is one of the largest CNI dioceses, situated in the State of Maharashtra on the western side of India. It has 117 pastorates and 455 congregations. Being primarily rural many of its people are Dalits, and its 1996 report states 'Unless the needs of rural people are catered for we would not be doing justice in the sight of God.' It goes on to state the Diocese's commitment to **Holistic Mission**, *which means 'we should be interested in the total human being', and that 'our love must go beyond just giving some charity to constructive development action and working for social justice'. The Diocesan Bishop is George Ninan, who previously worked with the Christian Conference of Asia and the General Synod of the CNI, and who has supplied much of the vision behind the diocesan initiatives.*

Rich peasants are the dominant political lobby in Maharashtra, explains the report. The right-wing State Government has assisted the commercial interests in

78

the urban areas and allowed the well-off peasants, normally non-Dalits, to dictate the economic development of the countryside. This means for example that the irrigation requirements of a cash crop like sugar-cane which needs ten times more water than a cereal crop - come before those of local villages trying to feed their people. Hence, 'the marginalised have been further marginalised... the status of the weaker sections like Dalits and adivasis has been one of facing cultural and political annihilation'. The adivasis are India's tribal peoples who, at 8% of the population, number some 70 millions throughout India; some have said the situation facing them amounts to genocide.

There is little hope for the poor. The report points out that in the new 'liberal' economic policy the Indian Government has been forced to adopt, 'the prevailing development process ruthlessly integrates nations and societies purely on the logic of markets and capital'. This 'atomises' local communities, the young leave for non-existent jobs in the cities, the poor have to travel to what amounts to the bonded labour of sugar-cane cutting, education is seen as a waste of time and the children are taken off to help cut the cane. 'Many do not find their names on electoral rolls... they may cease to be citizens of India.'

The Diocese has sought to take a proactive role within this situation. Among its various initiatives is the **Nasik Diocesan Society for Holistic Development (NDSHD)**. This has a range of programmes, including community development, technical education, health, women's groups and assistance for farmers. It seeks to empower people to find their own solutions to their problems, reasoning that no matter how much the Diocese does, or how many resources it brings in, it can never more than scratch the surface. Hence alongside health, literacy and farming skills people are taught how society operates, who holds the power and what they might do about it.

In one area a doctor - who now calls himself a health worker, to demystify the medical role - works in twelve villages, covering 30,000 people, and focusing on preventative rather than curative health care. Most of the villagers are Dalits. The health team spends some time getting to know villagers then selects someone, usually a woman, to train as the village health worker. In the meantime they talk about such things as the need for 'soak pits', which drain away water on which otherwise mosquitoes would breed, diet, the importance of clean water and the medicinal properties of local herbs - much cheaper than imported drugs and often as effective. The village health workers come together each fortnight, for further training and to talk over common problems.

In the villages discussion often turns to the difficulties of access to water, land and farmer-support, especially animal health care. The field staff are able to point out that the State has a responsibility to provide animal immunisation, no-one knew this and unfortunately caste officials deemed it unnecessary to tell them. Then there are Government programmes for land, water and agricultural assistance. The team explains who are the responsible officials, and how to go about contacting them, but ensures that the people themselves make the approach, and invite the officials to come and visit. By the end of 1997 the villagers were able to set up a meeting with the most senior local State officer, with some 200 representatives of the 12 villages concerned.

Such work is not always without opposition. In 1995 diocesan staff came to the village of Antarwale, and discovered the traditional caste structure operating in the village, with the Dalits living on the periphery. Two generations ago some 68 acres of land had been given to the Dalit villagers under a land scheme but they had not had the initiative to develop it. Now, with the support of the field staff, they began to do so. Opposition came from the non-Dalit villagers and from another local village. However the Dalits resisted this, and after hard work and a good monsoon, the land produced a very satisfactory crop, including extra cattle fodder. This meant there was a milk surplus which has initiated a Dalit milk co-operative. However, as is often the case, there is no access to the main road from the Dalit area - a road was sanctioned years ago but work never started. The Dalits are now agitating for this. They are also fighting off the relatives of someone who had donated a piece of land for a Dalit cemetery. Despite the registration documents the relatives tried to prevent further burials and regain the land, something the Dalits were able to resist, although in 1997 burials were still being carried out with a police presence.

In the twelve-village area the Diocesan staff have a wary relationship with the largest local landlord, who is also a sugar baron and elected representative in the State Parliament. He had to be persuaded that the people needed health care, then that they had to become literate in order to read the health information. He also wants the people's votes however, and the field staff were careful at an early stage to build up a sufficiently strong relationship with enough villages for it to become difficult for them to be dislodged. The Diocese has also raised the Dalit question as a matter of public debate, and in September 1996 held a national seminar on the problems facing the Dalit community.

Opposition sometimes come from within the Dalit community also, especially when women's development is involved. In the village of Nagapur the field staff had to face the anger of local men when the women began to meet together to discuss their common problems. One of the women was actually the Sarpanch, the 'mayor' of the village, but this made no difference. The men destroyed a hut in which the women had begun to meet. Then one evening when a female member

of the field staff was walking to her lodging she was threatened and abused by two
drunken men. With support from other staff she put in a complaint to the police.
The women's group demanded police protection for their meetings, and two
officers were assigned to their next meeting. This gave the women confidence and
their membership shot up to nearly fifty. Thus Dalit women also continue to fight
for their rights.

The Nasik Diocese is an example of what can be done when solidarity with the
poor is taken seriously. There is opposition from within the church, but the energy,
vision and determination of the diocesan leadership carries the work forward.
Warnings are also sounded in its report about national economic policy and its
effects at the grassroots. 'Globalisation' and its outworkings in liberalisation and
privatisation are seen as providing development for the few and destruction for the
many. Meanwhile globalisation makes the rich countries richer, hence the living
standards in the West have an increasingly direct relationship with the poverty of
Indian Dalits and tribal peoples.

e)   Against Women

It is said repeatedly by those engaged in the Dalit struggle that women
suffer a further degree of oppression, they are 'the Dalits of the Dalits'. They
must work harder, carry responsibility for children, manage on less money
and suffer sexual exploitation, in addition to the normal battles of being a
Dalit. Says N.G. Prasuna, in an essay in *Frontiers* on 'The Dalit Woman':

> She looks after the family. She walks miles and miles to fetch water,
> fodder, fuel and so on. She gets up before the cock crows. Her day
> starts by sprinkling water which is mixed with cow dung in front of the
> house. With the sunrise she goes out to work in the fields. She comes
> back in the evening and starts her routine household work. She eats
> very little, she sleeps late in the night and she wears patched clothes.

i)   Patriarchy and religion

As in Western society religion in India has been used to undergird male
comfort and domination. Although there is a marked improvement as one
crosses the border from the Islamic Republic of Pakistan, women still
remain second class citizens in India. Gabriele Dietrich in a paper on
patriarchy recalls Engels' use of the term which links property, patriarchy,
family and State in a power network but remarks that as such relationships

81

have been created they can also be dismantled. She says that some Indian feminists have associated patriarchy with colonialism, ecological destruction and the development of Western capitalist technology, and although this may be true Dietrich believes patriarchy in the Indian context cannot be fully understood without seeing caste as part of the problem, and therefore its eradication as crucial to the solution.

M.E. Prabhakar in his *Frontiers* essay defines patriarchy as a 'power relationship in a male-dominated society by which woman's labour, her sexuality and her fertility are controlled', resulting in her subordination. These relations of inequality have shaped the social ideology of the Indian people and 'caste, production and reproduction have constructed a closed structure to preserve land, wealth, property, women... within it'. Such control of women also ensures purity of caste. The design for a patriarchal caste-class system, says Prabhakar, was developed by brahmins who 'were obsessed with maintaining caste purity through their wives'. Apart from her husband, 'the wife has no existence within the brahminical patriarchy', women obtain their salvation by assisting men to achieve theirs, and by so doing they may acquire the 'karma' to be reborn as men.

We may recall Ilaiah's comments about the Hindu gods and goddesses, and how Brahma's wife Saraswathi is understood as the goddess of learning and education even though she cannot read, as brahmins did not allow women to read their texts. The Ramayana narrative is another means of subordinating women by asserting that wives must be subject to their husbands. Christians may have heard that elsewhere. Ilaiah feels such teachings must be put behind us if we are to defeat patriarchy.

In her essay also in *Frontiers* Kamal Raja Selvi describes Dalit women as 'fourth class citizens'. She tells how in some Christian communities the women have stepped forward to fill gaps in leadership. A woman may even have a white-collar job. But at home she has still all the dirty jobs to do. Being educated or employed does not offer freedom, it can even make life worse. Of course, 'Christian men know and accept that all are equal and that all are made in the image of God', but if they put that into practice they undermine their easy life. Men pay all kinds of compliments to women and proclaim their freedom but at home the woman is 'an unpaid servant, a child-bearing machine'.

The roots of Indian patriarchy go deep and include the **devadasi** system. 'Devadasis' were women maintained as temple staff some thousand years ago who were initially, according to Romila Thapar, a venerated group of women attendants. They later became part of the temple entertainment, some of them undertaking the very demanding dancers' role. Devadasi literally means 'female slave of the gods', and as the system began to crumble in many temples the devadasis simply descended into prostitution. Many of them were Dalits. Their place became symbolic of the patriarchal system in Indian society. Dr Ambedkar tried to draw attention to their situation, and addressed meetings of devadasis and prostitutes in Bombay saying prostitution was a dark blot on society. Godwin Shiri found the practice still in place in his studies in AP and Karnataka, although there the women are called basavis. His survey revealed 12 cases of Basavis among Christian Dalits. It seems that the devadasi system and sexual violence by caste men against Dalit women feed off each other and off the social system of male domination, and are undergirded by Hindu religious practice.

Prasuna observes that patriarchy also has deep roots in biblical tradition. A 'male-dominated cultural context' is given religious authority by its presence in Scripture. Hermeneutics and theology are a male preserve, 'it was men who taught... and interpreted the Bible'. She believes interpreting the Bible entirely as patriarchal however is wrong, there are many texts which suggest women's liberation. Christians need to challenge those notions of God which are based on power, especially the power of patriarchy, which reinforces Hindu patriarchy and in the Indian context causes both religions to be used to justify discrimination against women.

ii)   Economic control

The two most effective ways of controlling women are by refusing any kind of economic freedom and by the use of harassment and violence. Both are practised on Dalit women, sometimes by Dalit men, reinforcing the experience of women as 'Dalits of the Dalits'. N.G. Prasuna begins a section on 'Economic Status' saying 'The financial position of the Dalit woman is very adverse', and goes on to comment that there is no restriction on the kinds of jobs Dalit women can do, they are free to do any menial filthy job from which caste women are kept away. In addition Dalit women contribute 80% of the social labour in the Indian economy. They often find themselves in the position of bonded labourers, having borrowed money for marriages, house improvements, animal purchases and other purposes, which they cannot repay. When they die their children take their place.

Mechanisation and economic liberalisation have made the Dalit woman's life worse. Jobs are even more difficult to come by. Prasuna divides employment into two categories, the formal and the informal. Both include agricultural, industrial and service sectors. Most Dalit women operate in the informal sector, in low-paid unskilled jobs. Prasuna gives four reasons for this poor education and training, the power of tradition in women's jobs, growing use of technology in the formal labour market and ease of entry into the informal category. In rural areas 80% of women work in the informal agricultural sector, on land preparation, irrigation, threshing and storage. They are on a casual daily wage, while trying to grow food for their families and cash crops to sell.

In industry labour can be divided into factories, mines and plantations. Factories offer jobs in printing, food-processing, pottery, fishing, weaving, carpet-making and plastics. In the informal industry sector women do domestic work, fuel collection, sales, construction and cattle-tending. For the same work women get paid less than men and there are no benefits or holidays. Many have health problems in relation to continuous heavy labour or work with chemicals, or eye problems with jobs like lace-making or embroidery. There is little self-employment or entrepreneurial activity. Kamal Raja Selvi in her essay on the Dalit woman as 'Fourth class citizen' adds the consequences of widespread deforestation, which removes wood for cooking from the vicinity of villages - and sometimes moves entire villages as well.

Kancha Ilaiah describes the roles of male and female Dalitbahujan workers, but says women can fairly easily take on the role of men if need be, something which would not be possible for brahmins. He adds, 'a Dalitbahujan woman is a very much a political being, a social being and an economic being'. Finally he draws attention to a phrase from the Gita that particularly affects Dalitbahujan women, 'you have a right to work, but not to the fruits'. The fruits are directed into caste families.

Kumud Pawde, writing on the position of Indian women in *Indigenous People* reiterates how insecure is a Dalit woman's work. There is no protection for their wages, and in many cases no guarantee of even semi-permanent employment. One or two per cent have Government jobs due to the policy of reservation, and perhaps five to ten per cent imitate the life of the middle classes. Up to five per cent take advantage of Government loans. The position of some has changed due to post-independence Government policies.

One of the ways economic control is maintained is through the denial of education to Dalit girls. Even in the state-sponsored schools begun for

Dalits by Jyotiba Phule in the mid-nineteenth century there were very few girls. Reformers kept trying to educate more girls but without great success. Urmila Pawar in an essay about what the Dalit movements have offered to women in *Crossroads* lists a number of efforts in the first half of the twentieth century to draw Dalit women into education. She remarks that only initiatives by the Ambedkar movement made any headway, the most important thing was to persuade parents of Dalit girls to send them to school, 'even today the drop-out rate of Dalit girls is very high'.

Kumud Pawde quotes figures showing that the 1981 Government census showed Dalit women's literacy rate to be 35.9%; in her own survey in the slums of Nagpur in 1993 it was 37.15%. Up to 5% of the latter women had enroled for university education and most of them were conscious of the educational needs of their children, especially the Christians. Shiri's survey shows that, among Christian Dalits in his area, 87% of women were illiterate compared to 65% of men. Only 7% of women had primary and only 3% higher primary education. When asked why this was 40% of the women blamed poverty while another 40% blamed gender discrimination. They recognise that at least some of the power to overcome high illiteracy is in the hands of Dalits themselves.

An overall Government education survey in 1981 suggested that literacy among Dalit women is just under 25%. They tend to drop out in middle school. N.G. Prasuna says that Christian Dalits are more likely to send their children to school, and most likely their male children. Hindu Dalit women bother least about their children's education, because their main aim is to earn their living for which education is not needed. Girl children have to look after the younger children when mother goes out to work.

iii)   Harassment and violence

Stories of abuse and violence against Dalit women are widespread. The underlying dynamic appears to be that caste men have a 'right' to out-caste women, and in order to demonstrate their superiority and dominance over out-caste men they continue to exercise this so-called right. In time past, especially in south India, Dalit women were not allowed to cover their breasts, though this prohibition has largely ceased. It is an extraordinary fact that, although contact with Dalits is supposed to pollute the caste person, when it comes to sexually assaulting Dalit women such 'pollution' magically disappears. Violence against women runs deep in India. Girl babies are more likely to be killed at birth, or even before birth now scanning enables the prediction of gender. Also, although experience of 'sati' (or suttee) - that is the self-immolation of a widow on her husband's funeral pyre - is outlawed it still occurs very occasionally and a woman who undertakes it may be lionised and sanctified. Dowry murder, where it is judged that insufficient dowry has been provided, is another form of such violence.

In her *Indigenous People* essay Kumud Pawde lists the violence meted out to Dalit women - raped because in the opinion of the caste people they have no morals, slain for taking drinking water from caste people's wells, beaten for defecating in caste people's fields when there is nowhere else, burnt alive for violating the caste people's eccentric rules. Then they depend on caste people for their work and bread, this is 'the great problem of existence for them as they are bound between inhuman rules and dependence'.

Shiri's survey documents a wide range of sexual harassment from abusive remarks on the street to rape, even of young girls. Suggestive remarks are made to Dalit women working in the fields, where it is relatively easy to molest and even rape them. Sometimes the Dalit community reacts and tension rises. The caste men hurry to damp down emotions, and use their historical position of social dominance to discourage any action. Often, due to a lack of unity and determination, says Shiri, 'and because of their inherent fear psychosis and servile attitude', the Dalits accept a compromise. Perhaps some money is paid. That is why these incidents continue, unabated.

There are other indirect ways of harassment. Several examples were discovered in Shiri's survey area of Dalit women unmarried or even married - being kept as mistresses by wealthy caste men. There was even approval of such arrangements in some communities. In one village there was an alarming number of unmarried mothers among Dalit girls, due to the sexual activity of the village's more powerful non-Dalit males. Faustina comments on this in her paper on women in *Frontiers*. She says that when the rich caste man or landlord arrives, the rest of the Dalit family have to step outside their home and wait until he has finished. Also in some villages Dalit brides are still sent on their wedding night to the caste landlord.

In the same volume N.G. Prasuna lists incidents of violence against Dalit women in different parts of India. She mentions a village in the state of Madhya Pradesh where every Dalit family has at least one woman raped by a landlord, the state of Orissa where in 1995 330 rape cases were recorded within eight months and a village near Madras where 18 Scheduled Tribes women were raped by Forest Officers. Prasuma identifies the reasons for such behaviour as patriarchy sanctioned by religion, the caste-hierarchical structure of society (with Dalit women at the bottom), women's low education and economic status and the scattered nature of Dalits hampering the organisation of resistance. Further examples are given by WCC staff member Aruna Gnanadason in her essay in A *Reader in Dalit Theology*, she adds that when Dalits do dare to get organised, Dalit women bear the brunt of the caste people's reaction.

Kamal Raja Selvi goes more deeply into the dowry system. She states that whereas dowry was originally something the young man gave to his bride's parents as a symbolic replacement for her labour, due to rich caste people's practice of providing gifts towards a bride's sustenance it became a cultural trait for brides' parents instead to offer 'dowry'. Now many girls are forced to remain unmarried as their parents cannot afford dowry. Selvi tells of three sisters in Kanpur who hanged themselves together because their parents could not afford dowry. Some brides are sent back home after the marriage to demand more goods. Hardly a day passes without some story in the Indian press about dowry suicides, or murders passed off as 'stove-blasts'. 'Brides are for burning!' says Selvi.

A number of observers have remarked that, as in other situations involving Dalits, it was worse than useless going to the police, as they were just as prone to abuse Dalit women as anyone else. Urmila Pawar comments that the Dalit community itself needs to teach more vigorously against sexual harassment and rape, and to organise more effective support and rehabilitation for victims. In the meantime the degree of violence against Dalit women in particular in India is a disgrace to that society.

iv)   Women in the Church

Unfortunately it appears that Dalit women are no better off in the church than outside. Godwin Shiri's survey suggests that Christian Dalit women were as little supported as non-Christians. Kumud Pawde says the treatment of Christian Dalit women is simply traditional. If they come from an illiterate background, as most do, they follow traditional thinking, 'even in caste matters and women's household duties'.

Faustina, a former nun, describes the situation in 'From Exile to Exodus' in *Frontiers*. She points out that women's subordination is not only in 'social, economic, religious and political power structures', but is rooted generally in attitudes, values, language and thought. She tells of meeting some Dalit women on the way home late, from Mass. She sees they are tired and hungry and asks if they have been to work, but is told they have been sweeping the church and the priest's bungalow. She asks if the priest gave them some refreshment and is told indignantly that they were doing their duty and making reparation for their sins. When she inquires if the caste women also helped she hears they are not used to such work, and anyway they do not need to do it as they do not commit so many sins. When she looked at them sadly they tell her they have stolen firewood and food from the caste people' gardens - there was no chance for the non-Dalit women to sin in this way as they did not need to work in the fields for their food.

Says Faustina, 'I kept quiet for... this kind of faith and spirituality has been given to Dalit women by the hierarchical and caste-ridden church.' Religion reinforces caste women's beliefs that they are inferior and sinners. 'In the name of God, Jesus, Eucharist, faith and spirituality Dalit women are exploited in such a subtle way, they don't realise they are fooled.' Dalit women are not provided with a spirituality that is communitarian and liberating, they are subject to atrocities and told they are in mortal sin if they do not meekly accept the teaching of the Church.

Dalits and Dalit women in particular, says Faustina, like to live life with 'spontaneity, simplicity and sincerity'. They express emotion without hypocrisy, but instead of upholding the beauty of their lives religion alienates them by ignoring their culture and feeding them with 'imported pseudo-religious values and practices'. The articulation of their feelings and their relationships to other human beings and to nature are the core of Dalit women's existence but they are 'crushed and abused by the casteist politics and religion'. They exemplify the 'suffering servants' of humanity. Faustina stresses the importance of bringing Dalit women face to face with 'Jesus the Liberator', to 'kindle the fire of righteous anger' within them with the person of Jesus who came 'to set fire on the earth'. Jesus himself broke the rules and regulations of his society to relate freely with women. Dalit women need an exodus, out of the patriarchal religion and into the liberating life and teaching of Jesus.

Protestants claim to have rejected the inferiority of women believed in and practised - as they see it - by Hindus and Muslims. There are occasional reports of women taking non-traditional leadership roles in Protestant contexts. In 1884 a woman missionary preached at a funeral where hundreds of women were present. However Protestant Christian faith was communicated largely from man to man and only secondarily to women. John Webster admits the missionary literature of the late nineteenth and early twentieth centuries was 'amazingly silent' about Dalit women. This was partly because their work was dawn to dusk, and focused basically on survival. Perhaps the most positive gain for women in the Christian Dalit community was the opposition to divorce, which gave them some protection from abandonment.

Younger Dalit women seem to have adapted to the new faith more easily, and gradually Dalit women have begun to take a more active role. At the All-Religions Conference with Dr Ambedkar in Lucknow in 1936 one of the Christian speakers was a woman, Mohini Das. She said Dalit women had been given a new opportunity by Christ's teaching, which 'worked as leaven and revolutionised the position of women'. It was a force which still 'energised the living present'. Women are still however very much second class citizens in the Indian churches. They are a small proportion of the clergy. In the Roman Catholic Church there are many nuns, but only a tiny percentage are Dalits. Jesus's teaching has not yet revolutionised the place of women in the Indian Church.

Discrimination against Dalits is therefore wide and deep in modern India, and it is even worse for Dalit women. In the social, economic, political and religio-cultural sectors of society the caste people continue to fine-tune the system of oppression. M.C. Raj calls what has happened 'objugation', a combination of objectification - making others into objects and 'subjugation' - dominating them. But there is also resistance, and we shall hear about some of that in the next chapter. There are similarities, some of them astonishing, to the ideologies and systems of racism and apartheid with which Western readers will be more familiar. There are also differences, and perhaps the most profound is the concept and practice of uncleanness, pollution, which has been drummed into the collective Dalit psyche for tens of centuries. It is a wickedly conceived and executed weapon, but it is not going to be enough. Dalit people are on the move, the struggle is intensifying, and where there is active struggle there is vigorous hope.

3 THE CURRENT CONTEXT

a)   The response of the State

The 1947 Indian Constitution outlawed untouchability, and it should not really exist. As Indian social scientist Andre Beteille points out, 'we have gone further than most modern Constitutions, including the American, in inscribing the commitment to equality in ours'. Despite this however, he says, 'our practice continues to be permeated by inequality in every sphere', and goes on to describe the situation described in the previous chapter as 'the most manifest contradiction in everyday life in contemporary India'. The stories in the previous chapter illustrate the problems Dalits face. They have the worst land, the worst housing, restricted access to water, the lowest wages, the greatest difficulties in getting decent education or employment, the poorest health care and even the most tumbledown churches - when they have them at all. Sandeep Pendse, in his introduction to *Crossroads* says that today in India 'no-one can ignore the caste question'. It is there in every sector, because the struggles of the Dalits 'have forced this realisation on the rest of society'. Let us look then at how the Indian state has responded, the (rather less influential) response of the churches, the effect of 'globalisation', the progress of the Dalit movements and the reaction of Hinduism.

The main mechanism which successive Governments have developed to counteract the ignoring of the Constitution's provisions is the system of **reservation**, in which Dalits have set aside for them numbers of jobs or political places in proportion to their population, plus a range of other support schemes also. Reservation means, for example, that about a quarter of MPs in the Lok Sabha, the Indian lower house, should be Dalits or tribal people, out of a total of 542. The Bharatiya Janata Party (BJP), the most right-wing of India's larger political parties, which led a coalition Government between 1998 and 1999, might have about half of these. However, Dalit activists say such MPs are bought by their political bosses. They could never afford to stand for Parliament without the financial support of caste people. They are therefore firmly in the latters' pockets when it comes to policies and voting, and this is why nothing changes. There are also Dalits in the State Assemblies, they are known as MLAs, or Members of a Legislative Assembly, but are often still the creatures of the caste parties. One hears echoes in this of the 'Coloured' Parliament set up under apartheid to give a 'voice' to those of mixed race. Perhaps the main Dalit-supporting party is the Bahujan Samaj Party (BSP), founded in the late 1980s, about which we shall say more later.

John Webster in *The Dalit Christians* gives a detailed description of the Indian Constitution's basis for what he calls 'compensatory discrimination'. He outlines how originally Christians in the Scheduled Castes and Tribes would have received the same opportunities under the reservation system as Hindus, but even the Christian members of the Advisory Committee of the Constituent Assembly agreed that Christians - along with Muslim and Sikhs - would not after all qualify. The restriction on Sikhs has since been removed. The main reason Christian leaders supported this was to minimise Hindu concern over conversions to Christianity. If converted Dalits still had reserved access to jobs and political posts the 'politics of numbers' argument would reinforce Hindu opposition to conversion. The result however was that the great majority of Christians who were Dalits lost the opportunities that reservation created.

The Government's *1995 India Yearbook* spells out statistics based on the 1991 census. It says that at that time there were 138 million Scheduled Castes and 68 million Scheduled Tribes, nearly 17% and 8% respectively, and slightly up on the 1981 figures. There is a reservation for 27% of all civil service jobs for these sectors, and a further 10% for 'Other Backward Classes'. The Yearbook does not say how many of these are filled, and Dalit observers comment that appointments to these posts are mostly in the hands of caste people who decide when and if they will be made. Only Dalits willing to toe the line normally get such positions, and when some have been 'advertised' and are not filled due to various manipulations by the upper castes, non-Dalits are then allowed to apply.

In 1990 the Indian Government set up the **National Commission for Scheduled Castes and Tribes** to monitor what is happening to the Dalits and Tribals, to investigate particular situations and to report regularly. It has powers similar to the courts to obtain information, and has seven members. In addition there is a **National Commission for Minorities**, of which Christian Dalit Dr James Massey is a member, along with Muslim, Sikh and Hindu representatives. There is a Government scheme of grants to local bodies representing the Scheduled Castes, in 1993/4 these amounted to R75 million but in 1995/6 over R200 million was available if Dalits could successfully apply. A common complaint about such grants is that they tend to be administered and controlled by caste people and are hard for Dalits to access.

Another compensatory mechanism the Indian Government adopted is the **Protection of Civil Rights (PCR) Act**, which was strengthened in 1977. Over twenty States have made provision for legal aid to Dalits to make use of this law. There are 42 special courts, some mobile, which have been set up in the most incident-prone States such as Andhra Pradesh, Tamilnadu and Bihar. The Government also organised in 1979 a special central assistance scheme for socio-economic development, making 100% grants to States to support initiatives with Dalits. In the year 1994/5 funding available totalled R2,740 millions. There is a Government-funded Finance and Development Corporation for Scheduled Castes and Tribes, with capital of R3 billion, and education schemes including hostels for village children, scholarships and pre-examination coaching schemes to help Dalits with exams for the civil service. There are also promotion 'set-asides' for Dalit people, which again are all-too-often dependent on the goodwill of those who administer them.

Other laws which the Government has brought in to address aspects of casteism are the **Prevention of Atrocities Act**, in 1989, and the **Protection of Human Rights Act**, in 1993. The former was intended to generate more rigorous action against violent harassment, and connected Prevention of Atrocities Rules were published in 1995. The Protection of Human Rights Act set up the National Human Rights Commission, which is normally chaired by a judge and is aimed among other things at monitoring breaches of the international conventions to which India is a signatory. Some State Governments have set up their own human rights commissions also. The National Commission makes an annual report to the Indian Parliament, but a number of such Commissions make reports and these are often not actually debated. The Commission is pressured by such bodies as People's Watch in Tamilnadu, and now by the National Campaign for Dalit Human Rights, to live up to its responsibilities. Further legislation related to caste includes the **Employment of Manual Scavengers Act** (1993) and the **Panchati Raj Act** of 1994 which aimed to strengthen the representation of Dalits and other poor people in the panchayats, or village councils. There have also been efforts at land reform, a 1998 Oxfam report demonstrates both how vital an issue this is to Dalit communities, and how limited is the progress so far.

Ajit Muricken of VAK says that it was political mobilisation by the Dalits that helped to bring about these measures, to ensure some Dalit access to jobs, grants, protection and political representation. However they also had the effect of co-opting at least some of the articulate section of the Dalit community into the system. This in turn, says Muriken, led to competition between Dalit leaders for power and conflict between loyalties to party obligations on one hand and 'the real issues of deprivation, injustice and misery of the vast masses of Dalits' on the other. VAK also observes that the reservation policy has had an effect on the educational attainment of the Dalit community, leading to entry into occupations previously unavailable to Dalits, a 'toe-hold' in the middle class and the rise of a few individuals to 'positions of authority and influence'. Bas Wielenga of the Tamilnadu Theological Seminary and Centre for Social Analysis also comments that reservation, although not the answer to the whole problem, has provided an economic base for the improvement of some Dalits.

Webster provides a detailed analysis of reservation. He believes the potential benefits of the system have been undermined by focusing on access to jobs rather than land and using unnecessarily high standards to restrict the flow of Dalits into their reserved positions. He says this reflects a paternalism and incrementalism reminiscent of 'continued domination by the old caste elites'. The operation of the system kept Dalits divided and so far has changed 'neither the position of Dalits within Indian society nor the Indian social structure and its underlying value system'. He cites criticisms of the emerging Dalit middle class for cutting themselves off from their own people, being co-opted by the oppressors and controlling the remainder of the reservations. On the other hand, he says, 'it is from this group that the intellectual and political leadership in the continuing Dalit struggle for equality has come'.

Franklyn Balasunderam remarks on the difficulty of reservation schemes for those who hope to benefit from them. 'The politician, the police and the judiciary have an upper caste bias' (and he might have added the civil service), and Dalits have to declare their Dalitness publicly to get any possible preference. This can then reinforce their inferiority status. Kancha Ilaiah speaks of Dalits who make their way up in the police service because of reservation requirements and who then 'face the wrath of brahminical officialdom' and the caste business community, still being treated as untouchable as their families before them in village life. However Ilaiah says such police officers are becoming 'a source of inspiration' for many Dalits, giving them hope for future change. Padhy and Mahapatra in their *Reservation Policy in India* (1988) conclude that 'the principle of preferential opportunities must be accepted as justified, inevitable and also necessary' and state that such treatment is 'not a violation of the principle of equality, rather an attempt to make competition more equal'.

The most significant development of reservation for Dalits, according to Webster, has been the emergence of Dalit Christians from obscurity in church and society. Religious discrimination makes them aware of themselves as 'a distinct social entity', and encourages them to take collective action to address the problem. It has also pushed them towards more active collaboration with non-Christian Dalits, a necessity if real change is to be brought about.

One argument in favour of the Indian State's reservation system is that it actually enshrines in law a principle which anti-racists in Britain and other European countries have been pressing for some time, the principle of **positive action**. The basis of this is that where the playing field is not level, which it rarely is for minorities in any society, certain structures have to be introduced to make the field level, otherwise nothing changes. The UK has had 'equal opportunities' policies for decades but they have made comparatively little difference to the proportion of black and minority people still unemployed and absent from the corridors of power in British society. For example there are only tiny numbers in the judiciary, at senior management level in big companies or Superintendent level in the police. In Parliament there are only nine MPs of minority origin; by proportion of population there should be well over thirty.

In the United States 'affirmative action' has been successful in improving the educational standards of minorities, enabling access to better jobs, creating a range of minority businesses and launching a range of black people into senior roles in business, politics and the media. For example in the early eighties under black mayor Harold Washington the city of Chicago through a 'set-aside' system increased tenfold its contracts with minority businesses over a two-year period, thus leading to many more minority jobs. Under Ronald Reagan, however, steps were taken to undermine affirmative action, and some programmes were designated as unconstitutional by a Supreme Court gradually packed with Reagan nominees. Small minority businesses closed down and the unemployment rate for blacks began to rise again.

There are always repercussions from positive action initiatives; the key is to create structures leading to gradual but irreversible improvements along with an educational programme that sets out the gains in terms of a more balanced and less prejudiced and anxious society which is using the talents of minorities effectively. There is then a far greater likelihood of social peace. The Indian Government hedged for a number of years on the findings of the Mandal Commission which had reported in 1980 that the situation of Scheduled Castes and Other Backward Classes was not improving, despite all the facilitating schemes and programmes. It advocated a much more vigorous approach to the schemes and structures that were already in place. It was put on ice until 1990, when the V.P. Singh Government decided, no doubt in part for its own political reasons, that it should be implemented. There was an enormous reaction. Caste people actually committed suicide to demonstrate the strength of their opposition - and in practical terms their commitment to casteism. It was out of this situation that the 'Hindutva' movement, discussed in section e), emerged.

b)   Casteism in the Church

The battle against casteism has been ongoing in the churches since the missionaries arrived. Most observers say that, overall, casteism is more prevalent among Roman Catholics than Protestants. An example was the protracted court battle in Vadakkankulam, Tamilnadu, where in 1910 a Roman Catholic church had been built in two wings, with a wall one metre high separating the caste people from the Dalits. M.R. Arulraja tells the story in *Jesus the Dalit*, stating that the local priest actually demolished the wall in November 1910. The caste group in the church took him to Court, quoting a Catholic catechism published with the support of the Bishop of Pondicherry which stated that 'The existing caste system in India is quite consistent with the way of the world. The Gospel has no direct relevance to this. Therefore the Catholic Church abides by it.' The catechism went on to cite the Pope, who had ordained that 'the preachers of the Gospels had no commitment towards the task of either changing or removing those harmless traditions'. Arulraja explodes at this description of casteism as a 'harmless tradition'. The priest, with the backing of his own bishop (of Trichy), won the case, but it was left to two judges of the Madras High Court - one English, one Indian - to state that such separation in worship 'contradicts the fundamental doctrine of Christianity'.

John Webster in *The Christian Dalits* cites complaints in the early twentieth century against some Protestant missionaries for bringing Dalits into the church. The criticisms were that this lowered standards of baptism and turned away potential caste converts, thus 'making the development of a truly Indian church more difficult'. Such 'upper caste' critics, some of whom in 1914 formed the All-India Conference of Indian Christians (AICIC), demonstrated a 'highly-ambivalent attitude' towards the bringing of Dalit Christians into the church. They claimed they were obliterating class distinctions and contributing towards 'the uplifting of the animistic races and so-called untouchables'. But the members of AICIC could not envisage such people being represented on church councils; it was they who were best placed to represent the 'depressed classes', and 'better than any other community in India'. AICIC was careful to stay well away from the political and economic struggles of the Dalits, something for which caste Christians are criticised up to this day.

It was in the 1920s, according to Webster, that for the first time there were 'clear signs of Dalit rebellion against casteism in the Church'. In the south-western State of Kerala defiant Dalits formed their own indigenous churches. In 1924 in one town a vigorous argument broke out over the use of a Catholic church between its Dalit and caste members. There was rioting and bloodshed, the police had to be called in and some caste Christians reconverted to Hinduism when their privileges were not protected. The next year in Madras Dalits got a conference against untouchability to condemn both segregation by caste inside churches and the refusal of admission to some Dalit converts. The political dimension of the Dalit movement was developing, even inside the churches.

In the 1930s Dalit Christians were calling on Gandhi to help them overcome untouchability in the churches. Gandhi expressed sympathy, remarked that 'Christian harijans' was a contradiction in terms, and said his movement would help them drive casteism from the Church. However, as Webster comments, Gandhi's movement was one **for** Dalits rather than **of** Dalits, and they became increasingly impatient with a Hindu leader who in the end was not willing to attack the caste system itself.

In an essay written around 1938 Dr Ambedkar commented that casteism continued inside the Christian Church and that Dalits had the same problems after conversion as before. Even more important the Church did not encourage Dalits to tackle their social and economic discrimination. It was non-Christian untouchables who formed the movement to tackle this discrimination, said Ambedkar, not the converts. He said tha, despite the education of some of their leaders he had never seen Dalit Christians organising 'for the redress of their social wrongs', they were too dependent on the missionaries.

James Massey in *Downtrodden* describes how in worship services into the sixties, Dalit and non-Dalit Christians were separated in worship, and non-Dalits sat near the front so they could use the communion vessels first. Poornam Damel in his *Emerging Dalit Theology* essay describes how in the 1980s in some places Dalits were still segregated during the liturgy, and prevented from reading the scriptures, singing in the choir or serving at Mass. In some villages they were not allowed in the church for a family funeral and in some cemeteries there are separate areas for Dalits and non-Dalits. They could not participate in the church council or pastoral work and at festivals the parish procession would not pass down their streets. Few Dalits are invited to 'vocation camps', set up to test a call to the ministry or priesthood. On Maundy Thursday only the caste people have their feet washed by the priest.

Arulraja has a further story of Dalits at Thatchur in the Madras-Mylapore Archdiocese presenting a 23-point petition to the Archbishop. This related to the reddy sub-caste and protested against separate church seating and exclusion from any representative participation either in worship (like scripture readings and singing in the choir) or other church activities. The Dalits also sought the leasing of church land for cultivation, a minimum wage when cultivating reddy lands and equal access to the parish school. The reddies had claimed none of the Dalits were able to read - the scriptures or anything else - despite the fact that as long ago as 1965 the school had 240 pupils learning Tamil, Telugu and English. Says Arulraja, 'we can imagine how much the reddies (had) worked to ensure that the Dalits did not get educated'.

In many areas Dalits still work as bonded labourers to caste Christians. Damel describes one situation where the Dalits had to cultivate the land of the higher caste reddys. They got paid 3-5 rupees for 12 hours work, which was not enough to enable them to cultivate their own lands. The reddys, who owned on average 1,000 acres against the 40 acres of the Dalits, took the Government loans which were meant for the Dalits. They also controlled the Government co-operative stores from which all essential commodities had to be obtained.

In a personal interview Anthony Raj expressed his dismay over the proportion of Dalit priests in the Roman Catholic Church. He said that Dalits were around two-thirds of the church members, but only made up 3.5% of the priests and 2% of nuns, and the first Catholic Dalit Bishop was not consecrated until 1993. Poornam Damel says even this only happened because there was so much agitation by the Dalit Catholic community. He also gives an example of the Pondicherry Diocese where in 1990 Dalits were 80% of the membership but only 12% of the priests, and none of these in any position of responsibility. Damel mentions dramas being staged by vanniar caste Catholics which ridicule Dalits, and describes one he witnessed where a collection raised 32,000 rupees. Caste priests get posted to lucrative urban parishes, he says, while the Dalits are appointed to the rural areas. Damel says this 'is structured violence against the Dalit Christians'.

Webster says there has been much research into caste in the Church, but it is mostly concentrated in the south of India, where caste and Dalit

Christians live side-by-side. In the north, there are very few caste Christians. The general consensus, he believes, is that their Dalit identity is significant to Christian Dalits but discrimination against them is just as great as against non-Christian Dalits. Among issues which remain are the degree to which 'class' discrimination replaces 'caste' in the Church, and whether Christianity offers a channel of upward mobility to Dalits. He singles out Kerala as a place where casteism remains particularly strong, there were still no Dalit priests in the Orthodox churches in 1968 - after 1900 years of Christian history! He also cites a 1986 study of a Roman Catholic village near Bangalore in south central India where social segregation was extreme, including the use of offensive caste names and denial of the services of the village barber and teashop to Dalit Catholics.

Through certain Christian institutions however, especially in the fields of education and health, Christian Dalits have found some improvement. In a 1963 survey in UP in northern India 35% were unskilled workers, 28% skilled, 18% white-collar workers, 15% teachers or church workers and even 3% were managers. However caste people dominate the church leadership overall and control the employment practices, including the ordination and location of clergy.

Webster gives a number of examples of how this works, and also of Dalits leaving one denomination for another, or even setting up a new one. In 1964 one group under Revd V.J. Stephen left the Church of South India in Kerala to form the Travancore Cochin Anglican church. This is strongly reminiscent of African Americans and African and Caribbean Christians in Britain and other European countries who in response to racism have 'voted with their feet' and set up their own churches. In the Kerala Syrian Church, in the mid-1980s Dalits were holding demonstrations, pickets and fasts to demand a proportional share of all church positions. Some Dalits reacted even more strongly. In one study between 1980 and 1983 over 2,500 Dalit Catholics in the southern State of Tamilnadu were reported to have rejoined Hinduism, a similar thing happened in central Andhra Pradesh. Others converted to Islam. A Conference of Dalit Christians in 1982 vigorously criticised caste Christians' power to give their own people education and jobs at the expense of Dalit Christians. Webster's initial findings are that casteism is still strong in the south, but in northern India class is becoming more important. In the urban areas particularly lines are less sharply drawn, and class begins to dominate caste. However the struggle is intensifying because, while the Church has assisted in creating a 'Dalit Christian middle class', its control over education and jobs is decreasing, it cannot satisfy all aspirants and upper castes cream off the best places. Dalit

98

Christians are squeezed, there are few opportunities inside the Church and - because they are not 'Scheduled Castes' - even fewer outside.

Education is a key contemporary issue for Dalit Christians. They are particularly caustic about the prestige schools which were initiated by the churches in the nineteenth century and which the children of the upper-caste elite now attend. There are both Catholic and Protestant schools in this category. Massey quotes the 1978 report of the Jesuit 'Inculturation Commission', which admits that the image of the Jesuits is 'mainly derived from our... educational institutions'. These are centred on urban areas, the medium is English and they serve the privileged, the 'upper ten', or top ten per cent of society. I made an enquiry of one head teacher as to whether issues of caste and inequality were dealt with in such schools, and was given to understand that although non-Christian students attended Christian assemblies such matters were not addressed. It seems extremely unfortunate that the Church should have become identified with elitism, at least without presenting different values and extracting additional income to educate the poor.

Godwin Shiri, in *The Plight of Christian Dalits*, gives a searing analysis of the difficulties faced by the Christian section of the rural Dalit community. Some, including the Indian Government, still argue that Christian Dalits are better off than non-Christians because they have access to the resources of the churches. Shiri's detailed study demonstrates that this is not so. He studied 44 villages in an area on the borders of the States of Karnataka and Andhra Pradesh in southern India, with between two and 150 Christian households in each. The villages varied from a few hundred to some thousands in population. 560 people answered a very detailed questionnaire and also attended some discussions. Only 13% of them earned more than 5,000 rupees a year (about £80). Shiri found that Dalits suffer the same discrimination from caste Christians as from caste non-Christians. When the Dalits were asked why they thought this was, they replied that it was due to their untouchability, which makes them 'objects of repulsion'.

It is the detail of Shiri's study which makes it particularly revealing. He undertook it partly to give the lie to the supposed better opportunities for Christian Dalits. He noted that in those villages where there were Christian non-Dalits they had no social relationships with Christian Dalits, there was absolutely no 'eating and dining' and Christian Dalits were not allowed into non-Dalit Christian homes. The non-Dalits attended worship, but were not involved in any other activity which would bring them into contact with Dalits. In the small town of Bellary, Christian

Dalits who had migrated there for work and gone to the local church were ignored by the caste Christians. When they organised a Jathra, a kind of festival, the Christian non-Dalits did not come. Shiri says it ironic that while everyone comes to the Hindu Jathra, including the caste Christians, only Dalits attend the Christian Jathra.

Shiri also questioned his respondents about their relationships with their pastors. All the pastors were of Dalit origin, but seemed indisposed to live in the Dalit areas of the villages, receive hospitality in Dalit homes or invite Dalit members into their houses. The latter was felt to be because their houses were in upper caste areas and they did not wish to upset the neighbours, so the churches were now building manses in Dalit communities. Shiri concludes this part of his research by commenting that casteism within has 'caused much harm to the mission of the Church' and to the growth of the Christian Dalit community. Christian Dalits see little difference between the views and behaviour of caste people whether Christian or Hindu. Even the pastors, though from the same background, are prejudiced and the general negativity towards Christian Dalits has prevented them from receiving church resources or taking their full part in church life.

Hence casteism clearly remains a substantial hindrance within the mission of the Indian Church. The influence of the Church is limited, but arguably it is greater than its 2.5% of the Indian population. Attacks on churches and on Christians by right-wing Hindus escalated in late 1998, which suggests that despite its weaknesses Christian witness against casteism is having some effect. Those attacking churches said it was because they were a foreign influence, undermining the Indian way of life. Christian observers commented that it was at least partly due to their success in uplifting Dalits that was making them a target for the casteists. The attacks have had the positive effect of bringing together the different streams in Indian Christianity, including the Roman Catholics, Protestants and Evangelicals, into the United Christian Forum for Human Rights, and this could point the way to a new era of challenging caste both within and outside of the churches.

c)   The role of 'globalisation'

It would be a fair question to ask how globalisation effects what is happening to the Dalit communities of India, most of whom live in villages way out in the rural areas. Time and again however, in the conversations I had with Dalit activists, in the reading I was given and even in conversations (through interpretation) with Dalit people in the villages, the term 'globalisation' cropped up. What does the term mean, in this context? What it appears to mean is the process by which capital has become increasingly internationalised, so that no Government or national bank any longer controls its own interest or exchange rates, or the flow of money into or out of its borders. This flow happens by way of transnational corporations, international banks and other financial institutions, and currency speculators who are wholly disinterested in the economic structures of the countries through which they do business, especially of the poor in those countries, but concerned simply as to whether there is profit to be made. There will be more profit to be made where wages and costs are low, services are privatised and land is cheap. At the same time, if products can be internationalised, with brand names known the world over, costs reduce and profits rise.

The global financial principalities and trading powers are helped if a proportion of the population of a country where they want to do business have entered into the 'global culture', where certain products such as soft drinks, electrical goods, cigarettes, cars and other consumables are fully recognised as being important if not essential to a comfortable and meaningful life. In Sri Lanka, at the end of my visit to South Asia, I came across one good example of the results of this process while walking round Kandy Lake beside the Temple of the Tooth, one of Buddhism's most sacred shrines. Across the lake from the temple, set in this most beautiful of cities, was a four-star hotel which proclaimed on its large advertising board 'Japanese Karaoke, Italian Pizza, Carlsberg Lager'. There was clearly little if anything Sri Lankan in there, the assumption being that - even if there was - no-one with money could possibly want it.

Globalisation in Indian terms means a new economic order which, after keeping out Coca Cola for decades, finally had to accept defeat and let back in that most banal and over-priced of Western products in the early nineties. It means an economy opening up to 'the market', with the kind of results outlined above, where Governments lose control of their exchange and interest rates because they are decided somewhere up in the financial ether, depending on how good the country is for making money and have nothing whatever to do with the plight of disadvantaged communities like Dalits. It means that small farmers in certain areas are persuaded to leave their traditional crops because the soil and climate are right for growing a cash crop like cotton. Unfortunately, if they all do so, as they did in one region of Andhra Pradesh in central India, the result is too much cotton. The price goes down, and farmers kill themselves because they cannot sell their crop, they have not grown any alternative and they cannot feed their families.

Globalisation leads to liberalisation. This means that transnational corporations may come in and buy land cheaply, forcing the labourers who earned their living on it to head for the cities, swelling the millions who are trying to eke out a living on the swamps and under the plastic sheeting of the slums in and around Third World cities. Liberalisation means that such companies buy up small local producers of - for example - fizzy soft drinks, then replace their product with an international brand name, close small factories, sack the workers, advertise heavily and put up prices just enough to sell the right number of cans to make the maximum profit.

Liberalisation leads to privatisation, the sale of public services to private capital. This means that telephones, buses, electricity, trains, sections of the civil service, gas, water, even prisons, gradually fall into the hands of private business, which will almost certainly provide an adequate service for those who can pay but, by definition, has no interest in those who can't. Where this is most damaging in the Indian context is that large swathes of public services, which were subject to the policy of reservation, with all its flaws, now are so no longer. Hence the number of jobs available to Dalits through the reservation structure is shrinking rapidly, leaving them with even less choice and forcing them to desperate measures.

One simple example of this came my way when visiting a small school, set up and run by Dalit youth who themselves could find no jobs. The children, in a small village school along a country road some miles from the nearest town, were seated in lines on the grass to meet us visitors, and when asked to sing an action song gave voice to 'Ding dong bell, Pussy's in the well. Who put her in, little Tommy Thin, Who pulled her out, little Johnny Stout' etc. When asked why on earth Indian Dalit children in a small village school miles from anywhere were singing in English I was told that those in charge of the school believed it was essential for the children to learn English to have any chance of finding a job in the new 'global economy'.

In a Paper for a discussion on **A Search for Dalit Unity** at a conference in September 1997 Anand Teltumbde spoke of the new situation faced by the Dalits since India opened up to the global economy in 1991, saying we have to take two identities of Dalits into account:

i)   Dalits as the specific oppressed social group,
ii)   Dalits as part of the broad class of have-nots.

In the first identity there will be less jobs due to disappearing reservation, 'the future job-seekers from Dalits will face virtually closed doors, those

102

having jobs today could face... losing them'. In the second identity there will be a reduction of jobs and social security, increased consumerism and inflation and an onslaught on Dalit culture. At the same time the caste people will seek to keep them obedient and divided. One good thing that could come out of this, says Teltumbde, 'at the risk of sounding sadist', is that the loss of reservation and the resulting alienation might impel Dalits fundamentally to review their position, for example how they might overcome the difficulty of forming alliances with the Other Backward Classes, which they will need if they are to challenge the current trends. Shantaram Pandere in his essay on Dalit militancy in *Crossroads* believes it is the Ambedkarist Republican parties who can bring about this common platform. If they are to do so they will, as he puts it, 'have to do away with petty groupism' and develop a new effective programme for Dalit liberation.

A report from the Indian National Social Action Forum comments that the Structural Adjustment Programmes imposed by the International Monetary Fund (IMF) and the World Bank are generating a real squeeze on the poorest classes. These programmes reduce the funds available for health, education and housing. The Indian economy is linking up with world capital. Even 'forestry and agriculture... are parts of an international economic chain'. Control of forests, land and minerals is being concentrated in fewer hands, even the 'pathetically feeble' governmental efforts towards land reform will fade. The report quotes a recent relaxation of the ceiling amount of landholdings by the Maharashtra State Government as an example. The small landowners of the Other Backward Classes as well as the Dalits will be the losers. There will be little employment even as wage slaves. All that will be left is work in tourism, entertainment and prostitution.

The report goes on to point to the role of Hindutva in destroying any approach to a common identity of oppression among the Dalits, Tribals and Other Backward Classes. The history of the few successful struggles is being buried. Perhaps understandably, says Bas Wielenga, in a time of contraction people look to the needs of their own family and clan first. The efforts of Ambedkar and Phule at creating 'self-respect and cultural revolt' are forgotten. As we have seen in the previous chapter, women are the particular victims of this process, being even less likely to obtain work and finding that subsequently their status declines even further.

It is the case that some Dalits welcome globalisation; they believe it is creating new relationships of production and urban job opportunities, weaning people away from the land, and that these processes will gradually

103

undermine casteism. Many however disagree. Kancha Ilaiah summarised the situation as he saw it in a feature article in the *Hindu* newspaper in November 1997, entitled 'Dalits and globalisation'. He wrote of the 'post-capitalist process' in the market economy creating an 'unprecedented consumerism of the middle and upper middle classes', which is destroying 'the very existential basis of the poverty-ridden masses'. The old feudal relationships still exist in the rural areas, the market is dumping consumer goods into social structures which include caste and the lives of Dalitbahujans are being torn between growing aspirations on one hand and increasing deprivation on the other. 'While urban roads are full of cars and motor-bikes, and the middle class and rich houses are full of durable, western-fashion consumer goods, the children from a majority of SC, ST and OBC families are unable to even go to school and eat enough food.'

The crime rate rises and the State cannot control it. Suicides in the villages increase. Despite slightly improving education there are few jobs available. Dalits have no access to capital, which might allow them an entrepreneurial role. In India caste rather than class plays the role of social capital and 'there is no way the Dalit-Bahujans can survive in the competitive capital market'. Even the Marxist parties are powerless to maintain a state social security system. The Hindu approach is no better, it treats all labour as undignified and redundant. Globalisation needs less and less human energy, but that is just what countries like India have got. 'Dalits', says Ilaiah, 'have to evolve a programme to contain and fight the effects of globalisation. Let us not forget what the Buddha told us, "Consumerism and *sama sangha* (truly human society) are antagonistic to each other". Globalisation is turning us into consumerist beasts. Let us reject it and return to our humanitarian roots.'

Before leaving this topic it may be worth drawing a distinction between what some economists have called 'humanising globalisation', as opposed to 'dehumanising globalisation' which has the kind of effects outlined above. There are humanising effects of globalisation, including the ease of international communication via electronic mail, which can lead to increasing understanding and the possibility of earlier intervention in problematic situations. Perhaps what is needed is the control, even democratisation, of globalisation by acting upon the greater knowledge and understanding evolved through improved and more immediate electronic communication. The people and the governments of the West have both the possibility and responsibility to humanise globalisation and we discuss this further in the final chapter.

d)   Movements of resistance

There is a very long history of resistance to casteism, most though not all initiated by Dalits. Most of the earlier examples were what Valerian Rodrigues in an essay in *Crossroads* calls 'transformist' movements, led primarily by caste people. D.A. Mane in a chapter in the same book describes one such revolt from as long ago as the twelfth century in Karnataka, a central Indian state, about the time the 'Bhakti' movement began among Hindus. Mane says that a brahmin, Basaveshwara (Basa), led a rebellion against caste, and mobilised the lower castes to fight the social evils that made their lives a misery. He formed a 'house of the learned' and offered representation to all. Women from the oppressed castes also participated in his movement. Basa took the view that casteism could only be abolished by inter-marriage, so he arranged a marriage between the son of an untouchable and the daughter of a brahmin. However his opponents poisoned the ear of the King about his activities, some of his followers were tortured and Basa himself ended his life in disgust by jumping into a river to his death. His movement died with him, although Basa remains an example of those Hindus opposed to casteism.

James Massey points out in *Downtrodden* that the Dalit struggle dates from the period the Vedas were being written, 600 BCE. He says the original inhabitants of north-west India resisted the invaders, the first major movements were the Jains and the followers of Buddha some 500 years before Christ. Massey comments that the Muslim era, from the 8th century BCE to the 17th CE 'brought no substantial change' for the Dalits. The Sikhs challenged untouchability, but it is Massey's view that the real turning point of Dalit resistance came around the time of the Indian Mutiny against the British in 1857. He goes on to describe a number of other Dalit initiatives which emerged during the nineteenth and early twentieth centuries.

Kancha Ilaiah in *Why I am not a Hindu* outlines the Vemana and Veerabrahma movements in the seventeenth century. Balasunderam describes a number of caste groups and organisations who worked with Dalits, including the Brahmo Samaj (or Society), the Arya Samaj and the Depressed Classes Mission. The Brahmo Samaj was formed in 1828. It was mainly an elite movement for upper castes and operated in English, but it did have a programme for Dalits. This mostly consisted of opening schools, organising a library and intercaste dinners, and promoting widow remarriage which was banned by brahminism.

Jyotiba Phule was perhaps the leading figure in anti-caste activity in the nineteenth century. Believing that making education accessible was one of the most important things, he founded a school for untouchables in 1852. According to Shantaram Pandere in *Crossroads* Phule made available to the out-castes his home water supply to demonstrate their equality as human beings. The movement inspired by Phule was known as the Satyashodak Samaj, and is said to have used popular anti-brahmin religion as its ideological base. It offered more participation to Dalits than some other anti-caste movements.

The Arya Samaj, founded in 1875 by a Hindu monk, operated in Hindi and became a more widespread movement. It worked mostly in the north, for example among the sweepers and chamars in Lahore and Delhi, but also had branches in Madras and Madurai in the south. It repudiated caste and opposed child marriages, opened schools and gave untouchables the right to wear the sacred thread, sign of the 'twice-born'.

The Depressed Classes Mission was started by V.R. Shinde in Bombay in 1906. It aimed to teach untouchables hygiene, sanitation and temperance, and offered free medical care. It opened night schools and hostels and sought to provide jobs. By 1913 it had thirty educational institutions. It spread across the centre of India to Madras. In 1918 Shinde proposed to the Indian National Congress that there should be reserved seats for Dalits in decision-making bodies but this was not accepted. The Congress had been formed in 1885, but did little on matters affecting Dalits until passing a 1917 resolution to remove 'all disabilities imposed... on the depressed classes' (33), but this was not effective. It was not until the arrival of Gandhi in 1920 that the Congress began actively to confront the effects of the caste system. As we have seen elsewhere however, Gandhi only challenged untouchability, not the system itself, and at least a part of his motive, as with the other examples above, may have been to stop the drift of Dalits into other faiths or political groupings.

Most of the above initiatives are placed by Rodrigues in the transformist category, attempts 'to reorder the existing relations from above by reorganising the elements constituting these relations'. A second category is 'participatory', which requires the involvement of 'those hitherto excluded from deciding issues concerning them'. Ambedkar is the key figure in this category. Another category is 'revivalist', which focuses on the idea that Dalits are all the descendants of Buddhists, and they need to revive their origins to escape from the Hindu caste system. Rodrigues' fourth form of resistance arises from a class analysis based on Marx and

106

Weber. There are three positions within this latter category, says Rodrigues, one argues that caste is the primary social relationship in India, a second that it is class and caste is subservient, the third that the two are intimately linked - there is a high correlation between caste and economic status but they are not always the same.

In order to oppose brahmin domination in southern India some non-brahmin 'forward' castes joined together in 1917 to form the Justice Party. This Party lay somewhere between the transformist and participatory categories, and included a number of Christians. In the 1920 elections it co-operated with the British authorities and won a majority of seats. Once in power, however, transformist tendencies took over. It gradually excluded the Dalits, and exhibited little interest in social reform. Balasunderam quotes one commentator as saying that the Party's aim had been to 'supplant the brahmins, while keeping the untouchables at a good economic, educational and political distance'. Its leader, Sir P.T. Chettiar, rejected the idea of a law against untouchability and in 1923 Dalit leaders like M.K. Raja left the Justice Party.

E.V. Ramaswami Naicker, later known as 'Periyar', was born in Erode in south India in 1879. He had only five years of formal education but gradually joined the struggle against casteism and for the opening of temples to untouchables. He joined the Congress Party but left it because it would not accept a fixed quota of seats for non-brahmins and in 1925 founded the 'Self-Respect Movement'. Periyar eventually became extremely critical of all religion, especially Hinduism, becoming convinced - says Balasunderam - that 'casteism and Hinduism were one and the same thing'. He wanted a new set of values where people of whatever caste enjoyed mutual respect. The first congress of his Movement in 1929 called for a boycott of brahmin priests, the removal of caste names, the eradication of untouchability and easier divorce - perhaps with persecuted women particularly in mind. From these initiatives came the Temple Entry Act (a step in the struggle for the elimination of untouchability), a campaign for the admission of Dalits to the priesthood and the movement for proper representation for Dalits and other backward classes at all levels of society.

Periyar developed his movement in 1944 by initiating a political party, the Dravida Kazhagam (DK), the Dravidian Federation or Front. Later one of his followers, C.M. Annadurai, split from the DK to form the Dravida Munnetra Kazhagam (DMK), the Progressive Dravidian Federation. Annadurai (who came to be known as 'Anna' or 'elder brother') was more sympathetic to religious belief than Periyar. He developed his party to the point that it won

Madras (now Chennai) in 1967. Anna's funeral in 1969 attracted three million people. He was succeeded by M. Karunanidhi who, after splits in the party cost him subsequent elections, re-emerged as leader and chief minister of Tamilnadu. Karunanidhi has vigorously promoted the Tamil language and culture, to a degree opposed caste and attracted some Dalit support. A further split from the DMK created the All-India Anna Dravida Munnetra Kazhagam (AIADMK), which has no obvious ideology and is now the political vehicle for entertainer Jeyalalitha, who helped to bring down the BJP Government in April 1999 by making continued impossible demands for her party. Selvanayagam says that 'in the wake of coalition politics in India... the Dravidian movement is becoming more and more vulnerable, wanting a clear ideology, mass mobilisation and steady leadership'.

It is to Ambedkar that one must continually return, however, in the field of Dalit resistance. He more-or-less defined the 'participatory' category, according to Rodrigues, and saw that the assertion of the deprived at individual and collective level, leading to a reorganisation of relationships, 'can alone break the ties of dependency and servitude'. In the first phase of his work Ambedkar mobilised around such issues as temple entry, opening up common drinking wells and the condemnation of 'sacred' texts supporting untouchability. In the second phase he began to view Dalits as a separate social group. However he was unable to win the social reforms for the Dalits which he sought. This pushed him to seek separate representation, the issue which brought the confrontation with Gandhi in 1932.

By the early 1930s, Ambedkar had come to believe that the Dalits should concentrate on their political identity. He devised a two-pronged strategy for this. Firstly, Dalits should seek the social and political skills required to participate in society and, secondly, the social structures should be redesigned to allow sufficient participation by Dalits. He adopted the slogan of 'Educate! Agitate! Organise!'

Ambedkar, as he moved towards his most influential piece of work in drafting the Indian Constitution, struggled with formulating the most effective structure for democracy. Democracy is not only a set of rules and institutions, says Rodrigues, it is 'an ethos'. Values and structures of the past may not fit with hopes and expectations of the future. Ambedkar believed traditional social structures in India militated against democracy, he feared that the Gandhian agenda would 'reinforce traditional obscurantism'. Rodrigues feels he probably hoped there could be a legal and constitutional coup from above, supported by some kind of movement from below. The belief grew in Ambedkar that Buddhism could be the philosophy and provide the energy for the move towards a true ethos of democracy. Buddhism would also 'bear witness to social and economic injustice', and defeat 'brahminism'.

It was in 1935, in a long speech to a conference of 10,000 people near what was then Bombay, that Ambedkar made the unexpected statement that, although he had had the misfortune to be born an untouchable, 'I will not die a Hindu because this is within my power.' The conference members subsequently passed a resolution that they would leave Hinduism and join any religion that offered them equality. The reasoning seems to have been that the Gandhians had failed to end untouchability, there was an intellectual and emotional need of the Dalits for self-respect and Ambedkar was seeking to place the initiative in the Dalits' own hands. There was a vigorous reaction, not least by other Dalit leaders who did not agree. Invitations came to Ambedkar from the Muslims and Sikhs. The Christians however, says Webster, were more cautious in their response.

Webster feels that some Christians did however understand Ambedkar's move. They challenged Gandhi's statement that untouchability was 'on its last legs'. Bishop Azariah of Dornakal said that true religion would bring social uplift, and Christianity had shown this. A Roman Catholic Archbishop appealed for an end to casteism in the Church, to show 'Christianity was a religion of equality'. The prospect of sixty million people changing their faith was, according to Webster, 'stunning in its impact'. Through the later thirties various faiths courted Ambedkar, while progressive Hindu bodies pressed him to stay. For the All-India Depressed Classes religious conference in 1936, Sikhs prepared the food, Muslims entertained the delegates and Lucknow Christian College provided the venue. Fourteen spokespersons told of what their faith could do for Dalits, unfortunately neither of the Christian speakers was a Dalit.

Christians however featured prominently, according to Webster, in the national debate about conversion. Gandhi reserved his most vigorous attacks for Christianity, and also revealed his view that Dalits were incapable of understanding the Christian message. Webster quotes his interview with John Mott when he asks 'Would you preach the Gospel to a cow? Well some of the untouchables are worse than cows in their understanding.' It was probably the continuing problems that Dalit Christians had within the Church that turned Ambedkar away from Christianity. Ambedkar noted that 'caste Hindus were the chief beneficiaries of Christian educational and medical work', and that casteism continued in the Church. Christianity was not 'the distinct, cohesive and political entity Ambedkar was seeking', says Webster, so eventually he became a Buddhist. This move never enhanced Dalit political power in the way Ambedkar had hoped.

However, many believe Ambedkar's legacy is still evolving. The key chapter in Gail Omvedt's *Dalits and the Democratic Revolution* is 'Ambedkar: the Theory of Dalit Liberation'. Omvedt believes strongly that 'Ambedkarism' is a living force today, both in India and beyond, and remains the ideology of the Dalit movement. She herself offers a Marxist analysis, often comparing Ambedkar and Marx. One disappointment which comes through her writing is that the Indian communists failed to see the revolutionary potential in Ambedkar's thought, and allied Indian communism with Nehru and the Congress Party rather than with Ambedkar. Omvedt defines the six themes of Ambedkarism as first 'an uncompromising dedication' to Dalits which required the 'total annihilation of the caste system', second 'an almost equally strong dedication to the reality of India' - which he sought to wrest from the imposition of a 'Hindu' identity, third the conviction that the eradication of caste meant the repudiation of Hinduism as a religion, fourth a broad economic radicalism interpreted as socialism but with a dedication to individual rights, fifth a 'fierce rationalism' which took 'liberation theology' forms, and sixth the importance of linking a 'firmly autonomous Dalit movement' with an alliance of the socially and economically exploited.

Such an approach meant that, when the fairly powerful communist parties opted to support the battle for independence as part of what they saw as 'the socialist revolution', Ambedkar felt that while visionary revolutionary leaders seek a socialist revolution, Dalits have to get on with bettering their lot, so should fight for the 'democratic revolution'. Ambedkar was not against Marxism but, believing that Buddhism was more effective in the abolition of private property, felt it was superior to Marxism. Ambedkar was keen to reconstruct the Dalit identity and, according to Omvedt, linked with Phule and Periyar to 'construct an alternative identity of the people, based on... low-caste perspectives, critical of the oppressiveness and claims to antiquity and superiority of the dominant Hindus'. He argued for a late origin of untouchability and therefore its less-difficult eradication. 'brahminism' and 'capitalism' were the main enemies and had constantly to be challenged and fought. He advocated an alternative political force to undertake this, but neither Congress nor the communists were able to support him. He therefore moved first towards creating the Scheduled Castes Federation, and later the Republican Party, but unfortunately died before the latter could be brought into a proper existence.

India is one of the few countries where Communist parties are still electable. There is however fragmentation among these parties. The Communist Party of India-Marxist (CPI-M) is the largest, and holds or has held office in the states of Kerala and Bengal. The Communist Party of India is now quite weak; the Communist Party of India-Marxist/Leninist (CPI-ML) is active but fragmented. One of its best-known factions is the People's War Group (PWG), which is a semi-Maoist group most active in the eastern states of Bihar, Orissa and Andhra Pradesh. The PWG seeks to work with Dalit and tribal people in struggles on land and other issues at local level, but one criticism is that it leaves them exposed. For some time in Bihar there have been battles over particular pieces of land, and some landlords employ (illegal) private armies to protect their interests. On 1st December 1997, in Bihar, one such private army raided a village where cadres from the CPI-ML and the PWG had been supporting local peasants in a land campaign. They killed 61 people, including women and children, and it seemed that the PWG was unable to defend its proteges. A retaliatory raid in March 1999 left about thirty of the landowners' militia dead.

Kancha Ilaiah comments that Marxism is 'the most revolutionary theory that capitalist Europe has produced'. He believes that if colonial rule had produced anti-brahmin Marxist intellectuals, India might have had a 'Dalit-bahujan socialist revolution'. Hinduism would have become the religion of yesterday, and brahminism the ideology of the past. However, he says, colonialism produced only upper-caste intellectuals, and Marxism became the domain of the more reactionary social forces - brahmins and neo-kshatriyas. The caste links between brahmins inside and outside the revolutionary movement have prevented any real progressive change. Dalit observers also comment that, while Dalits were welcomed into the CPI and the others as members, they never somehow made it into the leadership. Rodrigues believes the Communist movement is yet another type of transformism, it does not really engage the Dalits themselves. It has not radically altered social relations, nor empowered Dalit people.

The beginning of the current phase of the Dalit movement can probably best be located in the launch of **Dalit Panthers** manifesto in 1973. This grouping, which took their name from the Black Panthers of the USA, grew up in the State of Maharashtra, inland from Bombay on the west coast. The Panthers' manifesto describes untouchability as 'the most violent form of exploitation on the face of the earth'. However much power structures change, it seems to survive, because Hindu feudal rule controls production, bureaucracy, army, police, land, jobs, capital - and even religion. The manifesto states that these structures must be understood, so 'we can... strike at the heart of this exploitation'.

The Panthers emerged out of the Phule-Ambedkar tradition. In a related fashion Dalit art, theatre and literature developed also, challenging the arts establishment. The Panthers began to burn the Manusmriti, the Hindu holy writings. Groups of their activists went to the scenes of atrocities against the Dalits, comforting the victims and threatening the caste people. They urged Dalits to organise against their oppressors. In *Crossroads* Shantaram Pandere quotes a Panther leader asking, in reference to the stripping of a Dalit woman, what the meaning was of a piece of cloth masquerading as the national flag in a country in which the cloth that a Dalit woman wore was not inviolate.

This militant approach created an inevitable backlash, and Pandere points to a key weakness of the Panther strategy in that they did not seek to isolate specific oppressions and build a unity of the Dalits and lower castes against them.This left the village Dalits exposed when the caste people attacked them. On the other hand the Panther movement did create a sense of pride in Dalit communities where there had been none before. They began to celebrate the anniversaries of Phule, Ambedkar and even Buddha. They flew a blue Buddhist flag and erected Ambedkar statues. Such changes, which occurred without any local or national government permission, were - according to Pandere - an 'historic step of Dalit militancy'.

The main study of the group appears as *The Dalit Panther Movement in Maharashtra* (1991) by Lata Murugkar. It concludes the Panthers' lack of ongoing success was mostly due to poor organisation which among other things failed to levy any subscriptions, allowed disruptive elements into its inner circle and failed to control 'obscene and abusive' leaders. However, says Murugkar, it was the Panthers who after Ambedkar had gone 'awakened the slumbering community of the Dalits again... galvanised them into action, made them stand with raised heads and clenched fists... and was successful in attracting the attention of the authorities and society towards their plight'. Murugkar believes the Movement had a revolutionary ideology which could not be put into practice because its leaders lacked the necessary revolutionary character.

Perhaps the high-point of the Panther period was the renaming of the Marathwada University in Maharashtra after Dr Ambedkar. A campaign to get the relative legislative bodies to agree was successful, but immediately created a vigorous backlash. Says Pandere, the 'violent character of the brahminical casteist forces was revealed for all to see'. Dalit campaigners were attacked, houses were burned and some were killed. This however brought together the progressive forces, there were demonstrations and hunger strikes, and hundreds of thousands went voluntarily to jail, in Gandhian **satyagrahi** (truth force) tradition, also practised by the Civil Rights Movement in the American South.

In the long run however the Panthers failed to come together with other campaigning groups in any joint analysis or ongoing programme. Gradually the movement fell apart into a number of individualistic factions with competing leaders. Similar fragmentation happened in the Republican Party. The tendency to individualistic and competitive leadership, which has frequently bedevilled Dalit initiatives and is encouraged by caste parties, struck disharmony into the heart of the post-Ambedkar crusade. Even now different sections of the Republican Party vie for Dalit support, in Maharashtra and beyond. Some attended the second national convention of Dalit Solidarity Peoples in December 1997, pressing their claim to be the true heirs of Ambedkar. Vestiges of the Panther movement remain however. Gita Mehra in her collection of essays published for the fiftieth anniversary of India's independence in 1997 describes a visit to a Panther poet in his plastic-sheeted shelter in a Mumbai slum. He rages against the political culture that is almost wholly interested in and dependent on money, and finishes by rejecting even Ambedkar's policy of changing religion. 'For people like us', he says, 'power can only come from the barrel of a gun'.

Statues of Ambedkar are one of the main signs of Dalit resistance today. Visiting the village of Thaiyyur (see Story 4 in Chapter 2) it was a statue of Ambedkar the villagers wanted to put up as a sign they had won control of disputed land. On the way to meet Ayyangali of Perungudi (Story 5) I passed large Ambedkar statues in Madurai and at a key road junction, festooned with garlands for a special feast-day. Sometimes caste people ridicule these statues. In July 1997 a poor community in Ramabai, Mumbai, rose up when sandals were hung round the neck of their Ambedkar statue as an insult. In the ensuing melee the police shot ten dead and injured 26, (reported in full in *Broken People*).

Another illuminating account of Dalit resistance is told by Ilaiah in *Crossroads*. It is the story of the Chundur rebellion, which took place in Andhra Pradesh in 1991. The Chundur Dalits had been among the first in

113

the area to convert to Christianity, but they had never really challenged caste. To the upper castes then, the Church was a place which saw some improvement in the literacy and dress of the Dalits but did not challenge - for example - the tradition that cattle had more rights to drinking water than the Dalits. However when religious consciousness began to be combined with political consciousness and the two main Dalit sub-castes, the Malas and Madigas, began to work together and erected an Ambedkar statue in the village, the upper castes got nervous. Also they discovered the Dalits were raising funds for education, and could see their cheap labour getting too clever to be exploited much longer.

The reddys were the main sub-caste in the area, and in mid-1990 they had arranged one of their regular street dramas, but as the play was about to begin Dalits came and insisted on sitting among the reddys, despite their objections. At this behaviour the reddys from surrounding villages began to collect funds for the Chundur reddys to help them teach their Dalits a lesson, and raised 50,000 rupees to buy weapons. Meanwhile the Dalits were challenging the caste system in all kinds of ways, in cinemas, queues, hotels and bus seats. The reddys began to spread propaganda about Dalit designs on upper caste women, a frequent prelude to physical attack.

In July 1991 Govatova Ravi, a Dalit student from Chundur, went to a cinema and bought a 'chair-class' seat, sitting next to reddy youths. One of them claimed Ravi's foot touched him, and his friends beat up the student severely. The Dalits retaliated, Ravi's father when he heard about the incident sent his son away for safety. The next day the reddy youth went to the school where Ravi's father was a teacher, dragged him out and tortured him to get information as to where Ravi was. They then beat Ravi unconscious. The whole Dalit community came behind the terrified family, and the reddys began to arm themselves.

The Reddys solicited collusion by the police, who went to Chundur and told the Dalits to flee to the west, saying only men needed to go and they should not carry weapons. The Reddys were waiting for them and as they ran through bushes by a canal the reddys axed their legs, speared eight of them to death, cut up the bodies into bags and threw them into the canal. The police meanwhile sat and smoked in the village. Their officers, and the public officials who should have conducted an immediate enquiry, failed to do so.

The Chundur Dalits fled to shelter in a Salvation Army church some way off, which pleased the caste people as they thought the Dalits would never come back, and would forfeit their land. However sympathetic forces also arrived at the church. The Dalits made their plans and decided that the next day they would take a large procession into the reddy part of the village and bury there the bodies of those who had been killed. The Government officials and landlords tried to prevent them, the latter even set fire to some of their own haystacks to cause a provocation, but the Dalits burnt some reddy houses and a landlord was also killed. The dead Dalits were buried despite the presence of the police, and the reddys themselves had to leave as their area had been polluted. Ilaiah finishes with the comment that the Chundur rebellion was a major victory, and stands as a permanent warning to the upper castes.

The Rural Education for Development Society (REDS), based around Tumkur in Karnataka, has developed a strategy of resistance by empowering Dalits, and assisting them to understand the nature of the globalisation and casteism which keep them on the periphery. The founder of REDS, M.C. Raj, has evolvd a philosophy of 'Dalitness', which emphasises a new dependence on Dalit spirituality, traditions and skills. It also challenges the outside supporters of Dalit liberation to a new kind of relationship with Dalit communities. Raj calls on Dalit intellectuals to come together to help reorientate the Dalit psyche.

A very recent analysis of the growing effect of Dalit resistance is offered by Aloysius in *Nationalism without a Nation in India* (1998). He argues that the allocation of the rise of political consciousness in India to 'uppercaste, urban segments... and the subsequent emergence of the Indian National Congress' is based on a very narrow political understanding of nationalism and a particular ideology. He says that 'uppercaste consciousness is so dominant among the intelligentsia that little research has been done on the egalitarian aspirations emanating from traditionally depressed communities'. He describes a number of movements from the base by Dalit peoples which shook the colonial system, including the Chandals in Bengal in the 1870s and 1880s, the Vaishnava movement in Assam in the 1920s, the Mahatos and Yadavas in Bihar and UP and the Noniyas and the Chamars in north India in the 20s and 30s. Aloysius argues that these movements of resistance were in fact the real independence movement; they promoted a genuine nationalism, not a replacement of the colonial structure with a neo-colonial, casteist system. The anti-Brahminical movements 'were in fact struggling for and supporting the process of birth of a nation'. The anti-caste Dalit movements were the true Indian nationalists.

e)   The 'Hindutva' backlash

There is, unsurprisingly, a vigorous reaction to the growing consciousness of Dalits among the traditional Hindu population, the 'caste people', and certain aspects of this are extremely unpleasant. Some observers of the Indian political scene at the present time are sufficiently concerned about the direction and approach of right-wing Hinduism to refer to it as neo-fascist. It is Kancha Ilaiah's view that violence has been Hinduism's principal method of control, hidden much of the time behind a consent system maintained through gods and goddesses who have been co-opted from the social base it exploits. Ilaiah describes in detail his upbringing as a kurumaa boy, specially trained in sheep-breeding, and gradually separated from his childhood friends in other sub-castes who were toddy-tappers, plough-drivers or cattle-breeders. The girls too were brought up learning different skills. Gradually he learned his group's place in the caste system. His parents warned him particularly to be polite to the higher caste landlord, who would otherwise 'hit us in our stomachs'. His sub-caste, the kurumaas, could however command malas, madigas and others who were untouchables lower down the scale.

Ilaiah's proposed alliance of Dalitbahujans - that is Dalits and sub-castes of the sudras, the fourth caste (OBCs in Government terminology) - should assist in opposing what he describes as the 'neo-kshatriyas', the new alliance of upper sudra castes like reddys and velamas. This alliance is attempting to take over the kshatriya role of political power within the Hindu framework, it is becoming the patron of 'Hindutva', literally 'Hindu-ness'. Hindutva, says Ilaiah in *Why I am not a Hindu*, is a modern form of brahminism which works in the interests of caste people 'to subvert the political assertion of the Dalitbahujan castes which form the democratic and secular social base of India'. Its blend of spiritualism and political power is rooted in 'casteised patriarchal authoritarianism'. It builds on the brahminical tradition of patriarchy, attempting to establish control over the institutions of the State and civil society. Its attitudes and behaviour towards those it deems as lower castes border on fascism.

The ideology of Hindutva is seen by many Dalits as the most dangerous development in India at the present time. James Massey describes it as 'militant Hindu revivalism' and quotes the 1996 BJP Election Manifesto referring to 'one nation, one people, one culture... defined by our ancient culture and heritage. From this belief flows our faith in 'Cultural Nationalism', which is the core of Hindutva'. It is this approach which led to one of the most unpleasant and dangerous incidents in the life of

116

independent India, the destruction - with several deaths - of the Babri Masjid in December 1992 at Ayodhya. This was a Muslim mosque, and not only were the BJP happy to see it destroyed but they wanted to replace it with a Hindu mandir, in the belief that there had once been a Hindu temple on the site, which had been destroyed by Muslims. There is as yet no real proof of this but militant Hindus are reported still to be preparing the construction of a mandir.

It perhaps needs to be reported that the Hindutva movement claims that it alone can uplift the Dalits. It points to the number of schools and hospitals it is running in north India to illustrate this. There are Dalits who support Hindutva in its strengthening of the Hindu identity. It was also of course possible to find so-called Coloureds and even Africans who supported apartheid, and African-Americans who regarded Martin Luther King and the Civil Rights Movement as Communist trouble-causers. It is very difficult to see how Hindutva could offer genuine psychological and spiritual freedom to Dalits.

In *Towards an Understanding of Indian Society* Gabriella Dietrich and Bas Wielenga from the Centre for Social Analysis in Madurai point to the dangers of 'communalism', the exclusive identification of one's own religion with the truth, the attempt to draw all members of that religion into a common approach and the determination to drive out, or destroy, those of other faith communities. It is important to understand the ideology of communalism, the belief that people who have the same religious interests also have common political, social, economic and cultural interests. Hence Hindus should unite as Hindus, Muslims as Muslims, etc. Thus in India the old brahminism is being superseded by a strategy of trying to create a pan-Hindu identity, into which all Hindus - including the Dalits - will be incorporated. Such communalism is fired up by attacking other faith communities, such as in the Ayodhya atrocity, to which the then-Indian Government turned a blind eye for its own political reasons.

There are other political and more shadowy groupings on the Hindu right-wing, promoting Hindutva. They include Shiv Sena, Vishwa Hindu Parishad (VHP) and the Rashtriya Swayamsevak Sangh (RSS). Some of these have even attempted to appropriate Ambedkar, by saying he was pro-Hindu and anti-Muslim. Many Dalits would not know this was untrue, so one task facing anti-casteists is a constant educational programme to communicate the true nature of Ambedkar's teachings. Groups like Shiv Sena and the RSS have been organising for some years to build up a national network of similar-thinking people, and are now becoming increasingly active. The media seem unwilling to expose them; no doubt media people have their own pressures, anxieties and fears.

A good example of the dangers of communalism occurred during my visit in the city of Coimbatore in central Tamilnadu. As is happening more and more widely there has been in Coimbatore an increasingly open relationship between the right-wing Hindu leadership, the police and sections of the business community. There was an incident between Muslim youth and the police on 29th November 1997 which led to a senior police officer threatening to shoot Muslims. The youth went back to their community, organised an attack and murdered a traffic police officer. Thereupon the police went out of control, attacking a number of Muslims including an MLA, burning his car, then shooting a number of Muslims and murdering others who were brought injured to the hospital. Witnesses heard senior police officers telling their men to carry out the latter task, presumably on the basis that those arriving injured must have been involved in attacking police officers. A report by **People's Watch** of Tamilnadu to Amnesty International within three days of the events analysed what had happened and the reasons for it. From the press however it was impossible to understand what was going on, much less that there was a strong communal element.

This type of communalism among higher caste Hindus also impacts on Dalits. A number of observers describe the intensity of right-wing Hinduism now as neo-fascist. Bas Wielenga notes certain comparable elements, including the 'glorification of virile strength and aggressiveness', a sense of humiliation in the past, projection of all that is bad on to the enemy (in this case the Muslims) and the symbolic use of certain images for mass communication and mobilisation. In a personal interview Franklyn Balasunderam agrees with Ilaiah's view that elements of the BJP and parties further right were fascist. Nalini Pandit in his *Crossroads* essay on 'Dalits and Hindu Communalism' describes the activities of Shiv Sena who, he says, organise the Backward Classes against the Dalits and get income from contacts with organised crime. Pandit goes on:

> Shiv Sena is openly for dictatorship and its ideology and tactics are those of the Fascists. Fascism is an ideology of the ruling classes in a time of stagnation and decline. Its main interest is to suppress discontent and divert it towards ethnic or cultural minorities. In India, where caste and class are closely related and caste is more in the consciousness of the people than class, Fascism can be used as antidote to class struggle.

To the extent that the ideology of Hindutva lies behind the philosophy and the initiatives of the BJP and its partners, therefore, it is a dangerous and destructive development. Casteism, like racism, in its more extreme forms spills over into fascism. The next Indian Government, if it really wants to make the reservation system work, end the ugly harassment experienced by the Dalits and enable them to play their full part in Indian society, will have to evolve a far more active and long-term education programme, ensure its criminal justice system is geared up to tackling casteism and demonstrate a much greater commitment to ending discrimination than it has thus far.

4 STRUGGLE AND HOPE

Like many other countries in the South there is increasing injustice, inequality and violence in Indian society, and casteism is a vital part of the ideology which sustains and encourages this. The degree of oppression against Dalits was reinforced by the March 1998 election results which brought the BJP to power in a coalition Government. The results of the fall of this Government in April 1999 remain to be seen. At the same time there is an increasing awareness among Dalits of their situation, and corresponding increase in writing, organising, cultural initiatives and praxis (actions-within-a-purpose). Some of what I saw and heard in India reminded me of the spirit among young black south Africans in the 1960s and '70s, a spirit which led eventually to the exposure of apartheid in all its venality and to its destruction. The struggle is on, and as with all struggle it benefits greatly from outside support and feeds greedily on the hope that lies within it.

Before exploring the movement that is taking place it is important to undertake some analysis. The account below draws partly on personal discussions while in India, partly on writings of social and political observers there and partly on comparisons with situations of struggle in other parts of the world. There is finally some comment on what inevitably is the relatively minor role which the Christian Church may have in Dalit liberation.

a)   Analysis

What exactly is going on in Indian society, with respect to Dalits, and what are the causes? Some of the latter may be internal and some external. Firstly the population is continuing to increase, putting ever greater pressure on the social infra-structure and the environment. Secondly inequality is also increasing, the rich are getting richer and the quality of the poor's life is declining. Thirdly the process of 'globalisation', the latest manifestation of monopoly capitalism, is gathering pace with its accompanying dynamics of liberalisation and privatisation which place more and more public resources - including land and jobs - in private control. Fourthly this process is in turn forcing more poor people, especially Dalits, off the land and out of relatively secure if low-paid jobs and into the urban slums. What happened in Zaire in 1997 and Indonesia in 1998 illustrate a possible outcome. Lastly the greatest burden is borne by women, who have to continue with badly-paid casual work while seeking also to build a home and bring up the next generation.

120

One of the most active debates among social and political analysts in India is whether caste or class has the most powerful effect, or whether a new type of 'claste' analysis is appropriate, incorporating both class and caste analysis. Bas Wielenga, a European social analyst who has worked for many years at the Social Action Centre related to the TTS examined this topic in the context of a lecture on the centenary of Dr Ambedkar's birth. He observes that many Indian Marxists limit themselves to a class analysis and explain caste away as 'the superstructure of feudal class society'. Their strategy for change has been to concentrate on class struggle against landlords and property-owners, and assume that caste will wither away. Wielenga however argues that a complete analysis needs to take account of all dimensions of social consciousness and is best done within the Marxist dialectic. This requires, for example, taking account of Dalit women agricultural labourers who suffer discrimination on grounds of caste, patriarchy and class. To address their situation they need a trade union, a women's movement and a Dalit organisation.

Wielenga notes that Ambedkar, confronted with the harsh reality of the effects of the caste system, follows Marx in documenting what happens to real people. So the massacres of Dalit agricultural labourer families in various places around India highlight the way caste is used to maintain the structures of power. He says Ambedkar bases his analysis on his own experiences as well as on theory and thus makes it contextual, particularly with respect to religion. For example when Ambedkar wrote a paper on 'Annihilation of Caste' for a 1936 conference of caste Hindu social reformers, he placed the emphasis on the need for either a radical reform of Hinduism or a different faith. On another occasion Ambedkar engaged with communists and socialists in and around the Congress Party, arguing that economic reforms are only a partial answer; social status and religion must also be tackled. In an address to a Dalit conference the same year Ambedkar exclaimed, 'You have nothing to lose but your chains, and everything to gain by changing your religion'. The allusion to the Communist Party Manifesto linked class struggle to a change of religion. Ambedkar's over-riding concern, Wielenga goes on, is how the Dalits can escape from the 'isolation imposed upon them by the caste system'. Omvedt offers a similar analysis.

Wielenga believes Ambedkar was correct in including caste and religion in his analysis, as well as class and economic structure. Ambedkar wanted to replace Hinduism's 'religion of rules' with a 'religion of principles', which would include liberty, equality and fraternity. It sounds like he had the same kind of trouble as Jesus did with the Pharisees. However, says

Wielenga, Ambedkar did not see religion as a weapon in the struggle so much as contributing to a vision of the future, the 'basis for a wider community in the new society to come'.

Poornam Damel SJ debates a caste, class or 'claste' analysis in his reflections on the Dalit struggle for liberation in *Emerging Dalit Theology*. He first makes a number of harsh observations about modern India, that it has a capitalistic government of the rich for the rich; that rather than a democracy it is a 'mammonocracy' where politicians are made and bought by money; that big companies are getting richer while nearly half the population live below the poverty line; that agricultural surplus is diverted to industry forcing peasants to head for the city; that a recent survey of 200 villages showed 95% of government development grants were used up in administration and that the laws supposedly protecting 'untouchables' are a farce. Damel quotes Nehru's fine words about Indian socialism involving 'vast and revolutionary changes', with the ending of private property and profit for a 'higher ideal of co-operative service'. This would actualise the inter-relatedness of all humanity, says Damel, and it is against this larger canvas that 'the evil of caste oppression suffered by Dalits... has to be seen'.

Damel's view is that 'an exclusively caste-based approach to the liberation of Dalits... will be suicidal'. He observes that removing injustice in the wider social structures 'through a class-based organisation of all the oppressed' would, although difficult, be the best hope for causing present injustices to wither away. He notes that some suggest organising initially on a caste basis then switching to alliances with all the oppressed, a 'claste' approach, but feels the effectiveness of either will be best determined through actual praxis.

In the same volume Maria Arulraja SJ observes that the 'Indian Marxist comrades' regard Ambedkar's religious conversion as a disservice to economically deprived Dalits. These comrades however are not involved with or committed to Dalits at the base. He quotes Ambedkar who observed that people will not join a revolution for equalisation of property if they are not going to be treated equally themselves, 'You cannot have political reform, you cannot have economic reform, unless you kill this monster' (i.e. casteism). Drawing on Mao's teachings Arulraja comments that Dalits 'as the leaders of the Indian revolution should understand the existential animosity between the Backward Classes, Other Backward Classes (OBCs) and 'untouchables' as the 'non-antagonists contradiction'. In other words Dalits and all other 'backward classes' have much more in common than sets them apart, and need to identify their 'common principal enemy' in the march towards 'the new heaven and new earth'.

Mohan Larbeer of the TTS Dalit Resource Centre offers a similar perspective. He is a founder of the Federation of Dalit Action for Liberation (FeDAL) which had its first major conference in December 1997 in Madurai. Larbeer believes Dalits need to build alliances with tribals, OBCs, women and environmentalists to develop a sufficient power base to effect change. This is controversial as, especially in Tamilnadu, some Dalits see the OBCs as their worst enemies. On this analysis key aims must be the removal of untouchability alongside addressing the psychological oppression of Dalits, and persuasion of OBCs that alliances with Dalits are in their interests. Larbeer views the growing violence in Tamilnadu as dangerous and believes that if it has to happen it needs to be more controlled and strategic.

Kancha Ilaiah also believes that Dalits have to ally with other disadvantaged communities. He challenges the 'Hindutva' ideology, which claims all Indians not belonging to another specific religion are Hindus, including Dalits. Ilaiah, from a sudra sub-caste, argues that Dalits, sudras and ati-sudras should unite as Dalitbahujans, against the common ideology of the three 'upper castes'. He points to the ideological conflict now going on between the brahmins, baniyas and neo-kshatriyas whom they have co-opted, and the Dalitbahujans who have now discovered Marxism and Ambedkarism. Ilaiah believes the neo-kshatriyas, the managing class, are now becoming the pillars of Hindutva and neo-fascism. He says, 'it is only a conscious Dalitbahujan Liberation movement which can 'step by step, decasteise society, socialise the means of production and finally create humanitarian socialism in India'.

From the Mumbai-based VAK comes a similar perspective. In *Crossroads* they reprint the Statement of the Indian National Social Action Forum (INSAF) Commission on Dalits and other oppressed castes. INSAF argues that there are common factors between Dalits and OBCs. Their resources are expropriated, they are both victims of exploitation and oppression, they are denied social well-being and political power, they are denied their share in what society produces. In order to gain some control over land, water, jobs, education and health they will need to join together. Violence is used to deny them these things, and the 'higher' castes operate a divide-and-rule policy among the SCs, STs and OBCs. Jobs are a particular problem, as privatisation is taking jobs out of the public sector where they are subject to the reservation system. The same is beginning to happen in education. The Hindu Communalist forces seek to deny the cultural identities of tribal peoples (adi-vasis) and Dalits. They seek to absorb them into Hinduism and distort or eradicate the tradition of struggles and movements among the oppressed. The INSAF's Commission argues that unity is vital, among Dalits, with other 'Oppressed Castes' and with all other oppressed groups 'with transformatory potential'. Hopefully that might that include the churches.

VAK sets the whole problem in the context of globalisation. Ajit Muriken, VAK co-ordinator, points to IMF and World Bank policies which reduce the money available for education and health. Privatisation means less jobs, rural labourers flee to the cities. TNCs buy land and concentrate on crops for export, which further displaces rural populations. High-tech industries appear, creating jobs but only for the highly-trained. Mechanisation in sugar and other rural industries and railways puts hundreds of thousands out of work. Wealthy business people begin to ally with politicians and both with organised crime. Communalism is whipped up by conservative religious parties to ensure retention of political power. Muriken supports the suggestion in an earlier chapter that behind the BJP is the RSS, which has been building its power and influence over decades and represents extreme right-wing Hinduism, with its 'Hindutva' ideology.

The situation needs to be addressed at the emotional and psychological level as well as the intellectual. Dalits are in particular need of gaining their self-respect in order that they can respond to the calls for action and change. For Christians there is need for a liberation theology which deals with the psychological dimension as well as those of economics and politics.

There is an ongoing debate, particularly among external supporters of Dalits, over the parallels between casteism and racism. Should Dalits like minority communities elsewhere claim a separate racial or ethnic identity? How strongly should they argue the parallels of their situation with native Americans, black South Africans, Australian aborigines or black and minority communities in Britain? Bas Wielenga suggests pressing this too strongly would be a mistake. It could leave Dalits with even less claims in Indian society; it is better for Dalits to argue they are an integral part of the Indian community and deserve equal treatment. The Indian authorities are however sensitive about suggestions of racial discrimination. The 'Hindu' newspaper on 9th December 1997 reported the Indian Government as rejecting a US suggestion of 'racial and ethnic strife' in the country in relation to the Bihar massacre of 61 Dalit and tribal people, and retorting somewhat ingenuously that there were 'instances of social tensions which sometimes result in violence'.

The vision for India has to be one of equality, freedom and justice for all, within the one society. In terms of international organisations and conventions, Dalits need to be seen as a persecuted minority as well as suffering a form of ethnic or racial discrimination. This would bring them within the orbit of the United Nations Human Rights Committee, the Working Group on Minorities and the Committee for the Elimination of Racial Discrimination, as well as the Commission on Torture and other appropriate bodies.

b)   Signs of hope

In a five-week visit one can only see parts, even fragments, of reality. However these can be set in a wider context and most observers of contemporary India to feel there is real movement today in the struggle against casteism, although at the same time there is a long way to go. There follow here some of the fragments of hope I saw or heard about. They can be only a tiny sample of what is going on in the complex social, political and economic relationships which make up modern India. Casteism is beginning to crumble but the emergence of a BJP government demonstrates that there is a great deal yet to do.

i)   Psycho-cultural and religious

Perhaps the most important area to be addressed is the Dalit psyche. The damage caused by 4,000 years of psychological oppression is enormous. It is a long-running war of attrition. There are constant irritations for Dalit people. In a new place they will be asked where they are from, what is their name, who are their relatives. If they are known to be Dalit they will be denied a chair, or excuses made not to offer a drink or share a meal. If they return to their village with a successful career they will still be treated as an out-caste. Yet more and more Dalits are embracing their identity and celebrating their roots. This helps others to develop pride and self-respect.

The growth of Dalit culture is a significant sign of the strengthening of Dalit identity. Drumming and dancing are the foremost Dalit skills and are now being turned into educational tools as stories of oppression are written and choreographed to help generate resistance. There are powerful examples of these at Dalit festivals, one of the most memorable experiences in my visit to India was attending the annual Dalit Cultural Festival at TTS. Although unseasonal rains forced the event indoors, the spirit and commitment in the dancing, music and poetry were considerable and it was the younger dancers and poets who demonstrated the most vigour and feeling. That year the Festival majored on poetry, with a score of Dalits poets reading their work. Even without understanding the language it was easy to observe how angry and outspoken are the younger generation. Much of their work is on casteism and its effects, the violence and inhumanity expressed towards Dalits and the commitment to establish Dalit identity as fully human.

I was often told Dalits are 'emotional people', they need opportunities to express their feelings. I was struck by a similarity with African people; in the resistance to slavery and apartheid and the battle for civil rights, music and songs were crucial to lift the spirit and express the intensity of the struggle. In AP, as I travelled among villages with Dalit organisers the 'colony' people always wanted a song - like the one in the Introduction - to end the visit.

Some papers on Dalit literature and poetry appear in *Dalit Solidarity* (1995). J.H. Anand has an essay on Dalit literature as literature of protest. He notes that Indian literature is predominantly religious but that the Indian scriptural epics are all written in Sanskrit and that for caste people Sanskrit is the classical language. The next most important language of communication is English. However Buddhist Scriptures were written in a regional language of the people, Pali, and when Dr Ambedkar started the modern movement for Dalit consciousness in 1927, the Sanskrit Manusmriti was burnt as a protest. Dalit literature began to blossom in Ambedkar's language of Marathi. Anand says that some Dalit writers are linked to a particular ideology, like Marxism or Buddhism, others are not. But some of their poetry and short stories have shaken up the Indian literary world. Anand also cites *Akkarmasi* (Bastard), the autobiography of a 35-year-old Mahar, as being the best Indian writing of 1992.

The same book has an essay by Achintya Biswas on Bengali Dalit poetry. He writes of a Dalit revolution way back in the 11th century, out of which poetry was composed in vernacular languages and in 'deliberately distorted Sanskrit'. This was the beginning of a Bengali Dalit tradition which has produced literature for the ordinary people. He describes the influence of the Ambedkar movement on Rabindranath Tagore, who wrote poetry in which can be seen 'the anti-caste thinking of this great soul', and says Tagore's 'Pratham Paja' is some of 'the best Dalit poetry ever written by non-Dalits'. Anand notes there was a movement in the first quarter of this century from which poetry of protest appeared, and there was more in the '70s. But we should not assume that all those of Dalit origin write genuine Dalit poetry, 'without Dalit consciousness one cannot be a Dalit poet'.

Dr Ambedkar felt that as well as culture one of the keys to undermining caste was inter-caste marriage. One bishop told me that Christians were still more likely to marry across faith than across caste. Some of the destructive passions in this area are illustrated in Arundhati Roy's Booker Prize-winning *God of Small Things* (1997). Some felt there was a growth in inter-caste marriage, although there is also resistance, from both sides. When a 'higher' caste man wants to marry a Dalit woman the woman's family are often anxious for her, and how she will be treated by her in-laws. If the woman is upper caste the man's relations fear for his safety. These are some of the same dynamics as when in European society a white woman becomes the partner of, or wants to marry, a black man.

According to former TTS Principal Kamber Manickam it is the young who are pressing to break down the marriage taboos. He and others challenge caste people who protest that they want to live as 'brothers and sisters' with Dalits, 'What we want you to do', he says to them, 'is live as brothers and sisters-*in-law*!', that is, marry Dalits - a much tougher proposition. Godwin Shiri estimates that some 10-15% of marriages may now cross the caste barrier. One inter-caste couple spoke to me of their difficulties, how long it took to persuade the girl's family despite the young man coming from a highly respectable Christian Dalit background. It was the arrival of children which seemed to make the difference.

New understandings of Dalit religion are another positive sign. There is frequent discussion among Dalits about the nature of Dalit religion, and its degree of separation from Hinduism. Most Dalit deities are female, and independently so, unlike the female deities of Hinduism who are reliant on the males. In a number of villages I visited I was told about their goddess, and shown the shrines. It appears that earlier observers may have misunderstood the true nature and racial content of Dalit religion, or perhaps it was hidden from them for fear of the wrath of the caste Hindus.

In an essay in *Revisioning India's Religious Tradition* (1996), published in honour of Methodist missionary Eric Lott, Sathienesan Clarke of the UTC, Bangalore, presents evidence for the argument that Dalit religious tradition is not in fact simply a shadow of Hinduism but has its own dynamic and its own very different perspectives. He gives an account of the religion of the Paraiyars (Pariahs) of Tamilnadu from his own observations over several years in Chingleput District, where the great majority of the Dalits are Paraiyars. Clarke focuses on Ellaiyamma, the goddess of the Dalit 'colonies' or village-sections. Ellaiyamman has not been co-opted by caste Hinduism. Her name means either 'Mother of all' or 'Mother of the boundaries' and her image is often found protecting the boundary of the colony. It is the distinctiveness of Ellaiyamman, says Clarke, which demonstrates 'the Paraiyars' resistance to the expansionist and overpowering nature of caste Hindu hegemonic forces'. He sees the goddess as 'an iconic representation of the resistance of Paraiyars to the conquering tendencies of the caste Hindu world'. The fact that a set of beliefs so opposed to mainstream Hinduism has survived, and is now becoming more widely known, seriously undermines both the picture of Dalit religion as merely an element of Hinduism, and the argument of the BJP and others that all Indians are originally Hindu. It is a further indication of hope for the Dalit struggle.

The importance of Dalit spirituality is also emphasised by M.C. Raj. He states that it has survived in 'the realm of a personal and family relationship with the dead'. It has no commandments, no specific rituals, 'no sins, no rebirths, no heaven and hell'. Dalit spirituality is 'a continuing experience of benevolence, protection, nurturing and angry reprovals from nature'. This spirituality has helped to create a community strength which has withstood the 'terrible oppression of the caste system'. Withstanding this for, literally, thousands of years demonstrates what Raj calls 'the spirituality of resilience'.

Increasing self-esteem and religious independence among Dalits enable greater possibilities of organising and resisting the worst levels of oppression and violence. Unity however is still difficult to create. There is a need for new symbols, new values, new language to assist in the process of creating unity and it is here that songs, poetry, literature and religious practice can help, and have begun to do so.

ii)   Political

There are also some signs of hope in the political sphere. The installation of a Dalit, K. Narayanan, as President of India has symbolic importance. Dalit politicians can rise to high places, they can only do it however with the support of their political party - which may be casteist but also needs Dalit votes and is therefore willing to elevate Dalits. There are severe limits as to what the president can do, and if he goes too far in advocating unpopular causes, his sponsoring party may well drop him extremely quickly. Some say having a Dalit president masks the ongoing exploitation of the caste system.

There have also been some successes lower down in the system. Perhaps the greatest in the last decade has been the Bahujan Samaj Party (BSP) which was founded in 1984, primarily by Kanshi Ram, himself a Chamar - a Dalit sub-caste, though not from a totally unprivileged background. The party has campaigned hard to link together Dalits and the OBCs as a 'Dalit-Bahujan' party. It won three seats in the 1989 General Election, two in 1991 and 11 in 1996, but fell to six in 1998. In the 1996 State elections in Uttar Pradesh it won 67 seats. In 1995 it was already strong enough in UP to enter an electoral pact, albeit with the BJP, and when Mayawati took over as UP's Chief Minister this saw the first Dalit woman to fill such a post. However to achieve this she had to ally with the BJP, who had their own reasons for ousting the previous Chief Minister, and when it suited them they withdrew support from her also.

The BSP has some claim to be regarded as a national party but the BJP, the Congress Party and other larger parties are constantly nibbling at its edges and seeking to entice its MLAs and MPAs into their own folds. It suffered a number of defections in UP in the mid-nineties and again prior to the 1998 national elections. It did not fare well in those elections, Kanchi Ram lost his seat. However Mayawati was re-elected, and a seat was gained in the state of Haryana, where the BSP had none before.

There has been a similar initiative in Maharashtra, where the Bahujan Mahasangh Party has sought to bring Dalits, minorities and OBCs into a coalition against the BJP and Shiv Sena. It has won a few local Council seats, and achieved reasonably well in the 1998 General Election when the BJP lost ground in both its strongholds of Maharashtra and Rajasthan. This is also the area in which the Republican Parties, set up by Ambedkar but subsequently prone to splitting, have their base. Dalits in other parts of India want to see them reunite, a single Republican Party would have much more influence on the national scene, but the situation in late 1998 was that there was a 'near total split' in the RPI.

To the surprise of some the BJP made gains in 1998 in Karnataka and Tamilnadu, in the latter by what local anti-casteists regard as a questionable alliance with the DMK. However one Dalit politician Mr Dalit Ezhilmalai, a member of the PMK (People's Labour Party), a largely sudra party which has four MPAs and had formed an alliance with the DMK, found himself national Government Minister for Health and Family Welfare. This was because the BJP and its allies were desperately looking for Dalits to serve in the coalition Government they were stitching together, but which fell in spring 1999.

A further development in Tamilnadu has been the success of the Puthiya Tamilagam (PT, New Tamil Home), a Dalit-based party initiated by

K. Krishnaswamy, which defeated a number of those who claimed to speak for Dalits but did not really do so. Krishnaswamy states that his six candidates in 1996 averaged 35,000 votes, and that the PT will seek alliances with Christians and other oppressed groups but will not compromise on its commitment to Dalit power. According to local church leaders it is a genuine Dalitbahujan party which came from nowhere in 1996 to win an MLA seat for its leader. Hence there are a number of signs at state and national political level which suggest that Dalits are gradually moving towards becoming a national political force.

The development of Dalit political consciousness at a local level was the subject of an article in the *Hindu* newspaper during the March 1998 election. The writer first remarks how special Dalit schools had been built closer to the caste people's area of the village, and when he asked why was told that they doubled as polling booths and it was easier for the caste people to control them at election time. He then describes the problems faced by some Dalit voters who had to walk for several kilometres in the hot sun to vote. No vehicles were allowed on the road by police for fear of 'poll capturers' who come in and forcibly take over a polling booth and its votes. Some Dalits who came to vote discovered their votes had already been used by caste people. In other cases the 'zamindar' who controls the village land and tax system instructed them how to vote. Also, the BSP voting booth was less accessible to voters. Nevertheless, said the article, 'Dalits are voting in larger numbers than before; more Dalit women are voting too. The Kanshi Ram-Mayawati phenomenon has surely helped produce this effect.' When the reporter asked one old woman why she had walked so far she puffed, 'Victory here could ride on a single vote.' Echoes again of blacks beginning to assert their political rights in post-1992 South Africa.

iii)   Self-organisation

Some examples of organising and networking outside the party political structures are offered below, though this is certainly not an exhaustive list. The first ones are entirely Dalit-led. The Dalit Solidarity Programme, now renamed **Dalit Solidarity Peoples (DSP)**, evolved in the early nineties and held its second five-year convention in Delhi in December 1997. During this time the DSP has sought to bring together Dalits from differing religious backgrounds, aiming to build alliances between Dalits from Christian, Muslim, Buddhist, Sikh and Hindu communities. It has organised regional conferences and training events, including for women and youth, all over India. Its 1994 report gave an account of a national women's conference held in Delhi, which was addressed by the Minister for Education and Culture, and a western region conference in Mumbai. The 1995 report recounts a visit by the World Council of Churches' General Secretary Konrad Raiser, village-level meetings in north-west India and an international team visit to Europe. 1996 saw more of a focus on the south and west regions of the country.

The 1997 DSP convention attracted 300 delegates and appointed a Working Committee of 51, of which 17 were Hindus, 15 Christians, 13 Buddhists, four Muslim and two Sikh. Sixteen are women and two are tribal people, providing links with the Scheduled Tribes, which are formalised through the Joint Council of Dalits and Indigenous Peoples of India (JACDIP). DSP's programme priorities continue to be education and communication, but human rights is a significant new area of work. According to the WCC observer at the convention, Bob Scott, this reflected concern at the increase of violent actions against Dalits. The convention sought continued links with the WCC to help internationalise the Dalit struggle. The DSP has no paid staff; all its resources are fed into bringing Dalits together and building up wider solidarity.

Also in December 1997 the **Federation of Dalit Action for Liberation (FeDAL)**, held its first conference in Madurai, Tamilnadu, in south India. Some 160 delegates were present, only a small proportion Christian. The conference identified brahminism, patriarchy and capitalism as the main forces oppressing Dalits. There was keen debate about the possibility or desirability of alliances with OBCs. As in Tamilnadu they are often seen as the Dalits' worst enemies. Supporters of such an alliance agreed it would need to be a long-term strategy and would be dependent on the eradication of untouchability. For many delegates village campaigns for land and political representation were more important. There was also an increasing interest in human rights, due to the rising violence. FeDAL is a federation of Dalit activists, including people like Jawakhar (see Story 2 in Chapter 2). Mohan Larbeer believes the churches need to take their lead from Dalit activists and give them all the support they can.

In the eastern state of Andhra Pradesh the cutting edge seems to be in the **Agricultural Union** (Story 6 on PAN), which includes both agricultural workers and small farmers. Activists linked with the Dalit Action Resource Centre (DARC) and the PAN have evolved a strategy of encouraging the formation of union branches in the Dalit section of each village. Both men and women can belong and gradually strength is building. The organisers wait until a branch is strong enough before tackling local issues, so there is a good chance of winning, whether it is access to water or land which is legally Dalit land, or transport, or 'tea-glass apartheid'. They have sought to build branches in neighbouring villages so if a crisis develops and there is confrontation with the caste people or the authorities, supporters can be quickly brought in and it made clear that the local Dalits are not alone.

The union tries to insist that the local panchayat takes up complaints, so that Dalits get used to using the proper channels, but it gives them legal advice and support. Organising brings its problems. In one area the union organiser's car was stopped and he was badly beaten. However he pressed his complaint and now seven caste people are facing charges. In some areas the Dalits remain divided, and the union cannot help even when major acts of violence take place. The activists are trying to develop a structure in each 'mandal', an area covering a town or a number of villages. One had built up a membership of 2,800 by the end of 1997, each paying 12 rupees a year (20p). In that way, gradually, the union will become self-sufficient, and no longer have to depend on outside support.

Out of this work has developed an emphasis on human rights which local activists say needs to be expressed at national and international level. In late 1998 the **National Campaign for Dalit Human Rights** was formed, of which Paul Divakar is convenor, launching an international petition for Dalit human rights. Key supporters of the Campaign include DARC, REDS and DLET. At the same time the Indian Catholic Bishops Conference, the National Council of Churches of India and the Evangelical Alliance of India came together to form the United Christian Forum for Human Rights as a reaction to the attacks on Christians, many of whom were Dalits or were working with Dalits and tribal peoples. In a particularly brutal attack a missionary and his sons were burnt alive in their car in January 1999. Attacks on tribals and Dalits have been particularly bad in the Dangs area of Gujarat and the eastern state of Bihar.

An initiative based in Tamilnadu is the **Dalit Liberation Education Trust (DLET)**. This was formed in 1985 by Henry Thiagaraj, a former Tamilnadu state civil servant. DLET focuses particularly on the training of youth and women, believing this will have the most long-term effect in the Dalit communities. It has developed an Education Facilitation Centre, and also five local rural centres, where Dalit youth are brought together for self-awareness training and community organising. There are also cultural programmes, which use music and dance to help Dalit youth rediscover their history, and sport for recreation and team development. DLET helps young people with legal aid when they face court cases and, with advice from lawyers, teaches them how to take on the system. By 1998 DLET had taken over 2,000 people through its training camps and had begun to develop a human rights emphasis in its work, including the formation of a Human Rights Education Movement. It produces videos and a newsletter, and is another of those initiatives contributing to a liberation consciousness among Dalits.

There are many struggles going on at local level - examples appear in the Stories, in some the church is involved, in others not. Story 7 recounts some of the activities of the Nasik Diocese in the Church of North India. In the Church of South India the Madras Diocese has been quite active, largely through the energies of its recently-retired Dalit Bishop, Masilamani Azariah. He has now been succeeded by another Dalit, V Devasagayam, formerly of Gurukul Theological College. I visited one local church in this diocese where the local pastor was struggling to persuade a rather unsympathetic congregation to pay more attention to Dalit issues. Bishop Azariah was urging the search for a new spirituality, which finds its outworking in self-realisation, self-reliance and self-respect. To encourage local churches to take this seriously he developed the 'BBC' campaign, where better-off urban churches encourage poorer, largely Dalit churches with 'BBC' gifts, a Bible for self-realisation, a Bicycle for self-reliance and a pair of Chappals for self-respect. The sandals are to encourage Dalits to wear something on their feet in defiance of casteism. There is also an education campaign, where Dalit school drop-outs are urged to come for the basic skills of language and arithmetic and other students can get an extra hour's tuition in diocesan schools after formal lessons are over. Bishop Azariah also raised funds to provide a team of five workers in each local church to carry out a social, pastoral and evangelistic programme.

Behind effective organising at national or local level, good research is required, and there are a number of examples of this, although here we find more groups not run by Dalits. The **Christian Institute for the Study of Religion and Society (CISRS)** is a research group originally based in Bangalore. It helped to initiate much of the early work on Christian Dalits and supported the development of the Christian Dalit Liberation Movement. There was also a largely Roman Catholic Dalit Christian Liberation Movement in Tamilnadu in which Anthony Raj was involved, but in 1998 both of these were at a low ebb. Further south is the **Dalit Resource Centre** currently based at TTS in Madurai, which has probably the most complete collection of material. It provides information and backing for local activists, FeDAL and the Dalit cultural celebration held annually in Madurai. In Mumbai there is **Vikas Adhyayan Kendra (VAK)**, which like most effective research groups in the countries of the South is an 'action-research' operation, where information is gathered and processed in relation to programmes of training or local campaigns intended to change people's lives. There is also the Jesuit-supported **Indian Social Institute**, with offices in Bangalore and New Delhi.

Some Dalits are developing alliances with women's groups, environmentalists and other people's initiatives. One such network is the **National Alliance of People's Movements (NAPM)** although thus far anti-casteism is not high on the NAPM's agenda. One ongoing debate in NAPM has been that, although it supports reservation, this does perpetuate a vested interest by caste identity which is in conflict with the ultimate aim of eradicating casteism. There is also a tendency by ecological movements to shy away from the controversial issues surrounding Dalits. Gabriele Dietrich, who is involved in NAMP and also works at TTS, feels environmentalists need to become more social justice orientated both for the sake of their own causes and for the alliances they need. She believes alliances between Dalits and the women's movement are mutually beneficial as they can fight together for labour legislation and programmes on resource conservation which could create many new jobs. They have common interests too in challenging violence and in 'cultural subversion' by foreign media and the forces of Hindutva. Alliances with women's groups could also sensitise Dalit male leadership to women's issues. However Dalit activists say NAPM will have to become more overtly anti-casteist for these benefits to flow.

iv)   Among women

A very positive sign of hope is the increasing consciousness among women. Men still rather idealise the Dalit male-female relationship, they argue that women are more equally treated among Dalits than in caste communities. Kancha Ilaiah is one, suggesting that male and female work is freely interchangeable in Dalit villages. Dalit women are less sanguine. They still have a considerable struggle with their own menfolk, never mind the caste people. They start 'thrift and credit' schemes because they cannot rely on men for money. They have to campaign against alcohol abuse - one woman was locked out of her home for 15 days for persistently trying to stop her husband drinking, before he gave in. Gambling is another target; I heard of one village where the women got so fed up with their men losing the family's money they got together, marched to the house where the gambling was going on and when the men took no notice of them proceeded to break the place up.

The women's worker with PAN (see Story 6) explained how she only got her education because her father happened to have progressive views, although she said things are better in the new generation. PAN helps women to form their own societies in the villages, and where they face conflict, to link up with the union to deal with it. Micro-credit schemes are helping with the purchase of animals, setting up small shops or roofing a house. For the younger women there is leadership training, economic self-help classes and courses on hygiene and reproductive health.

Karam Raja Selvi in her *Frontiers* essay puts forward a series of demands that Dalit women are making, including the right to work and to equal wages, property ownership in the name of the man and woman and the need for cràches for working mothers. Also the introduction of new technologies should always be accompanied by training for both genders so alternative work can be found. She says that even Government agencies do not offer equal opportunities and wages to women and the Government must set a better example. Dalit women are becoming much more outspoken in their demands and their self-confidence is increasing.

c)   The role of the Church

Perhaps the most crucial theme in the history of the Indian Church is that of Dalit conscientisation. It has been of very great benefit, both to the Church and to Dalits. Without it the Church might not exist in India today, apart from small enclaves of caste people gathered round educational or medical institutions. The Dalits too have benefitted as the Gospel, when lived and communicated as it should be, has led to a social and psychological liberation for many Dalits. There may therefore be much to be gained, were the Church to commit itself more openly and vigorously to the development of Dalit awareness and the struggle for Dalit liberation.

i)   Dalit awareness

Godwin Shiri's survey gives a very useful insight into the way Christian Dalits see their faith. They were asked how they understand 'sin' and responded with a list of individual, social-ethical sins such as robbery, lying, gambling and debauchery. However, says Shiri, their perceptions also relate to justice and they do not appear to place undue emphasis on original sin or human depravity. Their understanding of sin carries a strong 'corporate' as well as a 'justice' dimension. Similarly 'salvation', which Dalits understand as doing good, helping the poor, living justly, liberation from bonded labour. There were some who saw salvation in a traditional 'spiritual' sense, including repentance and forgiveness of sins, but the overall picture indicates 'a significant social justice element' in the Dalit understanding of salvation. Hence Dalits' existential situation 'has quite deeply affected their faith perceptions', they perceive a 'spiritual solace' in Christianity but also a yearning for social liberation. This points to considerable mission opportunities for the Church.

Telling the story of the Chundur uprising, recounted above in the section on harassment and violence, Kancha Ilaiah explains that there were three inspirational factors for the Chundur Dalits, Ambedkar, growing economic self-sufficiency and Christianity. The Chundur Dalits were the first in the area to convert to Christianity, but they had never challenged the authority of the caste people. Their dress and literacy had improved but they still sat on the floor in schools and theatres, they did not touch water in tanks and reservoirs and they stood in the buses without touching a caste person. Jesus 'never became anathema to the upper castes'; in fact in some areas the caste people were converted to Christianity. When, however, the political consciousness inspired by Ambedkar combined with improved education and employment opportunities and a religious awareness that encouraged the two main Dalit sub-castes in the area, Mala and Madiga, to work towards Dalit homogeneity, the caste people attacked. The reaction of the Dalits in burying those killed was unprecedented. Ultimately, it seems, the self-belief which their faith had given them emerged and Jesus did become 'anathema to the upper castes'.

There are signs of the awareness-building role of the Church among Dalits in many places. The Stories give some examples, see especially Story 1 about the 'Christian Society for Health and Education'. It provided a forum for Dalit consciousness to grow, but seemed not to be popular with the local Church of North India authorities, as it dealt with subversive issues. This appears not untypical. The report of the CNI Board of Social Services for 1996-7 refers to an impressively wide range of initiatives, and lists almost 300 programmes the Board supports in 18 dioceses. However only one of them mentions Dalits and as Dalits are the majority of the rural poor this is surprising. It is true that within the texts of some of the Synod reports reference in made to Dalits and tribals but only in three or four cases. It may well be that Dalits are part of other Synod programmes but they do not say

136

so. There is a positive comment in Bishop George Ninan's Foreword about 'achievements in consciousness raising, awareness-building and progress of movements of Dalits, Tribals, Women, Children'. It appears however as if Dalits are to a degree invisible in official church programmes and the reason for this is unclear. One exception to this is Bishop Ninan's own diocese of Nasik, which is more overt in its commitment to Dalit liberation.

The importance of overt policies in programmes for Dalit awareness and liberation is illustrated by the final section of Shiri's survey. He argues that for Dalits 'a path of struggle appears to be the only way out of the present situation', but asks whether the community has the 'much-needed tools for such a... long drawn-out struggle for liberation', and 'what kind of restructuring would the church have to undergo in re-orienting its priorities and programmes'? Those may be questions not only for the churches in India but for those who assist them from outside. Shiri goes on to make certain observations.

Firstly the Dalit Christian community has much inherent potential, its world view is based on communitarian cultural roots. Dalits, although often illiterate, are very socially aware. Their docility is a self-protective mask (shades of South Africa). They sense a discriminatory and oppressive society and state, and an indifferent church. They also understand they need both social and spiritual empowerment and that the wider society, including the church, could contribute to that empowerment. From the Church they want education, economic assistance and pastoral care. In general Christian Dalits, despite some bitter experiences, still hope in the church. They converted to Christianity not as 'rice Christians' but 'to seek liberation from serious caste oppression', and the fact that they cling to their faith, despite the economic and other sacrifices involved, demonstrates its 'superior quality'.

Secondly anti-Dalit discrimination in the church is undeniable. Christian Dalits may soon lose hope and give up their faith, which would be a great loss to both them and the Church. This requires urgent restructuring within the church, giving priority to pastoral ministry with a Christian education component and lively worship, giving Dalits a 'spirituality for combat'. There should be effective programmes for self-reliant economic empowerment. Schools and technological education are essential. Pastors should be properly equipped with skills in theology and social analysis and action. The churches should also be involved in the wider Dalit struggles against discrimination by the police and state authorities. Links with secular Dalit movements should be supported. Finally, to play an effective role in the Dalit liberation struggle, urban Christians and the church leadership should 'undergo a sincere change of heart' - or, in theological language, repent. This should lead to a sharing of resources and an involvement of rural Christian Dalits in the training opportunities and decision-making structures in a way which has so far been denied them. Hence, though Shiri does not say it, might the Church rediscover its own soul.

Such an analysis is supported by Roman Catholic observers also. Poornam Damel comments that the liberation of Dalit Christians will come basically through people's action, but the churches must listen to the 'small voice of dissent', confess and condemn the discrimination against Dalit Christians within their own fold. He says more ecumenical research is needed to document what is really happening to Dalits and to ascertain the extent to which foreign money flows in to caste people, Christian or not. He proposes that 'a one-day closure of all Christian institutions in India will be an impact-making symbolic action of solidarity with Dalit Christians'. Ultimately caste Christians must share power with Dalits, says Damel, or 'the writing on the wall portends' that it will be forcibly removed.

ii)   Dalit theology

The theology for this struggle is already being written. Several volumes of Dalit theology have appeared over recent years, one of the first was *Emerging Dalit Theology* published jointly by the Madras Jesuit Seminary and Tamilnadu Theological Seminary in 1990, soon to be followed by *A Reader in Dalit Theology*, edited by Arvind Nirmal and published by ISPCK in Delhi. There have then been the series of Summer School reports from the Gurukul Lutheran Seminary in Madras. One important question is how much this published theology is linked with praxis among the kind of rural Dalits whom Godwin Shiri surveyed. There seems some relationship but it was not possible on one short visit to examine this in detail. Nor is it possible in this brief section to do justice to the range of Dalit theology now appearing. It is essential that interested readers undertake this for themselves. The importance of Dalit theology in challenging the Church on casteism is stressed by Eric Lott in an essay recently published by Gurukul College.

Let me just however try to whet the appetite, as it were, with a brief survey to complement James Massey's 'Theology' chapter in *Downtrodden*. Massey's view is that three elements play an important role in Dalit theology, the aspiration of Dalits for fuller liberation, the recognition that God is on their side and the conviction that Christ is the model for the struggle, a struggle which continues today through the Holy Spirit. He notes that the history of Dalit oppression is much longer and deeper than that of African Americans, Latin Americans or Korean Minjung, who have also developed liberation theologies. He believes Dalit theology has an additional role, to make non-Dalits aware of Dalit suffering and pain. It should also raise the consciousness of the wider Christian community, enable ordinary Christians to play a role in the Dalit struggle and create the possibility of 'a full liberation or salvation, based on the Christ-event of redemption'.

A *Reader in Dalit Theology* contains essays by eleven writers including Massey, Nirmal, Bishop Azariah and Aruna Gnanadason of the WCC. V Devasahayam, formerly of Gurukul College, focuses on 'Pollution, poverty and powerlessness', pointing to the profundity of the pollution issue and how it affects both the Dalit community itself and the attitude of the caste people. He concludes by calling for 'religious revival', one suspects in Hinduism as well as Christianity though he does not actually say so. God is the hope of his people, he aligns himself with them in struggle. Nirmal himself outlines the path 'Towards a Christian Dalit Theology', arguing that such a theology must be developed by Dalits themselves. It is part of the process of developing a consciousness which is vital for the next stage of the struggle. The 'Exodus experience' for Dalits is a coming out of untouchability, out of the oppressiveness of Hinduism, into the liberating experience of Jesus Christ. 'The Jesus of India is in the midst of the liberation struggle of the Dalits ', and the God whom Christ revealed and of whom the prophets spoke, because he is a servant God, is a Dalit God.

Arvind Nirmal points to Isaiah 53 as a paradigm for the Dalit experience and links it with Jesus' words in Mark 8, 9-10 about the suffering and redemption of the Son of Man. He also draws the parallel between Jesus' cleansing of the Temple in Mark 11, and the denial of access to temples which the Dalits have continually experienced. And, as the Holy Spirit came upon Cornelius and other gentiles, urging them towards baptism, so the Spirit comes upon the supposedly 'unclean' Dalits today.

In his essay on 'Doing Theology in India Today' Bishop Azariah quotes Roman Catholic theologian S. Kappen saying 'The Asian theology of the future will have to be one that expresses the mute longings of the downtrodden and unwanted of the earth.' The economy must be restructured, power returned to the people and a counter-culture created consonant with human dignity. A relevant theology 'is more likely to emerge from those Christian thinkers and activists who in loyalty to Jesus have inserted themselves in the life of the people as partners in their struggle for justice'. A Dalit theology will be founded in Jesus of Nazareth who 'made his preferential option for the poor and oppressed, the Galilean peasants, publicans... Samaritans, the children and the women who were... the outcastes of society in Palestine'. It was these 'for whom he died on the cross as a true Dalit'. Theology has therefore a liberative role that can induce and introduce into the soul of the Dalit person and the Dalit community the word of hope.

Kothapalli Wilson, who is a philosophy professor in Hyderabad, argues in *Towards a Humane Culture* that Dalit Christians need to escape the 'sense of dependency which is the natural outcome of religious consciousness'. Jesus refused to be part of a religious hierarchy and his followers need to seek to become 'authentic human beings', throwing themselves into the cause of humanisation. 'To expect an entry into the Kingdom of God is the nature of a religious Christian' says Wilson, 'but to struggle to bring it about is the mode of an authentic Christian.' And wherever people suffer oppression, exploitation and humiliation in the name of caste, race and religion... an authentic Christian plunges into incarnating these sufferings and aspirations. Dalit Christians have to work out for themselves 'what the cry of humanity is in contemporary India', and decide whether the way forward is a religious way, or 'caste struggle'. Dalits need to become part of the Dalit liberation movement, and use this cultural unity to create a common platform with non-Christian Dalits for a larger struggle. 'All this demands politicisation of the Dalit Christians', it also requires a true liberation theology for the Indian Christian Dalits of today.

Emerging Dalit Theology comes primarily from the Jesuit stable, though it also includes Nirmal's classic essay on 'Towards a Christian Dalit Theology'. Some essays have been quoted from above, including those of Roman Catholic priests Anthony Raj, Poornam Damel and M.R. Arulraja. In his contribution A. Stanislaus argues for a 'counter-culture Dalit theology'. He sees the roots of this in the conversions to Buddhism and Jainism in the sixth century BCE, the eleventh century embracing of Islam and simultaneous development of the Bhakti cult, the neo-Vedantic movement of the nineteenth century and Ambedkar in the twentieth. The source of Dalit theology however, says Stanislaus, is the Indus Valley civilisation. This 'very first protest of the Dalits against the Hindu scriptures-based principle of purity and pollution in the sixth century', sowed the seed for a counter-culture theology. According to Stanislaus there are five stages in theologising - conscientisation, identification, historicisation, demythologisation and trans-culturation. In the last of these the Dalits 'in their struggle for their original faith, culture and God, begin to share the common platform of oppressed people of other countries, faiths and religions'. Being rooted and also able to transcend, says Stanislaus, is most important for the future internationalising of the Dalit issue.

Gurukul College has begun to hold an annual conference on Dalit theology and to publish the papers. In 1997 it was held jointly with theologians from South Korea on the similarities and differences between Dalit and Minjung theology. The 1996 title was *Frontiers of Dalit Theology* and included 25 essays, a number of which have been quoted above, and eight bible studies by V. Devasahayam, the organiser and editor for the conferences. Devasahayam points out in his introduction to *Frontiers* that, 'The contemporary theological scheme in India is.... characterised by a crisis', the old theologies are on the way out but the new theologies have not yet arrived. Both Indian and liberation theologies are insufficient, 'they have failed to relate the idea of God to the all-pervasive caste reality', to analyse the structure of oppression or to recognise the world of the most oppressed people, the Dalits. The old theologies have legitimised the present social and ecclesiastical order, and have served as 'a means of enslavement'.

Devasahayam says his Bible studies are intended to reflect the 'human face of Dalit theology, its matriarchal basis, redemption of the body, reclaiming the pleasure principle, rationality and priority of cultural factors over economic'. Dalit theology needs to be rooted in Dalit culture and identity, and challenge 'caste consciousness and caste culture within and outside the Church'. It aims to encourage, comfort and inspire in the struggle for liberation, and enable all 'to participate in the glorified humanity of the risen Lord'.

In the exchanges during the 1996 Summer School, says Devasahayam, the caste, class and patriarchal forms of oppression were analysed, the need to recognise Dalit women as equal partners recognised and the necessity of re-writing Dalit history emphasised. The importance of Dr Ambedkar's praxis was highlighted and the need to verbalise Dalit theology in a community with a high rate of illiteracy. A presentation on pollution revealed the role of pollution 'as a means of exploitation and oppression' and included a challenge to revise the concept of the purity of God. The work of the Holy Spirit was understood in Dalit theology as 'recreation, resurrection, revolution, liberation, maternal care and empowering the weak and oppressed'. Evangelism and mission are seen as the proclamation of the Kingdom by 'confronting structures of oppression by the grace of God'. For Dalits there is a greater need to convert caste Christians than 'pseudo-evangelism' among people of other faiths.

It is impossible to do justice to the rich and varied perspectives of this collection of papers and bible studies in a few short paragraphs, but each contribution has perceptions and insights which can contribute to the development of a genuine theology in the European setting also, to help put behind us the arrogant, patriarchal and eurocentric theology of the past and much of the present. The final essay in *Frontiers* on 'Eschatology in Dalit Perspective' by M. Gnanavaram reminds us that eschatology is to do with wholeness and completeness, and any oppression which creates incompleteness is a flaw in creation. The hope of freedom in eschatology strengthens us in the struggle, and the eschatological mission of the Messiah is 'to redeem and liberate the marginalised and oppressed'. And it is therefore ours. One of the challenges to the Dalit theology movement is to popularise it through regional languages such as Tamil, Kannada, Telugu and Hindi.

Jesus the Dalit is the title of a critical and challenging volume by M.R. Arulraja SJ. He describes casteism as 'worse than apartheid' and his book is a compilation of stories and reflections, with thought-provoking references to biblical passages and the early Fathers. His central theme is untouchability, its reality in biblical times and how Jesus dealt with it. He explores the way Jesus must have gradually analysed and understood his own society. He concludes 'Jesus found that the religion of his time was blind to the problems of the workers, the jobless and the poor'. The law had become a burden to working people, it had also divided people into pure and impure, based on rituals.

Jesus challenges the pure/impure dichotomy, especially in Mark 7, where in verse 19 he declares everything eatable clean and thereby ends also 'the division of the people as clean and unclean based on food habits, a direction that leads to the practice of untouchability'. Arulraja also explores how Jesus overcomes his own racial and religious prejudices which were inculcated in him by his upbringing. He cites the encounters with the Roman centurion and the Canaanite woman as bringing about a change in Jesus' own perceptions, a process which 'is easily understood and much appreciated by the Dalit Christians'. Arulraja goes on to probe the story of the Good Samaritan, illustrating it with an account of an 'atheist' law professor who often risked his life investigating murders, rapes and other atrocities committed against Dalits. He concludes 'Jesus was not telling the story of the one bad priest... he was condemning the priestly class and upholding the class considered untouchables'.

There is constant reference to practicalities in the book, and examples taken from the life of the churches. Arulraja challenges Roman Catholic teaching and practice in particular, and analyses where the papal encyclical 'Veritatis Splendor' gets it wrong. He concludes with a very sharp analysis of a pastoral letter written by the Catholic hierarchy to address casteism. Sadly, he says, the whole document 'smacks of the caste bias which the Catholic bishops have unfortunately not shed'. According to Dalits this is true of the wider Indian church leadership and may well strike chords with Christians elsewhere. Dalit theology challenges us all in the degree and quality of our commitment to the excluded, oppressed and untouchables of our world. It is very important that we read it for ourselves.

iii)   Christians and the wider struggle

Dalit theology points the way for the Church to be involved in the wider struggle for Dalit liberation. In fact it strongly suggests this is the path to salvation for the Church. Putting things in the context of Jesus' own manifesto in Luke 4, if the blind caste people are to be enabled to see, if the lame - the victimised Dalits - encouraged to walk, if the poor are to have the Gospel preached to them and the oppressed go free, and if the Church's raison d'etre in mission and evangelism is to be manifested then - whatever else Christians are involved in - Dalit liberation is crucial.

VAK in Mumbai has offered a useful analysis of the churches in India in a paper 'Church and Development'. In the past, it says, people of all communities would agree that the Church through the work of missionaries has been a pioneer in the fields of health and medicine. It has also contributed to women's greater freedom. In terms of the struggle for Indian independence however the Church's contribution was minimal, partly due to its close ties with the occupying power. Politically the Church falls between the ruling class and the marginalised. Particularly in India it is a 'passive domesticated community' with a burden of unproductive land, dilapidated buildings and obsolete institutions. Now however the Church has a unique opportunity to demonstrate its solidarity with the oppressed and become a 'church of the poor'. There is a strong movement both theologically and in social action to 'make the Church a movement for justice, peace and integrity of creation'. It is the largest social organisation in India with such a network of communication and organisation.

Hence the Church needs to commit itself to Dalit liberation both because Christian Dalits are still discriminated against and because all anti-Dalit discrimination is morally and ethically unacceptable. The Church also needs to engage in the struggle against communalism - so far it has seemed reluctant to get involved. The activity of certain Christian action groups in these fields show how great is the Church's potential in the struggle for social change. In order to be effective, however, the churches need to speak ecumenically. The VAK paper observes that the Protestant, Orthodox and Mar Thoma Churches have quite close relations with one another, while the Roman Catholic, as the largest, is 'very selective' in its relationships. It notes that the CNI, the CSI and Mar Thoma Churches have a joint council, that the National Christian Council of India has 27 member churches and a major development agency, CASA, and there are various study and training centres promoting Christian participation in development and social transformation.

There are also a number of Christian-based networks and groupings which have grown up with support from ecumenical groups inside and outside the country. According to VAK these are regarded with some suspicion by the established churches. They include some of the organisations mentioned above - DSP, FeDAL, DALT, National Campaign on Dalit Human Rights, CISRS, the Christian Dalit Liberation Movement, and presumably VAK itself. Increasingly such networks are working with non-Christians; in some of them non-Christians are the majority. VAK says that in the Indian context, where fundamentalism and communalism are major threats, it is vital that social action groups 'transcend religious boundaries and identities and form democratic alliances to meet the new challenges'. VAK cites INSAF, the Indian National Social Action Forum, as one example. To move in this direction however would require a transformation of the churches' own theological self-understanding and a radical reorientation of its mission. The 'structural bondage' of so many in contemporary Indian society is unrecognised. The churches need to develop a theology which promotes 'meaningful participation with others in social transformation'. The churches with their resources and experience should be able to work closely with movements for change, VAK concludes. They need to be seen 'in solidarity with the marginalised who form the majority... this is the challenge before the Church in India today'.

This accords closely with the writings of Dalit theologians and the activities of many Christian networks. M.R. Arulraja talks of the 'new ecumenism' needed in today's India. Dalit Christians of all denominations must come together to challenge the power structures in all the churches. At present ecumenism is most visible when 'the Christian churches gather, once every year, to sing lullabies to put the infant Jesus to sleep'. There are still few occasions when the churches join together 'to pressurise the

144

Government to include the Dalit Christians in the Schedule to the Constitution', i.e. the State discrimination against Dalits which still exists.

In its new guise the WCC-supported Dalit Solidarity Peoples (DSP) will continue in its five-year programme agreed in December 1997, to bring Dalits of different religious communities together, maintain an emphasis on women and youth and develop further links with the adi-vasis, or tribal peoples. One suggestion however from some Dalit activists is that DSP could make more integrated links with those in the forefront of the struggle who face threats and violence. This could mean a more active presence in rural areas, especially in the South where many of the atrocities against Dalits are committed. The unionising of agricultural workers in AP and the developing Federation of Dalit Action for Liberation are example of Dalit Christians working with non-Christians to develop serious and sustained analysis and activity for social transformation. It has to be said that when activists in some of these networks are asked if they are supported by the church the response is one of some surprise, as if it had not occurred to them that the church might be interested.

Anthony Raj is one who has experienced direct threats from caste people and questions from his religious authorities over involvement in Dalit liberation. He was accused of being a key organiser for Dalit activism in Tamilnadu. This was partly, says Raj, because it was thought Dalits were unable to organise for themselves. He believes that it is those without money or even food who are the most effective in the struggle. Once Dalit leaders obtain money they become less interested and less committed. Christians need to prod the churches to call on caste people to repent, and offer to help train them in anti-casteism and how to support the Dalit liberation struggle. Only in this way, says Raj, will the Church rediscover its mission.

Kancha Ilaiah argues that the Church and the whole of Indian society needs to undergo a process of 'Dalitisation'. This involves learning directly from the Dalit communities. It challenges for example the current approach to private property. The non-productive life of many caste people survives, according to Ilaiah, only on private property. Dalits believe property should be communally owned. Also Dalits have a very different attitude to the land; it is not there to be exploited, for individual profit, but there has to be a relationship with the land and what it produces so that it is not destroyed. The relationship between men and women is different among Dalits, as is the practice of democracy. Dalitisation was resisted in 1990 over the Mandal struggle and again in 1993 after the UP elections. Dalitisation of civil society, and the state and administrative apparatus is not going to be easy, says Ilaiah, and it should be achieved without violence. However caste people are maintaining their power by violence. The best approach may be through women, who also prefer change without violence and are more conscious than men of structural oppression. Dalitisation must be handled skilfully, 'we should aim for a cultural revolution that will avoid the loss of life'. Dalitbahujan intellectuals must work out a long-term strategy to restructure social, political and economic relations in a massive way.

This is echoed by M.C. Raj, who speaks rather of 'Dalitism', which he outlines in 19 theses at the end of *From Periphery to Centre*. He proposes Dalits prefix 'Dalit' to their name (in the manner of the previous Health Minister, Dalit Ezhilmalai). He says Dalits should all use a particular greeting 'Jai Bheem', with raised fists, African liberation style. Dalits should celebrate beef-eating, fix a price for their labour - including removing dead animals and digging graves and claim the right to water supplies, land and public access. Their music and drumming will be reestablished under their own control, non-Dalit religion rejected and Dalit religion redeveloped - the goddess Shakthi 'will be the source of our strength'. Dalits will reconvert to Dalitism by developing leadership at the intellectual, the community, the religious and the political levels. Says Raj, 'We shall expect you to sit with us as equals.... we shall not any more tolerate your domination.'

Sometimes people speak of the 'Dalit movement', but it appears as yet there is no single movement. There are a variety of dimensions to the movement, in terms of sub-castes, languages, geography, religion, strategies and objectives. Perhaps it is best to speak of 'a movement of movements'. There are many Dalit movements - some small and local, others widespread - over whole states and in some cases more or less national. New forms of struggle keep emerging. One of the most recent is in the field of human rights. It is felt by those initiating it that this will help internationalise the Dalit struggle, especially if evidence is given to relevant UN and other international bodies. It will reveal to the outside world the kind of pressures and atrocities Dalits experience daily in modern India from caste people and from the police and other authorities who are supposed to provide protection.

The struggle is becoming more violent as Dalits grow more articulate and explicit in their demands, so the caste people - often hiding behind state authorities - react more viciously. It is time now, perhaps long past time, for the world outside India to get involved. Casteism is the apartheid of today and it needs the same commitment and some of the same tactics and strategies from the world community to challenge it and root it out. The

World Church must challenge the Indian Church as - eventually - it challenged the South Africa churches in the '60s and '70s. But above all the Indian Government must be challenged. Dalits are a heavily persecuted minority and they are everywhere within Indian society. It is not acceptable, at the dawn of a new millennium, when the 'Third World' is supposed to have come of age, for scores of millions of one country's population to be consistently and continually marginalised and downtrodden. Solidarity for the Dalit 'movement of movements' must be spread around the world.

5   MESSAGE TO THE WEST

It is quite an experience when asking Indian villagers about the problems they face to hear, mixed in with the Marathi, Telugu or Tamil they are speaking, a familiar word like 'globalisation'. Rural Dalits are increasingly aware of the economic forces affecting their lives, and if there is no local word to describe them they use an English one. Local activists and researchers are helping them to understand why it is that there are even less jobs, land and other resources available, as capital of all kinds is sucked up into a global financial system which is fundamentally structured to benefit the rich and take from the poor even the little which they have. This process is the logical development of capitalism now that the alternative system of communism is discredited. Arguably however global market capitalism has a potential capacity for destruction much greater than communism ever had, chiefly because of its global nature.

There follows an overall look at the origin and effects of globalisation, as they affect the poor of the world, including the rural people of India. There is then an indication of some of the possible responses to capitalist-led globalisation, including localisation and 'Jubilee Economics', an approach which might enable those who are failing the opportunity to make a fresh start. The responsibility of funders is examined, the delicate balance between allowing the people on the spot to set the agenda but at the same time ensuring that the Dalit question is always addressed, at a fundamental level. Then come the aims and objectives of an initiative to offer solidarity to Dalit people in their struggle, and a discussion of some strategies which could be employed, being cognisant all the time that non-Dalits must check their perceptions and proposals with the Dalit movements themselves, so that they control the nature of the struggle.

Finally a brief theological perspective is offered, as to why Western Christians should be willing to support the Dalit struggle, and some of the issues which then arise. M.C. Raj stresses the importance of outsiders, saying that their efforts should support Dalit dissent at what has been happening to their communities. They must aim at 'strengthening the awareness and organisational base of the Dalit communities' throughout India.

a)   Addressing globalisation

It is not easy to find a simple definition of globalisation. The word itself is neutral, almost friendly. It smacks of the '80s' phrase 'global village', when we all began to talk of being much closer to one another in the new era of expanding inter-continental air travel and mass telecommunications. Marcos Arruda, the Brazilian economist, puts a qualifying adjective before the term speaking of 'competitive globalisation', over against what we might call 'humanising globalisation', in which Christians and humanitarians might want actively to be involved.

Social researchers like Ajit Muriken of VAK have observed the destructive affects of competitive globalisation in India and beyond, during the '90s. The loans contracted in the '70s and '80s need to be repaid. The World Bank and IMF have pushed forward Structural Adjustment Programmes (SAPs) which require poorer countries to open up their economies to the Trans-National Corporations (TNCs), including privatising many of their services. Countries are also required to adjust their production towards the export market, growing and selling commodities which will bring in foreign exchange. Such items can include flowers and exotic fruit and vegetables for European and American markets to the detriment of the local agricultural economy. In the meantime TNCs come in and buy up land, displacing agricultural labourers who then have to migrate to already overcrowded cities to seek survival. Muriken says this kind of thing is breaking up families and centuries of social structures within a decade.

In India this means that private companies are taking over public sector services. The latter had by law to operate a system of reservation, so at least some Dalits got jobs. This requirement does not apply to private companies - usually owned or managed by caste people - and they are not interested in providing Dalits with employment. They also want to reduce the number of workers. Hence the number of jobs available is decreasing, and the numbers of jobs available to Dalits is decreasing even more. The Nasik Diocese in central India (see Story 7 in chapter 2) has opened a Jobs Information Service in Ahmednagar especially targeted at Dalit youth. Parents give everything to provide a child with education, then it is very hard to find positions even when the young people have managed to qualify. The diocesan workers pressurise the responsible Government officials to go out to the villages and assess the situation. They also offer training in English as this is a much-prized qualification in the private sector. Muriken comments that the new technology is displacing people from factories; the job growth sector is in sales and marketing and for that spoken English is felt to be a vital asset.

Jawakhar, the village activist of Story 2, remarked that globalisation in his context means that the Government provides each village with a television, and adverts seduce Dalits from their own culture and towards consumerism. The diet of TV and cinema feeds a male-dominated patriarchal system. Many programmes are imported from the USA. There are none uplifting Dalit culture - painting, literature, drumming, poetry. Revd Isaac Mann, a Dalit Methodist minister in north-west India, spoke of going into villages and seeing local people transfixed for hours by small screens offering fuzzy images speaking in a language which hardly anyone in the village could understand.

What then is 'globalisation'? One definition, by Mbekou and Nziki, quoted by Beatrice Kersten, is 'a complex interlinking of the production of goods and services organised on an international scale. It is based on technical innovation and progress in the transport and communications sectors assisted by an international financial market which allows speedy movement of financial investments which greatly exceed the flows in the real economy.' It thrives on the dismantling of trade barriers, and it has repercussions in the fields of militarisation, employment, migration, effects on the biosphere and mass consumption and inculturation.

Marcos Arruda sees the seeds of the present global economic crisis in the events of the '70s where petro-dollars were cheap to borrow, inflation was low and there was a reasonably respectable exchange rate between the currencies of the North and the South. When interest rates began to rise as the result of the US Federal Reserve Bank decision in the late '70s to raise its interest rate by three times, the countries of the South found themselves in growing difficulties. The resulting processes have found a considerable number of countries saddled with debts which - because of falling commodity prices - they can never repay, and exchange rates which thoroughly embarrass the Western tourist with any conscience.

Competitive globalisation heralds immense changes in many parts of life. It particularly affects the poor, especially in terms of the debt crisis and the ways in which poorer countries are 'adjusted' to ensure they conform to what the wealthy countries require of them - primarily to pay their debt and thereby supply even more capital. The process of 'adjusting' to competitive globalisation is described by Arruda. The private sector was to be the engine of growth, and growth the means by which poverty would be eliminated. The World Bank meanwhile would assist debtor countries to adjust to the 'reality' of a world becoming global under the reign of transnational banks and corporations. 'Adjust' is a key term here, changing the structures of national economies to fit them for competitive globalisation. Power was transferred from national governments to international financial institutions, the focus of the economy was shifted to exploiting agricultural and mineral resources for export and manufacturing in sectors where low pay and weak unions were an advantage. Poor countries, says Arruda, 'scrambled to compete with one another in international markets. The result was a massive collapse in the prices of their exports.'

This whole process has led to a locking in of the productive sectors of the economies of poorer countries to the global market system in order that they can be exploited further. Meanwhile international structures such as the World Trade Organisation (WTO) and the Multilateral Investment Agreement (MIA), laying down rules for how TNCs will invest in certain countries, have been developed to undergird the onward march of competitive globalisation.

John Madeley, a development journalist, has listed the 'seven deadly sins' of competitive globalisation. It is a serious threat to jobs, as manufacturing moves wherever it is cheapest and computers take over many roles. It threatens democracy, as the requirements of free trade as envisaged by the WTO take over from the wishes of the people. It hands enormous power to TNCs, for example the MAI which increases the rights of TNCs even to sue governments. It leads to poverty by concentrating power in the hands of the wealthy. It widens the gap between rich and poor countries by removing protection from the commodities of the poor, eg Caribbean bananas. It damages the environment by demanding export crops which require fertilisers and pesticides and denude tropical forests. And it has caused a huge expansion of debt, which redistributes resources from the poor to the rich. Controlling the effects of competitive globalisation, upon Dalits as other exploited groups in the world, must now be a priority for those working for equality and justice.

Vandana Shiva of the **People's Plan for the 21st Century (PP21)** based in the Indian state of Karnataka describes in a paper called *Democracy and the Age of Globalisation* how competitive globalisation seeks control by capital of land, water and all natural resources. He sees globalisation as 'the expansion of the economic space controlled by corporations' at the expense of 'democratic space for citizens to determine and influence' their lives. Certain TNCs have been involved in setting up the Intellectual Property Committee to enhance the rights of corporations against people and even Governments; the Intellectual Rights Movement has therefore been set up in Karnataka to protect people's rights to biological resources. The World Bank is keen on ending land ceiling laws by which there is a limit on how much land one owner might control; activists therefore campaigned for the Alienation Act passed in the state of Punjab in 1990,

151

restricting the sale of agricultural land. The World Bank has recommended the creation of 'markets in tradable water rights'. Shiva says this will become a process for diverting water from small farmers to corporate 'superfarms' and lead to water monopolies. Thus local groups are having to fight the new Agricultural Policy of Karnataka inspired by the World Bank to privatise water supplies.

There is a more positive side to these processes which contributes to 'humanising globalisation'. People come into contact with those of different cultures and can communicate by physical and electronic means beyond any dreams of the past. For Arruda the challenge is to look beyond the economic sphere, and 'to accomplish a cultural, psychological and spiritual transformation... involving each and every human person and community in working for another globalisation, centred on the human being... on co-operation and solidarity'. Arruda points out that as well as TNCs globalising the conflict between capital and labour this process also creates the possibility for workers to organise transnationally. The global flexibility of production, the growth of the international finance industry, progress in telecommunications and the concentration of economic power all create challenges for people to organise their lives differently. They can respond by campaigning for greater democracy in all spheres of life, insisting on obtaining more information, setting up participatory and self-managed finance schemes, establishing direct contacts between grass-roots groups and communities, and reconstituting civil society. People can also to promote self-organisation and self-management in a way which marginalises the unaccountable power of the transnational banks and corporations. This is as relevant for India as for Arruda's native Brazil - or indeed for those concerned for justice within Europe.

Seeking an alternative to competitive globalisation one might hazard the definition of **humanising globalisation** as 'a process encouraging the growth of links, understanding, empathy and solidarity among the peoples of the world, acknowledgement of the existence of many cultures and lifestyles, celebration of those which most manifest liberty, equality and justice, and increased working together so that all human beings, regardless of gender, race or ethnic group, have access to food, clean water, shelter, clothing, work, education and healthcare'.

A helpful account of this crucial development in our world can be found in Rob van Drimmelen's *Faith in a Global Economy* (1998). He comments that competitive globalisation is in the tradition of colonialism, benefiting 'the powerful economic interests most'. He urges **internationalism**, saying that while globalisers accept world economic developments as inevitable, 'internationalisers want to shape and influence these developments'. He goes on 'Internationalism is based on the conviction that citizens should be able to influence government policies; globalisation erodes national sovereignty and can in the end threaten democracy and people's participation.' Internationalism and humanising globalisation are complementary.

Localisation is another process offering an alternative to globalisation. Vandana Shiva says that in India local people are organising to 'regulate commercial activity by asserting their environmental rights to natural resources - land, water and biodiversity - and their democratic rights to decide how these are used'. Localisation is the 'citizen's agenda for protecting the environment, and people's survival and livelihood' and presses for a shift in the power to make environmental and economic decisions from centralised states to local structures of self-governance. TNCs must be controlled, 'whether it is Cargill and Grace in Karnataka, Du Pont in Goa or Kentucky Fried Chicken in Delhi and Bangalore... Local communities are raising a common voice, "We will decide the pattern of investment and development. We will determine the ownership and use of our natural resources".' Localisation, says Shiva, is developing 'as an antidote to globalisation and to unrestrained commercial greed'.

A wider form of the global economy which is emerging to challenge competitive globalisation might be called **Jubilee Economics**. This idea has progressed most in the Jubilee 2000 Campaign for the cancellation of unpayable debt by the year 2000, but it has much wider implications. The Jubilee concept arises from proposals in the biblical book of Leviticus, chapter 25, that every fifty years land should be redistributed to those who owned it in the first place. This is because the land belongs not to any individual, no matter who they are, but to God. Such a mechanism prevents the rich becoming uncontrollably wealthy. It would represent a vigorous brake on the logic both of the growth of land ownership in ancient Israel and of competitive globalisation today. It gives the poor an opportunity to begin again. An occasion when a form of it was practised is recounted in chapter 5 of the book of Nehemiah when Nehemiah, having reconstructed the walls of Jerusalem, orders the entrepreneurs who during the period of the nation's problems have made themselves rich to return land, homes and vineyards to their fellow-Jews who originally owned them.

Clearly it will be very difficult to institute systems based on such a perspective, but it is vital to try. Mechanisms to regulate and where necessary block the competitive globalisation process need to be evolved.

Localisation is one such. Another could be a much more stringent control system over TNCs, including a code of conduct with real sanctions. The ethical investment lobby is a forerunner of this, publicity and boycott campaigns, and shareholder action help. Badly needed is the reconstitution of the United Nations Centre for Transnational Corporations which was evolving a code of conduct in the '80s when it was undermined and reduced to a small Geneva-based office, largely by US-linked capital interests.

One effect of competitive globalisation is the ridiculous and destructive flow of unproductive capital around the world, which is far greater than that being invested in practical enterprises, and simply seeks a tiny percentage point difference in exchange rates from which to make another few dollars profit. A far-reaching mechanism which has been proposed to deal with this is the 'Tobin tax', named after James Tobin, the economist who put it forward in 1978. Globalisation's driving force is international finance capital, held by transnational banks and corporations and mutual and pension funds which on the whole look for medium to long-terms profits in, say, construction industries or mining. However they also want faster and easier money. Beatrice Kersten quotes William Geister in *One World Ready or Not: the Manic Logic of Global Capitalism* as saying there is far more capital available than can be usefully invested in industry or infrastructure. Hence much human ingenuity is spent investing large sums of money based on speculation on future developments. Such investment is short-term and unco-ordinated. Such processes can lead to disaster, for example in the events of late 1997 and early 1998 in South-East Asia, where economies more-or-less collapsed under the weight of greedy expectation.

The Tobin tax proposes a tiny tax on cross-border financial flows. It would need to be just enough to slow down speculative investment in currencies which change marginally from day to day and push it towards investing in jobs and development for the poor - including the Dalits of India. 'Jubilee Economics' would provide a different kind of vision for the world. According to World Council of Churches development expert Israel Batista 'Jubilee' is an attempt to provide a comprehensive and symbolic vision during transitional periods, in which justice is an essential element. Jubilee means a new kind of beginning, a general overhaul of economy, culture and social life in order to restore persons, property and wealth to their rightful condition.' It is also celebration, 'an imaginative alternative to the prevailing criteria of exclusion'. The Jubilee Economy would include mechanisms such as localisation, debt cancellation, much more vigorous shareholder action and something like the Tobin tax in order to restore some human values into the rush to globalisation, to set the poor free from the chains of the past and to offer new hopes to groups like the Dalits in terms of education, land, health and work. The message to the West is that we are increasing our standards of living at great cost to the poor and the environment, and we ourselves need to adopt a 'Jubilee economy' for reasons both of justice and self-interest, unless we want to bequeath an even more chaotic world to the next generation.

b) Responsible funding

A constant theme in discussions with Dalits in India was the potential role of overseas funders regarding the Dalit issue. Franklyn Balasunderam noted that relationships with foreign funders in India often require some kind of loyalty from those funded. A rather static bilateral relationship can develop, focusing on the issues the funder is known to want to promote. Such relationships can lead to 'dynasty-building' in recipient countries where certain groups or institutions evolve a control over funding patterns. There is a need for continuing open discussion on these dynamics and on the Dalit situation. Balasunderam believes there should be a national ecumenical forum, convened by the National Council of Churches in India (NCCI), which would have a mandate to develop a medium-term programme to address Dalit issues. As it is I was informed that in mid-1998 only a small part of one staff member's work related directly to Dalits. Godwin Shiri, whose detailed work on rural Dalits in Andhra Pradesh and Karnataka is quoted above, commented that the Christian Dalit community was sometimes used in appeals to obtain foreign funds, but when the funds arrived they never reached Dalits.

Anthony Raj put forward the view that foreign funders are very cautious about controversial issues. They want to avoid such areas on the whole and to guide or even control the programmes of groups dependent on their support. If they are not very careful they can cause divisions in recipient countries, supporting the safer initiatives and therefore starving more radical initiatives of assistance. Funders need to ensure there is consciousness-raising as well as economic development - both are necessary. Agencies should also explore whether applicants are really working with and benefitting grass-roots groups. Church donors should ensure that secular networks are helped, often they are more militant and under more political pressure than those with religious backing.

Lecturers at the Tamilnadu Theological Seminary (TTS) with whom I discussed these matters had a variety of perspectives. Bas Wielenga of the

Centre for Social Analysis felt funders often contributed to fragmentation. Mohan Larbeer at the Dalit Resource Centre said on the other hand that it was often difficult for donors as, when movements split, each usually claims to be the true original. Accountability and transparency are very important in the provision and usage of overseas funds. The wider community needs to know how much is received by a particular group, from whom, for what purpose and how it has been used. Funders can encourage alliances and coalitions, in order to build up trust and patterns of working together. They might also want to discover which groups are experiencing opposition, even danger, in their activities. Kamber Manickam, the TTS Principal, felt it can be difficult for those outside India, including funders, to challenge casteism. However they could and should continue to ask questions of those they funded and of church leaders to ascertain what is really happening, especially with respect to caste. There needs to be much more openness in the churches on caste issues. Other activists commented that agencies are too cautious about supporting initiatives which are really seeking transformation rather than amelioration - this can be true of funders within the UK also.

K. Wilson in a hard-hitting essay written in 1982 bemoans that fact that Indian theologians are still living in the colonial era, 'it is insulting that even after 35 years of independence we find Christians who feel it prestigious to be called members of the Church of England' and that Roman Catholics are not able to express the word of Christ. There are brilliant Indian Christian thinkers but since the majority of them 'are tied to foreign mission institutions, depending on foreign funds for their sustenance', they are not academically or theologically free. And, 'if Indian Protestant Thought is conditioned by economic exigencies, Indian Catholic Thought is determined by ecclesiastical overlordship'.

Balasunderam in *Frontiers* also has some sharp observations on outside funders and their effect on Indian Christians. 'How many will talk about "Christian Dalit Theology" once the flow of money stops...', he asks. He goes on to comment that careful distinctions must be made regarding funding agencies, which is to say 'not all funding agencies are our friends'. The funding agencies which 'stress the "Christian" identity' need to be watched carefully. 'Who stand with the Dalits and who do not' is a crucial question for Balasunderam. M.C. Raj warns of how non-governmental organisations of both North and South can be seduced by what he calls the 'dominant powers'. He says that 'from a role of conscientising and building up of a critical mass of people, the NGO is consciously slipping into the co-opted role of poverty alleviation. In this the NGO is turning out to be more of a co-conspirator against the genuine interest of the people', because it treats its own survival as more important than that of the people. Northern NGOs are influencing NGOs in the South 'by effectively translating the strong-arm tactics of the Financial Institutions', i.e. the World Bank and the IMF, and perhaps also now, says Raj, the WTO or World Trade Organisation.

It is important therefore for any agency supporting development in India, governmental, non-governmental, aid or mission agency, to ask how the programmes it supports are challenging casteism. If they are not, they are failing to address one of the fundamental mechanisms by which the poor are kept poor. Programmes should be asked about their position on caste, what proportion of their employees are Dalits and what status these have within the organisations. A 1998 Oxfam report very honestly states that the organisation has not a single Dalit project officer. Agencies should also be asked how they make themselves accountable to Dalit communities and in what way they challenge casteism in the wider society and its institutions. Finally donors should seek to discover whether those funded are persecuted or under any form of attack, and for what reason. Often those of whom the authorities are most suspicious, or in the Indian context those who attract opposition from caste people, may be those doing the best work.

Agencies providing funds in the South Africa of the '60s and '70s gave less and less support to groups or organisations who were not challenging apartheid. They also found themselves funding groups and movements outside South Africa who were internationalising the issue and creating external pressures on the South African authorities. Sometimes they had to fund the most effective groups by non-public means. In the end Indians themselves have to destroy casteism, but those most actively seeking to do so deserve the greatest help.

c)   Nowhere without struggle

'Struggle' is a term which recurs continuously in discussions with Dalit activists about their situation and what is to be done. They see themselves very much as in a time of struggle, the level of which is currently intensifying. This can be established from such phenomena as the growing awareness of even Dalits in the villages about their situation, their increasing willingness to challenge it, the reactions by the authorities and other caste forces which are producing increasing violence against Dalits and the internationalising of the issue. The growing awareness is symbolised by the song quoted in the Introduction to this book.

What is now needed is for those in Western countries, and elsewhere, to support the Dalit struggle in the most effective ways. To assist in this it is important to identify the key areas of the struggle and then outline strategies which can be adopted to offer support and solidarity.

i)   The key areas of struggle

Perhaps the first of these is the conscientisation of the Dalit people themselves. Many Dalit activists say there has been a genuine increase in self-awareness among Dalits over recent years. One measure of this has been the growing interest in the works of Dr B.M. Ambedkar, especially since the Government of the state of Maharashtra began to publish them in an ongoing series of volumes. This has enabled many more people to study the thinking of the parent of modern Dalit consciousness. Ambedkar's observations, thought and wide-ranging analysis have given many Dalits both self-confidence and the intellectual undergirding necessary for effective struggle. The anxiety felt by caste people about the influence of Ambedkar are typified in an anecdote by Bishop Azariah, until recently Bishop of Chennai who says that before he became a bishop, when he worked for the NCCI, a senior non-Dalit bishop who had always supported him on Dalit matters only severely criticised him once, when he made reference to something Ambedkar had said, saying he should be quoting the Bible, not Ambedkar!

The increasing interest in Ambedkar's writings, the appearance of his statue and the regular garlanding of that statue are all signs of growing Dalit conscientisation. The plan of the Thaiyyur villagers in Story 4 to announce and celebrate their ownership of the disputed land by erecting a figure of Ambedkar is symptomatic of this. So was the incident in Mumbai in mid-1997, referred to in chapter 2, when a chain of chappals (leather sandals) were hung round the neck of an Ambedkar statue and the police subsequently shot dead a number of Dalits.

Conscientisation also appears in the focus on the history and identity of Dalits, the poetry and literature that is appearing, the more political content in dancing and drumming and, in the Christian sphere, the active growth of Dalit theology. This is the focus of Sathi Clark's book *Dalits and Christianity: Subaltern Religions and Liberation Theology in India* (1998) where he argues

158

that the recollection of the Dalits' religious experience assists in the recovery of their identity and strengthens their resistance. One particular item at the TTS-sponsored Dalit festival in December 1997 stands out in my mind where the story was told, vividly through drums and dance, of the landlord and his thugs who threatened and then beat a Dalit woman to get her off her land so they could take it over. Dalit communities are increasingly organising against such atrocities. Ultimately of course the struggle is about power, economic and political, and Dalits are awakening to this reality and the fact they have for so long been denied power. Hence solidarity activity which vigorously supports the conscientisation of Dalits and responds when they are under attack is an essential support mechanism.

Listening to Dalit activists it is clear that the fundamental objective of the struggle is the eradication of casteism. Whether that necessarily means an end to Hinduism is for Hindus to pursue. It may be that a form of Hinduism from which casteism has been removed can be developed. In the meantime Hindutva the neo-fascist ideology which drives right-wing, nationalistic Hinduism - must be totally opposed, in the same way that the heretical form of Christianity which undergirded apartheid was also confronted. Winning the psychological war around untouchability is crucial to undermining casteism, and outside support which celebrates Dalitness will help.

Next, Dalits strongly believe they are the original inhabitants of India and they wish to be recognised as such, or at least to see more detailed and objective research to discover the truth. Much of the anthropological and cultural evidence so far suggests that Dalits (or dasas) and tribal people (or adivasis) are descendants of the original inhabitants of South Asia. If this were established, or even if it were recognised that Dalits are descended from one of the original groups of the peninsula, this would contribute to Dalit self-confidence and pride. 'History from below' has been important in a range of other liberation struggles, in enabling oppressed groups and peoples more firmly to establish their identity. Research in this field is therefore something to be supported.

A further aim for those supporting the Dalit movements must be to encourage unity. There are many Dalit leaders working for unity, but there are constant efforts by the caste people to divide and rule, to offer modest immediate gains to put people off from more fundamental objectives, or to elevate one leader or group over against others. Such tactics have long been in operation, they can be seen most clearly in the machinations around the Republican Party, initiated by Ambedkar but not formally set up until after his death, where the Congress Party and other forces have been successful

159

in dividing the movement. Another example was the Bahujan Samaj Party when it gained some power in Uttar Pradesh in the mid-nineties and found some of its leading figures being seduced into other parties. Supporters from outside must seek to be as 'ecumenical' and broad-based as possible in their solidarity, having no favourites and supporting the kinds of alliances and coalitions which are likely to make gains in the wider struggle.

Solidarity work must not be naïve however. In the struggle against apartheid there were certain groupings based in South Africa which existed for tribal or sectional interests. There was also much activity by government intelligence departments, sowing doubt, division and disillusion in the liberation movements and their supporters. We learned subsequently how widespread, unprincipled and insidious that was. There must always be careful assessment of the real aims of any particular Dalit initiative, discussion with other Dalit organisations as to how they see its work, observation as to whether it has grass-roots support and inquiry as to whether its leaders are undergoing any sacrifice for their activities. Outside supporters must have the promotion of Dalit unity as one of their key criteria.

ii)   Strategies for outsiders

One of the main needs of which Dalits often speak is persuading, shaming or challenging the Indian Government actually to practice the policies of equality and human rights it has espoused and to make effective use of the laws and practices against casteism that it has promulgated. The laws on reservation, in terms of what Dalits are entitled to in relation to education, employment, access to grants and loans, housing and land development, protection by the police and the courts, are in many ways ideal. The problem is they are honoured far more in the breach than the observance.

It is important therefore for outside campaigners, for example, to acknowledge Indian anti-discrimination legislation and to seek information about its success. For example, how many Dalits have jobs in the public sector? What level of seniority have they achieved? Are all the 'reserved' places filled? What training is offered to those who may not make the grade for entry or promotion? Many of these questions are similar to those being put to UK and US employers regarding their 'equal opportunity' employment policies for the black and minority communities who suffer much higher unemployment rates than white communites. Other questions to the Indian authorities might include how many prosecutions have taken place under the 1989 Atrocities Act, how many have been successful and what kind of sentences imposed?

These kinds of questions can be put in different ways in different contexts. They may be put diplomatically Government to Government, or to State Governments, or addressed to the Indian Government's Commission on Minorities, or that on Scheduled Castes and Tribes. One important area for those concerned about the Dalit situation is that of international legislation and the fora related to it. A specific example is the Universal Declaration of Human Rights, and the United Nation Human Rights Committee which monitors it. Like all Governments the Indian Government has to make regular reports to that Committee, and others may also make submissions, as Dalit organisations have done from time to time. The National Campaign for Dalit Human Rights, launched in December 1998, has produced a Dalit Charter based on international human rights obligations. The UK Government has begun to ask for the views of NGOs when it is making its submissions to international bodies, and NGOs can make their views known to all Governments and make their own submissions in the international fora. They can be assisted in this by outside supporters, who may also disseminate their submissions. Other bodies in the general human rights field include the UN Committee on Torture, the Committee for the Elimination of Racial Discrimination and the Committee monitoring the Convention on the Rights of the Child.

As has been indicated a number of times above there are a number of similarities between apartheid and casteism, and it may well be that some of the mechanisms employed with respect to the former could usefully be employed against the latter. Apartheid was particularly objectionable because of the exploitation by a minority of settlers of a majority of original inhabitants and because of its racial basis. Casteism however is the systematic oppression of a minority by a majority and while the extent to which it may be a form of racial discrimination is not entirely clear the purity/pollution factor is as unacceptable as racism. In the 60s a special UN committeee was set up, the UN Special Committee Against Apartheid. Perhaps there is need for a UN Special Committee Against Casteism, in order to focus the world's attention on the equally unacceptable and systematised discrimination of the caste system.

A growing body of Dalit organisations are seeking a greater internationalisation of the struggle, and enlisting outside support. There is therefore an opportunity and an invitation to those - Christian or not - who wish to engage in the struggle for Dalit liberation to do so. One discipline must be to inform ourselves in much more detail about Dalit issues, to read what Dalits have written and where possible to hear from them directly. A second is to give time, energy and financial help to support the Dalit cause. Struggle involves sacrifice. For some Dalits this means putting their land, jobs, families, freedom, even their lives on the line. Those of us who wish to support the Dalit movements will also need to sacrifice if we want to enjoy the privilege of partnership in a struggle for justice. Such struggles are a crucial opportunity to bring into reality the oft-repeated prayer 'Your Kingdom come', and they offer us the opportunity for participation in the most meaningful dimension of human existence. As for Dalits so for Christians seeking the Kingdom of God: you get nowhere without struggle.

d)   A Theological reflection

Hopefully a Christian theological perspective has already become clear through the above, but let us in this last brief section make it more specific. Firstly it is essential to listen to the marginalised and oppressed themselves, their voice needs to be heard unadulterated. In an essay recently published by Gurukul Theological College, Methodist scholar Eric Lott argues for the principle of exclusiveness in Dalit theology. He remarks that 'Dalitva' or 'Dalitness' indicates 'courage, persistence, the refusal to give in, even the sheer celebration of life'. He looks for a Dalit 'counter-culture', a Dalit theology which offers 'a serious critique of the dominant Western secular model of cultural life', with its emphasis on male dominance, social aggression, economic competitiveness, ecological exploitation...'. In most instances that is the type of theology which is emerging.

Secondly, it can be said with confidence that for Christians exploitation and injustice in human relationships is rebellion against God's way for us, and is therefore sin. Clearly there is deep injustice and both psychological and economic exploitation in the Dalit situation and it is essential for Christians, both within India and outside, to do whatever they can to challenge casteism and eventually to destroy it. Such action also resonates with the 'option for the poor', initiated by the liberation theologians of Latin America, blessed by church leaders with varying degrees of enthusiasm, including successive popes, and upheld by hundreds if not thousands of church conferences, statements and resolutions. The biblical basis for such activitiy has often been spelled out. The continual demand for justice of the Old Testament prophets is well-attested. The earlier chapters of Amos communicate clearly and the message of Second Isaiah, with its themes of the despised and rejected who are God's servants and will eventually be recognised by him, is a source of comfort and inspiration for Christian Dalits.

However the 'praxes' (actions-with-purpose) of church bodies do not always fulfil the spirit of words - verbal or written. Many in the Indian churches are aware of the sin of casteism, indeed many are directly affected by it. However, as in Indian society as a whole, power in the churches is held predominantly by caste people and - as with combatting racism in western society resources for the fight against casteism are not easy to come by. Western churches need to support and encourage Indian churches when they take the 'option for the Dalits', and offer practical and prayerful support.

A third issue which arises in theological reflection on this situation relates to interfaith dialogue. If Hinduism is inextricably linked with casteism this makes Christian-Hindu dialogue extremely difficult. But any suggestion of attacking Hinduism may feed into the racism still actively present in Western Christendom; some Christians in the West need little excuse to decry other faiths, and may use casteism to oppose dialogue with Hindus. There are many positive principles in Hinduism, usefully encapsulated in a 1998 *Methodist Recorder* article by Eric Lott, including 'a strong sense of the sacred, the power of sacred places, peace to the whole earth as sacred Mother... the importance of sacred story and sacred books', together with forms of belief in God and exploration of how God is embodied on earth. Lott argues elsewhere that there is a 'liberationist' tradition within Hinduism, espoused by Hindus who are critical of the old brahminic structures and teachings, and their undergirding of casteism. It is a sensitive area, and Christians need to approach these matters humbly, cognisant of the fact that in its time Christianity has been used to justify apartheid, national socialism, anti-semitism and other unacceptable ideologies and systems, without the kind of outright and determined opposition from the churches that the circumstances required.

It is essential to continue the effort for interfaith dialogue. It is clear that the develoment of Israel's faith drew on the myths and legends of other ancient peoples, and the argument about the natures of Yahweh continues throughout the Old Testament. It is manifested in Second Isaiah's view of the Persian King Cyrus, as it is in the writer of Jonah's view of the 'foreign sailors' and the people of Nineveh. There is also the very important lesson Jesus learned from the Syro-Phoenician woman - 'we may be seen as dogs under your spiritual table, but we still have faith enough to enable healing'.

In dialogue with Hinduism, however, casteism is not an issue that can or should be bypassed. Hopefully a form of Hinduism is being developed, or indeed already exists, which in both theology and practice eschews casteism. There have been Hindu spiritual leaders who have campaigned actively and sacrificially against it. Christians must seek a form of Hinduism which can be respected and with which there can be authentic

163

dialogue. Yadav argues in *India's Unequal Citizens* that among Indian communities in places like Guyana, Fiji, Trinidad and Surinam 'almost all inter-caste barriers' have been 'obliterated'. He believes 'Hinduism will be strong and healthy if caste goes'. What it will be difficult if not impossible for Christians to do is to retain respect for a belief system in which caste is inherent. In particular the extreme form of Hinduism represented by Hindutva, which lies behind some of the attacks on Christians in late 1998 and 1999 and is described as neo-fascist by many observers, needs to be roundly condemned by Hindu and Christian alike.

Fourthly there needs to be some recognition, at least among British people, of our own complicity in the strengthening of casteism during the colonial period and our continued benefitting from the system since then in relation to our trade and commerce with India. There is an ongoing debate in the churches as to whether repentance is appropriate for acts committed in the past for which those who live in the present do not bear direct responsibility. To say such repentance is inappropriate seems a rather individualistic view of humankind, failing to recognise both our relationship with those who have gone before and the benefits we have received and continue to receive as the result of past injustices. Such a view also fails to recognise the corporate nature of sin and repentance, and to distinguish them from guilt. Repentance cannot be limited to particular individuals or contained within a given period of time. If our foreparents have failed in certain respects and been responsible for actions which cause others pain or from which we benefit, an active and continuing repentance is an appropriate response.

Repentance is a dynamic rather than a static concept. It involves turning, turning away from sin and towards God and, by implication, action to ameliorate or eradicate the effects of the sin. There is little point in expressing sorrow or pain about an event or situation without doing whatever can be done about it. Hence, given the failure of the British colonial administration to tackle casteism, and in many ways actually to capitalise on it in terms of keeping opponents divided, it would seem right and proper now for British Christians to do what we can to expose casteism in India and to support the Dalit movements which are challenging it. This may include some rather uncomfortable discussions with Indian church leaders, some of whom - not unlike church leaders elsewhere - sometimes seem more concerned for their own status than the status of the downtrodden of their society. It may involve some sensitive conversations with Dalit leaders also. They are not perfect, and suffer from the propensity of some from the base who experience a better lifestyle and want to keep it, even at the expense of their fellow sufferers.

The final theological comment relates to pollution and the absolute unacceptability in Christian terms of any human being regarding another as 'polluted'. As some Dalit theologians have pointed out there is a parallel in the New Testament with the attitude of the Jewish religious leaders to non-Jews, especially Samaritans. The verse in the story from chapter four of John's Gospel concerning the Samaritan woman at the well which speaks of Jews not sharing drinking vessels with Samaritans rings bells for Dalits. In fact they may be the only people in today's world who experience just that sort of discrimination, apart perhaps from those who are HIV positive. It is difficult to understand what is going through the mind of someone refusing to use the same plate or glass as another person, even after it has been washed.

The problem is also present in church buildings, even today. I was told that there are Christian churches where Dalits must sit in a particular place, or outside, or even not come at all. There is clearly an ongoing failure in Christian mission here which William Carey and others tried to tackle long ago and which the churches in India and outside need vigorously to address. However let none of us be complacent. How often do marginalised people - homeless or shabbily-dressed - venture into British churches, and what kind of welcome would they get? We have many ways of showing our indifference, and not long ago a friend told me of visiting a well-attended church on Easter Day and leaving with a mixture of sadness and rage because not one person had spoken to her - and she was white and middle-class.

Within this context the questions of commensality (table fellowship), and marriage need to be addressed. A particular means of Jesus challenging his contemporaries was by the company he kept at table. The Pharisees hated him eating with tax-gatherers - traitors to the community - and other 'sinners', nor did they approve of a prostitute anointing his feet. Again, the rules were that there were certain kinds of people you ate with and certain kinds of people you did not. But Jesus cut across all such human barriers, and ate and drank with whom he wished; every person is a child of God, and equal in His sight. But how long is it since any of us shared table fellowship with someone not of our class, or race, or faith? This is a matter we must try to address *together with* the Christians of India rather than in confrontation.

A further dimension of the 'pollution problem' is marriage advertisements in Indian church newspapers for 'fair' partners, the bishop who told me Christians would marry someone of the same caste from a different faith rather than a Christian of different caste, the stories of those who married across caste lines and the pain of trying to make peace with their families,

165

sometimes never achieved. Within a practice of marrying only 'one's own sort' lie suspicion, fear, even loathing of the other which have no place among Christians. The sense of the difference, the otherness, the actual pollution of the person of a different caste needs to be viewed without self-righteousness by white Western Christians, who are still struggling with their own racism, but it is so antithetical to Christian teaching that - like apartheid - it is based on heresy, and needs urgently to be addressed in the Indian Christian community. Many Dalit leaders believe that breaking down the 'eating and mating' barriers is the way to destroy the purity/pollution dynamic and thus the very basis of caste.

Casteism is an evil which it is time for Christians and all of good will to confront and to say 'we want an end to this'. It is the apartheid of the present time and should be addressed vigorously by the whole international community. It will be a struggle, but we shall find friendship, solidarity and comradeship along the way. We need to have faith in struggle for so often it is through struggle that we discover the meaning and reality of faith. That struggle needs to be alongside the poor, who provide our inspiration, and whose resistance continues to grow through songs such as that quoted at the end of the **Introduction**, and concluding 'We get nowhere without struggle.' And 'Caste out!' should be our cry.

BIBLIOGRAPHY

Akbar, A.K. Nehru: The Making of India Penguin, 1989

Aloysius, G. Nationalism without a Nation in India OUP, 1997

Amirtham, Samuel & David, C.R.W. Venturing into Life: the Story of Tamilnadu Theological Seminary TTS, Madurai, 1990

Ambedkar, B.R. What Congress and Gandhi have done to the Untouchables Thacker, Bombay, 1946

Ambedkar, B.R. The Untouchables, who were they? Amrit, Delhi, 1948

Ambedkar, B.R. Untouchables and the Indian Constitution 1948

Anand Mulk Raj and Eleanor Zelliott (Eds.) An Anthology of Dalit Literature Poems, New Delhi, 1995

Anandhi Dalits in Madras Indian Social Institute, 1995

Arulraja M.R. Jesus the Dalit: Liberation Theology of Untouchability Volunteer Centre, Hyderabad, 1996

Azariah, M. Mission in Christ's Way in India Today Church of South India, 1989

Ayrookuzhiel, A.M. Abraham The Sacred in Popular Hinduism Christian Institute for the Study of Religion and Society, Bangalore, 1983

Balasunderam, Franklyn Dalits and Christian Mission in the Tamil Country Asian Trading Corporation, Bangalore, 1997

Beteille, Andre Inequality Among Men OUP, Delhi, 1977

Beteille, Andre Backward Classes and the New Social Order OUP, India, 1981

Beteille, Andre The Idea of Natural Inequality and other essays OUP, Delhi, 1987

Beteille, Andre Caste, Class and Power: Changing Patterns of Stratification in a Tanjore Village OUP Delhi/University of California (2nd edition), 1996

Chanchreek, K.L. & Prasad, S. (Eds.) Mandal Commission Report; Myth and Reality HK Publishers, Delhi, 1991

Chellapa, Sadhu Caste System in India Agni Ministries, Madras, 1997

Chentarassery, T.H.P. Ayyankali, the First Dalit Leader Navdin Prakashan Kendra, 1996

Charsley, Simon & Karanth, G.K. Challenging Untouchability: Dalit Initiative and Experience from Karnataka Sage, Delhi, 1998

Clark, Sathienesan Dalits and Christianity: Subaltern Religions and Liberation Theology in India OUP, India, 1998

Das, Bhagwan & Massey, James (Eds.) **Dalit Solidarity** ISPCK, Delhi, 1995

Desai, A.R. **Repression and Resistance in India** Sangam, London & Bombay, 1990

Devasahayam, V. (Ed.) **Dalits and Women: Quest for Humanity** Gurukul Theological College, Madras, 1992

Devasahayam, V. **Outside the Camp: Bible Studies in Dalit Perspective** Gurukul Theological College, Madras 1992

Devasahayam, V. (Ed.) **Frontiers of Dalit Theology** ISPCK/Gurukul Theological College, Madras, 1997

Dumont, L. **Homo Hierarchicus: the Caste System and its Implications** Paladin, London, 1972

Dutt, N.K. **Origin and Growth of Caste in India Vol.1, 2nd edition & Vol.2** Mukhopadyhay, Delhi, 1968 & 1969

Fischer, Louis **The Life of Mahatma Gandhi** Granada, 1982

Forrester, Duncan **Caste and Christianity** Curzon Press, 1980

Galanter, Marc **Competing Equalities: Law and the Backward Classes in India** University of California, 1984

Hardgrave, Robert **The Nadars of Tamilnad: the Political Culture of a Community in Change** University of California, 1969

Hardgrave, Robert **India: Government and Politics in a Developing Nation** 1986 (4th edition)

Harris, Nigel **The New Untouchables: Immigration and the New Worker** I B Taurus, London, 1995

Hiro, Dilip **The Untouchables of India** 1982 (2nd edition)

Human Rights Watch **Broken People: Caste Violence against India's Untouchables** 1999

Irshick, Eugene **Politics and Social Conflict in South India: the non-Brahmin Movement and Tamil Separatism 1916-1929** OUP Delhi/University of California, 1969

Irschick, Eugene **Dialogue and History: Constructing South India 1795-1895** OUP Delhi/University of California, 1994

Ilaiah, Kancha **Why I am not a Hindu** Samya, Calcutta, 1996

Irudayaraj, Xavier (Ed.) **Emerging Dalit Theology** Jesuit Seminary, Madras, 1990

Jayaraman, Raja **Caste and Class: Dynamics of Inequality in Indian Society** Hindustan Publishing Corporation, India, 1981

Joshi, Barbara (Ed.) **Untouchable: Voices of the Dalit Liberation Movement** Minority Rights Group (US), 1986

Khan, Mumtaz, Ali **Social legislations and Civil Rights of Scheduled Caste** Uppal, Delhi, 1993

Kshirsagar, R.K. **Dalit Movement in India and its Leaders 1857-1886** M D Publications, Delhi, 1994

Koshy, Ninan **Caste in the Kerala Churches** CISRS, Bangalore, 1968

Manickam, Sundavaraj **Social Setting of Christian Conversion in India** Franz Steiner Verlag, Wiesbaden, 1977

Mahajar and Mann (Eds.) **Economic Development of Scheduled Castes in Punjab** Anmol, Delhi, 1997

Mahar, J.M. (Ed.) **The Untouchables in Contemporary India** University of California, 1972

Mehta, Gita **Snakes and Ladders: A View of Modern India** Secker & Warburg, 1997

Mendelsohn, O. and Vicziany, M. **The Untouchables: Subordination, Poverty and the State in Modern India** Cambridge University Press, 1998

Massey, James **Dalits in India: Religion as a Source of Bondage or Liberation** Manohar, Delhi, 1995

Massey, James **Downtrodden: the Struggle of India's Dalits** World Council of Churches, Geneva, 1997

Massey, James (Ed.) **Indigenous People: Dalits** ISPCK, Delhi, 1994

Massey, James **Roots of Dalit History, Theology and Spirituality** ISPCK, Delhi, 1996

Massey, James **Towards Dalit Hermeneutics** ISPCK, 1994

Murugkar, Lata **The Dalit Panther Movement in Maharashtra: A Sociological Approach** Popular Prakashan, Bombay, 1991

Nagaraj, D.R. **The Flaming Feet: a Study of the Dalit Movement** South Forum Press, Bangalore, 1993

Nirmal, Arvind P. (Ed.) **A Reader in Dalit Theology** Gurukul Theological College, Madras, 1991

Nirmal, Arvind P. (Ed.) **Towards a Common Dalit Ideology** Gurukul College, Madras, 1991

Omvedt, Gail **Dalits and the Democratic Revolution** Sage, Delhi/London, 1994

Omvedt, Gail **Peasants, Dalits and Women** 1994

Omvedt, Gail **Dalit Visions** Hyderabad: Orient Longman, Delhi, 1995

Padhy, K.S. **Reservation Policy in India** Ashish, Delhi, 1988

Pendse, Sandeep **At the Crossroads: Dalit Movement Today** Vikas Adhyayan Kendra, Bombay, 1994

Pickett, J.W. **Christian Mass Movements in India** Abinden Press, New York, 1933

Prabakar, M.E. (Ed.) **Towards a Dalit Theology** ISPCK, Delhi, 1988

Prakash, Prem **Ambedkar, Politics and the Scheduled Castes** Ashish, Delhi, 1993

Rajshekar, V.T. **Dalit: The Black Untouchables** Clarity Press, Atlanta, 1987

Racine, Viramma Josiane & Jean Luc **Viramma, Life of an Untouchable** Verso, London 1997

Raj, M.C. **From Periphery to Centre: Analysis of the Paradigm of Globalisation, Casteism, Dalitism** Ambedkar Resource Centre, Tumkur, 1998

Roy, Arundhati **The God of Small Things** Flamingo, 1997

Rushdie, Salman **Midnight's Children**

Scott, D.C. & Selvanayagam, I. (Eds) **Re-visioning India's Religious Traditions** ISPCK for United Theological College, Bangalore, 1996

Selvanayagam, Israel **Tamilnadu: Confrontation, Complementarity, Compromise** World Council of Churches, Geneva, 1996

Selvanayagam, Israel **Vedic Sacrifice: Challenge and Response** Manohar, Delhi, 1996

Singh, K.S. **The Scheduled Castes** OUP, India, 1993

Singh, Raajen (Ed.) **Globalisation: Impact on Dalits** Vikas Adhyayan Kendra, Bombay, 1996

Shiri, Godwin **The Plight of Christian Dalits** Christian Institute for the Study of Religion and Society, Bangalore, 1997

Spear, Percival **A History of India, Volume 2** Penguin, London, 1990

Srinivas, Mysore N. **Caste in Modern India** Asia Publishing House, Bombay, 1962

Srinivas, Mysore N. **Social Change in Modern India** University of California, 1966

Srinivas, Mysore N. **Dominant Caste and other essays** OUP India, 1994

Srinivas, Mysore N. (Ed.) **Caste: Its Twentieth Century Avatar** Delhi, Viking, 1996

Stanley, Brian **History of the Baptist Missionary Society** T & T Clark, Edinburgh, 1992

Thapar, Romila **A History of India, Volume 1** Penguin, London 1990

Theertha, Swami Dharma **History of Hindu Imperialism** Dalit Educational Literature Centre, Madras, 1992

Thiagaraj, Henry (Ed.) **Human Rights from the Dalit Perspective** Dalit Liberation Education Trust, Madras, 1996

Vakil, A.K. **Gandhi-Ambedkar Dispute** Ashish, Delhi, 1991

Van Drimmelen, Rob **Faith in a Global Economy: A Primer for Christians** World Council of Churches, 1998

Webster, John **Dalit Christians: A History** ISPCK, Delhi, 1992

Webster, John **The Pastor to Dalits** ISPCK, Delhi, 1995

Webster, John (Ed.) **From Role to Identity: Dalit Christian Women in Translation** SPCK, Delhi, 1997

Webster, John **Religion and Dalit Liberation** Manohar, Delhi, 1999

Wingate, Andrew **The Church and Conversion** ISPCK, Delhi, 1997

Yadar, K.C. with Singh, Rajbir **Indian's Unequal Citizens: A Study of India's Other Backward Classes** Manohar, Delhi, 1994

Zelliott, Eleanor M. **From Untouchable to Dalit: Essays on the Ambedkar Movement** (2nd edition) Manohar, Delhi, 1996